SWI...

W...

WARLORDS

ALSO BY KEVIN SITES

In the Hot Zone

The Things They Cannot Say

...ING
WITH
WARLORDS

A DOZEN-YEAR

JOURNEY ACROSS

THE AFGHAN WAR

KEVIN SITES

HARPER ● PERENNIAL

NEW YORK ● LONDON ● TORONTO ● SYDNEY ● NEW DELHI ● AUCKLAND

Some of the material in this book originally appeared in the October 2013 issue of *Vice*. Excerpts from the author's personal journals have also appeared in the *New Times* newspaper (San Luis Obispo, CA) from September to December 2001.

HarperCollins books may be purchased for educational, business, or sales promotional use. For information, please e-mail the Special Markets Department at SPsales@harpercollins.com.

FIRST EDITION

Designed by Michael Correy

Library of Congress Cataloging-in-Publication Data is available upon request.

ISBN 978-0-06-233941-6

14 15 16 17 18   RRD/OV   10 9 8 7 6 5 4 3 2 1

This book is dedicated to my father-in-law, Gary Smith,

who had both roots and wings and lived with the rare and

enviable grace of a man who always put others first.

CONTENTS

||||||||||||

SWIMMING
WITH
WARLORDS

CLEANSING CONFLICT

What is a saint? One whose wine has turned to vinegar.
If you're still wine drunkenly
brave, don't step forward. When your sheep becomes a lion,
Then come. It is said
of hypocrites, "They have considerable valor among themselves!"
But they scatter when
a real enemy appears. Muhammad told his young soldiers, "There
is no courage *before*
an engagement." A drunk foams at the mouth *talking* about what
he will do when he gets his sword
drawn, but the chance arrives, and he remains sheathed as
an onion. Premeditating,
he's eager for wounds. Then his bag gets touched by a needle,
and he deflates. What sort of
person says that he or she wants to be *polished* and *pure*,
then complains about being
handled roughly?*

* Excerpted from the poem "Cleansing Conflict," from *The Soul of Rumi: A New Collection of Ec-static Poems*, translation by Coleman Barks (Harper One, 2001). Rumi was a prolific thirteenth-century Sufi poet whose work, much of it focused on union with the divine, appealed to people on all sides of the religious divisions of his day and continues to inspire today. He was born in 1207 in the city of Balkh, in what is now Afghanistan.

Prologue
ENTRANCE

||||||||||||||

At the Kokol border crossing in Tajikistan, June 2013. My driver has asked the Tajik border guard how long it will take to repair the boat that will ferry me across the Amu Darya River into Afghanistan.

U nder cover of a moonless night in mid-October 2001, I found myself loading thousands of pounds of camera equipment and supplies onto a giant pontoon boat on the northern bank of the Amu Darya River. The pontoons were normally used to carry weapons to the Northern Alliance troops fighting the Taliban on the other side of the water. With all the gear and people, there wasn't any room left on that raft for allegory, but I remember feeling like one of the damned souls in Dante's *Divine Comedy* about to be ferried across the River Acheron to hell. The American airstrikes had begun, and I was headed into Afghanistan.

It was only one week after Osama bin Laden's Al Qaeda terror network struck the United States, crashing planes into the Pentagon and the World Trade Center. I was dispatched by NBC News to bear witness to America's righteous anger and retribution. It was swift and unrelenting.

In my first month in Afghanistan, I watched as the U.S. obliterated Al Qaeda's bases and, with the help of its Northern Alliance allies—a mix of ethnic Tajik, Uzbek, and Hazara Afghans—toppled the Taliban government that had hosted them. But the war, as we well know, did not end there and has not ended yet.

I went back to Afghanistan in the summer of 2013 for my fifth visit, on the eve of America's planned withdrawal. My goal was to try to understand what had happened to Afghanistan in the twelve years since I first traveled there, and what might happen this time after I left.

I reentered at exactly same place, crossing the Amu Darya River from southern Tajikistan into northern Afghanistan. The once busy Kokol–Ai Khanoum border crossing, through which weapons, spooks, Special Forces, and journalists like me had once been transported, was now just a dusty shadow of its former self. Today it's a remote outpost displaced by real bridges built or refurbished by the Americans and located near larger and busier population centers to help with the flow of commercial goods and war materials moving in and out of Afghanistan.

At the crossing, I found the pontoons moored on the bank, unused because so little cargo was moving back and forth. Instead, I stepped into an ancient, rusted motorboat one weld away from sinking and made the three-minute crossing a second time. As the boat chugged along against the current, I was certain of only one thing: the war I had found on the other side of the river a dozen years ago was there to meet me still.

WATCH A ONE-YEAR-OLD

Anger rises when you're proud
of yourself. Humble that. Use
the contempt of others, and your
own self-regarding, to change, like
the cloud in the folklore that became
three snake shapes. Or if you like
the dog-barking lion wrath, enjoy
the hurt longer. Watch a one-year-
old, how it walks, the slow wisdom
there. Sometimes a sweet taste
makes you sour and mean. Listen
to the voice that *says, It was for
you I created the universe.* Then
kill and be killed in love. You've
been two dogs dozing long enough!*

* "Watch a One-Year-Old," from *The Soul of Rumi: A New Collection of Ecstatic Poems*,
translation by Coleman Barks (Harper One, 2001).

PART I
THE NORTH

An Afghan National Police officer stands guard, prepared for possible violence between Uzbeks and Tajiks on the streets of Taloqan City.

1
OVER THE BORDER

||||||||||||

My second crossing of the Amu Darya River from Tajikistan to Afghanistan.
The rusted-out shell of a boat was more seaworthy than it looked. The Amu
Darya's strong current forced the captain to throttle hard against it in an up-
stream arc to ensure we reached our landing spot directly on the other side.
(Photo by Dost Muhammad)

Tajikistan, the poorest of the former Soviet republics, is one of the least visited places on earth, but in June 2013 I was on my way there for a second time. I had traveled there the first time in 2001, with my NBC crew. We had been stymied in our attempts to enter Afghanistan from both Iran and Uzbekistan; Tajikistan would be our final and most reckless attempt. We had traveled thousands of miles by every conceivable means, only to be blocked at each successive border crossing. Desperate to get to Dushanbe, the Tajik capital, we even bribed an entire Tajik flight crew to take a plane overloaded with our gear into the night sky. We thought we would be the only passengers, but after we boarded we were horrified to find that it was filled with other people—other people whom we might have gotten killed in a plane crash to reach a story that had started with plane crashes on 9/11.

Once in Dushanbe, we drove a few hundred miles south, and in the dark of night crossed the Amu Darya on pontoon boats, aided by Russian soldiers who had covered their faces with kaffiyehs. But the things we did to get there pale in comparison to the adventure that followed. Over the next hundred days, seven of our colleagues would be killed, I would videotape another being blown up by a Taliban mortar, and we would live in the house where legendary mujahedin commander Ahmad Shah Massoud was assassinated. In Kabul, we would unwittingly sleep next to an unexploded 500-

pound bomb and discover that our houseboy was being raped by the dirty fuck we had hired for security. I would watch B-52's drop 15,000-pound "daisy cutter" bombs on the Al Qaeda and Taliban fighters hiding in the mountains of Tora Bora, and in Jalalabad, on my final night of that first Afghan odyssey, I would be visited by what I believed was the spirit of a CNN technician who had died only a day earlier on the very mattress on which I slept.

This time Tajikistan wasn't a destination of last resort. I had specifically made it part of my story proposal to the editors of *Vice* magazine, pitching them on the idea of retracing the steps of my first journey twelve years later to see what, if anything, had changed in Afghanistan. To do that, I wanted to enter at the same spot.

While it added another plane, a car and driver, a Tajik interpreter, and hundreds of miles—and likely another thousand dollars to my costs—I believed it was essential to understanding my past and present experiences and for telling the full story of those I encountered.

I am fifty now, and had been in my first war zone, Nicaragua's Sandinista/Contra war, when I was half this age. I am still an obsessive-compulsive traveler, packing and repacking, clicking and zipping, the rip of Velcro pockets and flaps making those seated around me in the departure lounge at Dubai International wondering what it was I'd lost. But that couldn't be apparent to them—I'd lost my sense of order. When you have no control, I'd learned during a career reporting on war, you try to impose it on your surroundings.

All I had encircled me: a backpack bulging with cameras, cables, chargers, portable hard drives, my laptop—the tools of my trade—and a duffel bag filled with the necessities of life: food, clothing, shelter, body armor, Kevlar helmet, kneepads, first aid kit, ballistic sunglasses, a compass, broad-spectrum antibiotics like Cipro for the runs and Keflex for skin and respiratory infections. There were granola bars, peanut butter, packets of instant coffee, a water filter to get the dirt out and chlorine tablets to kill the bugs in it. While minimalist for most, some fellow war zone travelers might see my 60 or 70 pounds of gear and look at me disdainfully, as if I were a bubble boy who could not endure his hostile environment, wrapping himself instead in First World comforts and edibles to blunt, if not completely deflect, its impact. In truth, I simply wanted to be self-sufficient. And it was a lot less than what I used to bring. Ever-smaller digital gear and the go-light hiker revolution, after which everything from backpacks to sleeping bags to tents was made of wafer-thin nylon weighing about as much as dryer lint, made it possible to carry on my back everything I needed for a two-month trip.

Other things had changed, too. Unlike previous trips, this one frightened me. Maybe it was because my stepdaughter, usually as stoic as Demosthenes, started crying and didn't want to go to school the day of my flight so she could see me off. Maybe it was because almost everything had lined up for this trip too smoothly. Maybe I believed I was going to buy it because I had survived more than a decade of covering conflict without so much as a nasty scratch and it was finally time to pay up, to lose a limb or my life. I also believed, superstitiously, that now was the time such a thing was most likely to happen—when I loved my life, rather than being indifferent to dying.

But there were plenty of annoyances to distract me from that dark feeling. The travel itself, for instance. Unless you fly first class, international travel is a monumental pain in the ass. There is nothing easy or efficient about it. Even in the developed world it sucks—sweating while hauling luggage, flights suddenly cancelled with no explanation, arbitrary gate changes, managing the complex logistical flow of getting unorthodox things like body armor and satellite modems across continents to the places where you'll need to use them.

Fortunately, I had discovered a time-honored way to beat these oppressive systems like the airlines, security, customs, and the rules stacked against the common traveler: I flashed my pearly whites like they were lights on the Vegas strip. It was a smile that didn't come naturally to me, but I had learned its undefeatable power—that taking the time to fully acknowledge another human being could buy you vast amounts of goodwill.

Nasir, the beat-down driver in Dubai who had had to leave a wife and three kids behind in Pakistan ten years earlier succumbed to it, even cracked a smile of his own when I asked him to pose with a Hello Kitty figurine (a running joke in my family). Even dour Ansar at the Tajik Embassy was no match for it; perhaps he disdained the grinning idiot across the counter from him, but he nonetheless issued a short-notice tourist visa for me during a brief layover.

And so it was done. I was coming to you, my dusty, heavy, red velvet Tajikistan. You of few visitors, wearing too much makeup, scuffed shoes, and a cheap dress—but still, *your* smile was pretty, too, even under the sad weight of all that oppressive Slavic history.

Boarding the Somon Air flight, I pushed past the babushka moms holding babies already showing signs of five-o'clock shadow and men with hair so thick it looked like black moss. On the plane, a 737-800, the seats were in rows so narrow you more or less had to stand. My forward view was a scalp dusted with dandruff. But unlike flights in the West, I could freely block the aisle with my oversize bag just like everyone else on the plane, and when a flight attendant asked me to shut off my iPhone for takeoff she gently rubbed my arm with a finger rather than ramming my elbow with the drink cart. I smiled again, this time to myself, as the jet lumbered down the runway. I would be in Dushanbe by midnight.

Early the next day, after just a few hours of sleep, I met my fixer, Elena (which is not her real name—she did not want to be identified) in the lobby of my hotel. She was a dark-haired woman in her early fifties wearing an easy smile and a colorful Tajik version of a muumuu. I had attempted to hire someone by interviewing contacts at Tajik travel agencies and then triangulating those names with endorsements on

Internet message boards. It had still taken weeks of emails and phone calls to find her and a driver. Most car services demanded $500 or more for a day trip to the border, even without an English-speaking driver. Finally, one of my original contacts, an experienced pro who usually worked at rates double my budget, lined up both Elena and a driver for $300.

But that was only one of the hurdles in Tajikistan, the most trying segment of an otherwise smooth logistical operation. The agency I had hired in Los Angles to get both my Tajik and Afghan visas had secured only the latter, despite having an entire month and repeated appeals from me. Their failure, which I learned of only days before my departure, might have derailed the entire trip because of how tightly it was scheduled. I had six-weeks for on-the-ground reporting, then only another two weeks to write a five- to seven-thousand word magazine article. Theoretically, you could get a Tajik visa at the Dushanbe Airport, but I was arriving after midnight, when the visa counter would likely be (and actually had been) closed. Instead, I scrambled during a very short layover in Dubai to get one from the Tajik consulate there.

Arranging the travel from Dushanbe to the Kokol border crossing in the south had been just as troublesome. No one wanted to go to the crossing that connected the Tajik village of Kokol to the Ai Khanoum area of Afghanistan, an area whose commercial traffic was now mostly in illicit goods. Because of its remote location, it had once been a hotbed for transporting arms and other materials going to the rebel

Northern Alliance during the years of Taliban rule from 1996 to 2001.

With the Taliban toppled it is more or less irrelevant today, except for those with something to smuggle—guns, or drugs, or merely bags of cement and lumber for small construction projects on the Afghan side of the border. It was so remote that Elena and my driver weren't sure how to find it. We had left Dushanbe at 8 a.m., and six hours later I was losing faith that we'd reach it at all. At one point, the road disappeared into trackless sand.

"That's not a road, that's a direction," Elena said, pointing to the swirling sandstorm that seemed to be our path ahead.

Since I had only been there at night a dozen years ago I was little help, but finally, after another hour driving through dust and on rutted donkey paths, we found the entrance. The foothills that rose from the banks of the river looked vaguely familiar—more déjà vu then memory. The same pontoons were still there, along with the two rusted-out boats used to tow or nudge the rafts across. Not surprisingly, neither of them was working when we arrived.

We waited for the repairs on a ridge above the bank. Elena interpreted a conversation I had with a Tajik man named Muhammad who regularly transported supplies into Afghanistan for a hospital he was building in Khoja Bahauddin, a village about 10 miles to the east. It had once been a refugee village, the northernmost retreat of those attempting to escape the reach of the Taliban. It was also the headquarters of Ahmad

Shah Massoud, the Afghan mujahedin* commander who had fought the Soviets and become a leader of the Northern Alliance in its battle against the Taliban. And it was there that he was killed by two Al Qaeda operatives posing as a television camera crew on September 9, 2001—just two days before the terrorist attacks on the United States. Massoud's compound had become home for me and my colleagues for nearly two months after that initial crossing into Afghanistan in 2001.

On the ridge, I kicked up some rusted old .30-millimeter shell casings, likely from a Russian anti-aircraft gun once positioned on the border. Muhammad told me they were from fifteen years ago, fired at the Taliban by Tajik soldiers as makeshift artillery support for Massoud in his effort to hold on to one last piece of real estate in the north. To enhance the credibility of his information, Muhammad pulled up the sleeve of his shirt to expose a faded green tattoo of a soldier, the informal insignia, he said, of the Russian army unit he had been in when Tajikistan had been a Soviet republic. After decades of war in Afghanistan, remnants of battles past were everywhere, including neighboring states.

When the boat was finally fixed three hours later, the officer of the Tajik border forces invited us into a small metal shack where he checked our passports and our luggage. When he saw my camera and all my gear, he remained friendly but became suspicious. Elena told him I was a university professor, which was true, and that I was going into Afghanistan to

---

* A Muslim warrior engaged in jihad. In the West, the term had come to describe anti-Soviet fighters in Afghanistan following the 1979 Russian invasion.

conduct research—also true. I handed him a business card, which he couldn't read but that confirmed my credentials as an associate professor of journalism at the University of Hong Kong. He seemed satisfied, shook my hand, and ushered me out with a smile and instructions not to take any photographs during the crossing for security reasons.

Muhammad and I climbed aboard the ancient tug, surprised but grateful it floated. It looked like a metal quilt that had been patch-welded out of rusty corrugated sheets, and that one false step would result in lockjaw-inducing tetanus or a full breach of the rusty hull. But what the sad ship lacked in seaworthiness it made up for in horsepower. A large inboard prop engine drove the boat in a sweeping arc against the powerful current.

So little had changed here, I thought. So much water had flowed past these banks over the last twelve years, none of it able to wash away the memory and costs of this war. I had kept a journal during my travels in 2001. This is what I wrote of the crossing:

OCTOBER 2001

Shivering on a starless night. Waiting on the northern bank of the Amu Darya River. Waiting for a pontoon boat to ferry us to the other side. We are traveling with a thousand pounds of equipment and enough food and water to last us into December. This is where we cut the cord.

An old tractor engine mounted on the side of the raft spools up cable, pulls us toward the other side, pulls us

by the hand to the dance floor. Russian soldiers operate
the pontoon. They wear camouflage, wrap their heads
in Afghan scarves. We see only their eyes. They look
bemused as they ferry us across the threshold. A tiny chill
as we watch Tajikistan drift away. In this month-long
journey—15,000 miles by planes, cars, convoys, trucks,
and even donkeys, this narrow spread of water once
seemed uncrossable. No more. Tonight, in six minutes,
my boots will be covered with the dust of Afghanistan.

My interpreter Matin Sarfraz and my driver, his cousin Dost
Muhammad, wave to me from the shoreline. I was relieved to
see them, exactly where we had arranged to meet. Typical Afghan hospitality: they had arrived several hours early to make
sure they would be there to greet me had I arrived sooner. But
with all the delays, they ended up waiting almost half the day.

Matin had been a graduate student of mine at the University of Hong Kong (HKU), where he was on a special journalism scholarship for Afghan students. During his last semester
at HKU, I asked him to work for me during my time in the
northern Afghanistan; he was from Kunduz, a province in
the north, and his knowledge and contacts would be essential
in helping me complete my journey safely and successfully.
He agreed without hesitation, and we began meeting once a
week in the months prior to the trip, sketching out the journey with black markers on the dry-erase board in my office.
With his help, the boundaries and borders we had drawn on

my wall dissolved into this hot summer day. I had returned to the location of one of the most defining moments of my life.

Matin was a smart, thoughtful young man, a journalist of such high standards that the *New York Times* had hired him as their fixer and reporter in the north. He was just twenty-eight, married with three children and also supporting his parents, brothers, and sisters. He had a lot of responsibilities for someone so young but tried not to show the stress he was under. He was also in danger every single day in Afghanistan, unable even to use his own name in the bylines on his work.* Kunduz Province was one of the most conservative in the north, filled with Taliban and Taliban sympathizers. To work under his own name would make Matin and his family targets of extremists wishing to silence him and of opportunists hoping to profit by kidnap-for-ransom schemes, since local Afghans working for foreigners were always thought to be rich.

Because of my tiny budget (so typical for freelance reporters today), which had to cover all of my travel, accommodations, and food, Matin knew I couldn't pay him much. To make up for the shortfall, I told him that in addition to his salary I would give him all my video gear and an Apple PowerBook at the end of my trip so he could begin to produce short documentaries about Afghanistan on his own, something he had been inspired to do during his graduate studies.

I had also asked Matin to find me a traditional Afghan taxi, which would lower our profile on the road as we drove from

* He told me he wanted to forgo that anonymity for this story.

north to south. I grew a respectable beard in the month prior to the trip and asked Matin to get me a *shalwar kameez*, the long tunic and baggy pants traditionally worn in Afghanistan, Pakistan, and throughout Central Asia. In the past I had rejected dressing local, but Matin assured me that it would help me blend in and that even for those who did recognize me as foreigner, it would be seen as a sign of respect for local traditions and culture.

Since vehicles were licensed in their respective provinces, a Kunduz plate would get us stopped in Kabul, and finding a taxi we could drive everywhere proved difficult. Matin's solution was to ask his cousin, Dost Muhammad, to drive us in his own car. Dost was a minor celebrity in Kabul, an actor who also hosted several television programs, including one called *Mousetrap* that investigated political scandals.

Despite having not one, but two wives, Dost cultivated a devil-may-care-attitude that contrasted with Matin's responsible, family-man demeanor. Drive a Western journalist around Afghanistan? No problem! The car that came with him matched his oversize personality, a blue and white Toyota Corolla with the word *bahmani*—which in Persian means both "good purpose" and "avalanche"—emblazoned in bright red paint on the hood and both sides. In Dost's case, both meanings seemed to apply. On the dashboard, he had placed two plastic bobble-head tigers, one strumming a ukulele, so the vibrations of the car made it appear they were performing a hula dance.

In 2001, during my first taste of war here, it was difficult not to succumb to the romantic ideal of the intrepid foreign correspondent. Everything we reporters saw and did seemed to reinforce it. We rode on horseback to a series of World War I–type trenches where we watched Northern Alliance fighters chat with their Taliban counterparts on handheld radios, teasing and cracking jokes in between killing each other. Now, a dozen years later, my hair and beard were graying, the horses were gone—as were some of the colleagues—and the trenches were empty. I rode into the same war, but in the back seat of Dost's Bahmani-mobile. The romance, if not the danger, had worn off long ago.

After crossing the Amu Darya and reaching the Afghan shoreline, Matin and Dost helped me unload my gear and I took a long look around. What had once been just a tent and a few Northern Alliance soldiers was now a large, well-organized fenced-in compound, built by the Japanese and staffed by a company of Afghan border police. The setup seemed luxurious compared to the junkyard on the Tajik side, but given the investment in infrastructure that had been made in Afghanistan following the fall of the Taliban, I expected to see such basic improvements throughout the north, especially along the fortified border crossing.

We drove the winding dirt roads away from the river toward the district of Dasht-e-Qala; from the car window, I saw a farmer maneuver two large bulls behind a wooden plough, breaking up clods of earth. I felt a flush of nostalgia colored by the warm hues of sunlight and unexpected serenity. I was almost relaxed. It was very different from that first hour-long nighttime drive to our camp in 2001, when Northern Alliance fighters had run a price-gouging scam driving journalists from Dasht-e-Qala to Khoja Bahauddin using a fleet of Russian jeeps. Back then, an attempt by the driver to shake me down after our insane journey to the border had been the last straw:

From my journal:

OCTOBER 2001

Now I'm on the back of a bucking bronco. A Russian jeep really, but the same ride. We buck and heave through craters the size of the vehicle. The Perfect Storm *in dirt. There's an impact splinter on my side of the windshield. Forehead, I think, of a prior passenger. Least he softened it up for me. It's nearly midnight, and my vision feels like it's coming deep from within my head—like I'm looking through a mask. It's one of those instances where your momentum outpaces your mind. You are there, but in a dream.*

Before we reach the NBC compound in Khoja Bahauddin, our driver stops and turns off the ignition. He scratches his palm, then shows me two fingers. I pull out a twenty. He shakes his head. He writes on a scrap of paper, and by the orange glow of the gauge lights, I see these numbers appear: two, zero, zero. We have been shaken down at nearly every stop from Mashhad to Dushanbe. I'm rattle-cranked and full-body tired. All that's *left is anger and decibels. I crank up the volume, flap my arms, point a violent finger in his chest. He's surprised at my outburst. Finally, he turns the key again— for $100. A small victory, but even though no one can see it, I'm smiling for the rest of the ride. Even more so after we reach the camp and I learn that the going rate my colleagues were paying for the trip from the river was $200 per vehicle.*

2
CIVIL WAR

||||||||||||||

Dasht-e-Qala district police chief Imam Muhammad at his home
with bodyguards. He said he'd rather be a farmer than a police officer, but without peace he knows that's impossible.

Our first stop was the Dasht-e-Qala district police headquarters. The chief was a barrel-chested man named Imam Muhammad who had a kind but weary face. I removed my dusty boots and we were escorted inside his office. Matin gestured for me to take the seat to the right of the chief—the place of honor. Inside the room were Imam Muhammad's inner circle, officers he had handpicked, loyal friends or relations who also acted as his bodyguards. Another officer brought in two large watermelons and split them open with his knife, then used it again to grid the pink fruit into easily removable chunks. We reached down with our forks, jabbing at pieces and popping them into our mouths. I was parched from my travels, and the juicy sweet fruit helped revive me.

Matin spoke to the chief in between spitting seeds into his hands. Then he nodded toward me—my cue to talk. In an exaggerated pantomime I fall into when communicating with non-English speakers, I thanked Imam Muhammad for his hospitality, placed my hand over my heart as is customary in Afghanistan, and told him how happy I was to be back in Dasht-e-Qala. The chief smiled and nodded slightly as Matin translated, and then told him how I had been in the district in 2001 watching the battles from the trench lines, which weren't very far from his compound. After a few more minutes of polite conversation, we rose and headed back to the Bahmani-mobile. We were to meet the chief in a few hours at his home, where Matin had arranged for us to spend the night under his protection. It was a smart move, both for our own security and as a way to learn what had been happening in the region.

I was caked in dirt and sweat from the trip across Tajikistan, and Matin asked me if I wanted to take a shower before going to the chief's home. Most homes in Afghanistan, especially in rural areas, don't have running water, so Dost drove us to a small storefront in town. We were taken to a backroom lined with wooden benches and hooks on the wall for clothing. I pulled a towel and toiletry kit from my duffel bag and opened a door to a small, dark private stall. It had concrete walls and a white tile floor. A length of water pipe, painted green, had been secured against one wall and connected to form an upside-down L that ended in a sunflower-size white plastic showerhead. On the floor was a blue plastic basin. I stripped off my clothes and used the basin to wash them, rubbing them with a bar of soap, agitating and rinsing; it was a necessity when you had only three sets of shirts and pants for two months. I then rinsed myself under the cold water of the showerhead, scrubbing until what seemed like all the dust and dirt of Tajikistan swirled around the drain. There was a humility to the process that I appreciated, and I felt a small, ritualized transformation from the vanities and conveniences of the developed world to the challenges of this one. This I knew was, in part, what it was like to live like an Afghan.

Imam Muhammad's house was in the village of Ai Khanoum, near a cliff overlooking the Amu Darya. It was as close

to an Italian garden villa as I had seen in Afghanistan. While
the house itself was not so different from the single-story concrete bunker compounds of Afghan's better-off citizens (most
others lived in mud-brick huts), it was surrounded by copses
of fruit trees and flowers.

Ai Khanoum, which means "lady moon" in Uzbek, is a
historic place. In 1961, Afghan king Muhammad Zahir Shah,
while hunting near the village, discovered an ancient walled
city believed to be Alexandria-on-Oxus, a Greek town built in
the fourth century BCE in the wake of Alexander the Great's
conquest of the region. French archeologists began to exca-
vate the site in 1964 and continued until 1978, discovering a
palace in the city center, a temple to Zeus, a theater with seat-
ing for 4,000 to 6,000 people, a citadel with 30-foot towers,
and even a large gymnasium with a statue of the Greek god
Hermes. Other architectural artifacts were also found, including classical Corinthian columns and an ornate medallion depicting the goddess Cybele on a chariot being pulled by lions.
The excavations stopped after the Russians invaded in 1979.
During the civil war and the period of Taliban rule that followed, the exposed site became a magnet for looters, while
battles between Commander Ahmad Shah Massoud's forces
and the Taliban destroyed much of what was left. Sometimes
even history didn't survive Afghanistan's wars.

But Afghanistan's future, not its ancient past, was on my
mind as we gathered in Imam Muhammad's guest room.
Typical of those in most Afghan homes, the room was a large
rectangle, mostly empty except for the carpets covering the

concrete floor and small futon-like mattresses that guests could sit on while conversing and during meals and then sleep on at night.

Imam Muhammad's officers spread a large vinyl tablecloth called a *dastarkhwan* across the floor in front of us and proceeded to cover it with plates of food until none of it was left showing. We were served a feast of roast chicken, fresh tomatoes, peppers and onion, bowls of thin plain yogurt, and a traditional dish of meat and rice called pilaw that's eaten with fresh Afghan flatbread, as large and round as a spare tire. All of us were famished, and we wolfed down the dishes as if we hadn't eaten in days. Everything was rich in flavor—fresh tomatoes, rice cooked with saffron, the meat stewed tender in its own juices, the chewy, pillowy bread we wrapped around the roasted chicken and chunks of mutton and popped into our mouths.

Mealtime in Afghanistan is a relatively quiet affair; people prefer to concentrate on the food, saving conversation for afterward. This night was no different. When we had stuffed ourselves to capacity, the chief's men cleared the plates, removed the *dastarkhwan*, and brought out bowls of nuts and sweets and pots of tea or, as it's called in Central Asia, chai. In the north, unlike other parts of Afghanistan, they drink their chai without dropping in handfuls of sugar. As we sat back, full and comfortable, Imam Muhammad talked about the food he had just fed us as passionately as a chef on a TV cooking show.

"I would rather be a farmer than police chief," he told us. "I love the land. On my property I have *tarbooẓ* [watermelon], corn, everything you can imagine. All of what you ate to-night," he said, gesturing to the former spread, "came from my land."

He cracked almond shells by squeezing them in the palms of his large hands. Watching me struggle, he snatched them from me, cracked them easily, and handed them back, as if I were I child who couldn't figure out how to do it—all the while talking with Matin.

While he did seem to love his land and what it could pro-duce, there were other things that grew here too, crops much more profitable to cultivate. Drugs were a key part of the economy throughout Afghanistan. The commander gave us a lesson on the economics of opium poppy, which used to make heroin; Afghanistan is the world's largest grower.

"In Afghanistan, heroin costs $2,500 a kilo," he told us. "Across the border in Tajikistan, it doubles to $5,000. If it makes its way to Russia it turns into $13,000."

We asked him about another drug we had been hearing about called tabletka, a new and expensive, supposedly syn-thetic drug coming down from the former Soviet republics into Afghanistan. While most national drug officials seemed uncertain what it was, the effects—increased energy, height-ened chattiness, sexual arousal—seem to put it in the same category as the amphetamine MDMA, or Ecstasy.

He nodded his head and smiled—yes, he knew about tabletka. I asked him if his men were able to interdict any of the cross-border smuggling and if so, whether we could tag along to watch them.

"You have to go out very late at night and watch the river," he said dismissively. "You can sit there for hours before you begin to see them cross. It's very dangerous. They're not from this area."

It was an idea he didn't seem eager to entertain. And while drug smuggling was certainly a concern affecting the country's future, we had heard that something even more dangerous was once again moving across the borders into Afghanistan: guns. Some of the nation's most powerful warlords were openly admitting to rearming their own men to fight the Taliban on their own, unconvinced that the current Afghan National Security Forces (ANSF) could do the job after the scheduled withdrawal of U.S. troops in 2014. Imam Muhammad said he was not optimistic that he'd be able to retire to a life of farming anytime soon.

"I don't think the government will stay together," he told us. "We're already starting to see things pull apart. It's possible there will be civil war. Many of the local commanders don't have jobs. After 2014, they may have to fight again."

I asked him about the reports of warlords re-arming to fight the Taliban again and if he planned to do the same.

"If the central government doesn't stay together," he said, "I'll have to find a way to protect my people."

What he said was a bad sign. "My people" in Afghanistan means one's tribe. Very few outside of Kabul thought of themselves as citizens of the country—as Afghans.

Without a national identity, I wondered, could they ever really defeat the Taliban?

3
THE HOUSE OF MASSOUD

||||||||||||||

Afghan National Police take turns posing inside the room
where Ahmad Shad Massoud was assassinated.

The next morning, after having breakfast with Imam Muhammad, I drove east with Matin and Dost toward Khoja Bahauddin.

As we drove, the landscape washed over me like a childhood memory. I had traveled through it so many times in the past, driving from the Northern Alliance compound in Khoja Bahauddin to Dasht-e-Qala, then hiring horses to ride the last few miles to the front lines. The major landmarks looked the same—the mountains, rivers, and roads—but time had softened the sharp edges of war. I noticed cars and motorbikes and trucks filled with wheat and hay rather than soldiers. Where water had once been, sparse international assistance organizations had dug concrete wells topped with shiny metal hand pumps, visible every half mile.

On that first Afghan journey, I fell in love with my profession once again. Telling the post–9/11 Afghan story was a great privilege—a gift. There was nowhere else in the world I had wanted to be. Despite the hardships and fear, I had also felt a tremulous excitement every time we approached the frontline trenches, uncertain of what we would see that day.

I remained in love with my profession, but time had tempered both the recklessness and some of the excitement. In the past, I could work until I literally dropped from exhaustion and sleep wherever I happened to be. But years of this kind of living had taken its toll. Both my face and my mind had been indelibly changed by more than a decade at war. It was demanding, physical labor—donkeywork—and each year that passed my pack became a little heavier, the travel a little more taxing, slogging through endless hours of conversations and writing a little more challenging.

But with increasing physical liabilities had also come wisdom. The work felt harder, but I was doing it smarter. I understood the nuances of the environment. I had compiled an archive of knowledge and experiences during my travels, and the manic aggressiveness of my youth, when I had literally thrown myself at a story, had given way, thankfully, to a more considered and thoughtful approach. Patience and humility now trumped endless endurance. And most important, I had learned to look beyond the combat in war zones. While the guns were inherently dramatic, they weren't the only or even the most important part of a conflict. What happened to civilian society was the real barometer of war, and I needed to watch it closely.

When we reached Khoja Bahauddin, our first stop was again the district police headquarters. This, I had learned from Matin, was not only proper protocol but also afforded some measure of protection, as our safety would now become a matter of honor for the local police chief.

The commander's name was Asadi Noorullah, a man likely in his mid to late thirties. He welcomed us warmly. Chai and *tarbooz* appeared once again, and we talked while tucking in to the customary refreshments. After I explained to him that I had stayed at Massoud's compound at the start of the war, the commander smiled broadly. He had been a young fighter under Massoud, he said, barely out of his teens and engaged in the battle against the Taliban.

Noorullah said his forces were now much better trained and equipped thanks to NATO and the U.S., but despite this, he, like Imam Muhammad in Dasht-e-Qala, was deeply worried about the future.

"I have a big concern that when the U.S. leaves, we will not be ready to take over all security." Without a strong leader like Massoud, he believed the country would lack a center of gravity and that the old animosities among warlords would once again tear the country apart, allowing the Taliban to take advantage of the chaos and seize control, as they had in 1995.

I told him a bilateral security agreement (BSA)* was being negotiated between the U.S. and Afghan governments that would provide ongoing financial assistance and keep anywhere from two to twenty thousand U.S. troops in the country beyond the end of 2014. The commander nodded

---

* The White House is considering four options concerning the American troop presence and ongoing support for the Afghan government after 2014: In Option 1, a force of 10,000 American troops would remain in Kabul, Kandahar, Bagram, and Jalalabad until the end of 2015, with 5,000 NATO and other international troops based in the northern and western parts of the country as part of a NATO mission called Resolute Support. Option 2 would base a smaller troop contingent in Kabul and Bagram until 2016, but allowed for additional trainers and advisers for the Afghan forces. Under Option 3, only 3,000 U.S. troops would remain in Afghanistan and be restricted to Kabul and Bagram. Option 4, or the Zero Option, would be a complete withdrawal of U.S. forces. Karen DeYoung, "U.S. Examines Afghanistan Option That Would Leave Behind 3,000 Troops," *Washington Post*, February 24, 2014.

hopefully at the notion. But I knew at the time the odds of Afghan president Hamid Karzai signing the agreement by the end of the October 2013 deadline the Americans had set were not looking good. While a grand council meeting of Afghan leaders, called a *loya jirga*, overwhelmingly endorsed the BSA, Karzai was balking at making it official. Since his reelection in 2009, Karzai had become increasingly bellicose toward the United States, publicly criticizing the American military for the high number of civilian casualties he claimed it was causing. Karzai had also been calling for an end to American Special Forces night raids targeting Taliban leadership and complained the U.S. wasn't doing enough to bring the Taliban to the negotiating table. Indeed, to some observers, it seemed that Karzai wanted to sabotage the agreement outright; he had even arranged meetings with the Taliban without the knowledge of his American and NATO allies.[*]

In his January 2014 memoir, *Duty*, former U.S. defense secretary Robert M. Gates provided some explanation for the reasons behind Karzai's anger toward and distrust of the American government. Gates suggests that the Obama administration secretly helped Karzai's opponents in the bitterly contested 2009 Afghan presidential election, trying to ensure his defeat in "a clumsy and failed putsch."[†]

"The result was the worst of both worlds," said Council on Foreign Relations' Afghanistan expert Stephen Biddle to

---

[*] Azam Ahmed and Matthew Rosenberg, "Karzai Arranged Secret Contacts with the Taliban," *New York Times*, February 3, 2014.

[†] Robert M. Gates, Duty: Memoirs of a Secretary at War (New York: Knopf, 2014).

Foreign Policy magazine. "Karzai was reelected, and we now looked like we'd attempted to get rid of him and failed. Not good."* The White House denied trying to influence the 2009 Afghan election.

Another, more publicized obstacle for the BSA is the issue of immunity. The American government wants U.S. troops remaining in Afghanistan to have immunity from criminal prosecution in Afghan courts. Americans soldiers would be tried for crimes committed while on duty in Afghanistan under American law, in American courts. It was a sticky issue, one that had derailed a similar 2008 bilateral agreement with Iraq, leading to the complete withdrawal of American troops there.

The renewal of widespread violence in Iraq in the spring and summer of 2014, illustrated just how much was at stake. An Al Qaeda offshoot group of Sunni militants known as the Islamic State in Iraq and Syria (ISIS) was sweeping across northwestern Iraq, capturing major cities like Fallujah and Mosul and even threatening Baghdad. The country was in crisis mode. Perhaps recognizing that the lack of an agreement with the U.S. had left Iraq extremely vulnerable, Iraqi foreign minister Hoshyar Zebari urged Afghan president Karzai to take the bilateral security agreement deal in a meeting in Kabul in as early as December 2013.

According to the *New York Times*, Zebari said to Karzai: "Don't be under the illusion that no matter what you do the

---

* Yochi Dreazen. "Gates: U.S. Tried to Oust Karzai in 'Failed Putsch,'" *Foreign Policy*, January 9, 2014.

Americans are here to stay. People used to say that about the American presence in Iraq, too. But they were eager to leave, and they will be eager to leave your country as well."*

When we finished talking, Commander Noorullah insisted on providing us with an escort to the former Massoud compound, and twenty of his men piled into two green Ford pickups, which the U.S. had provided by the thousands—the official vehicle of the Afghan National Police. With a double cab, benches on both sides of the bed, and a mount for a light machine gun in the middle, it could easily carry nine or ten officers—and an intimidating amount of firepower—although open and without armored protection it was extremely vulnerable to roadside bombs, rocket-propelled grenades (RPGs), and even small arms fire. The Toyota HiLux, the pickup of choice of both the Northern Alliance and the Taliban at the beginning of the new millennium, had been replaced, it seemed, by the American-made Fords.

The entrance to the compound made it appear to be a fully functioning military base. Hesco barriers—wire and canvas baskets filled with rocks and sand—ringed the compound's outer wall, creating a maze through which entering vehicles had to pass. This allowed them to be stopped and searched for a explosives or insurgents. There was also a large sentry tower at the entrance packed with

---

* Azam Ahmed, "A Top Iraqi Official's Advice to Karzai? Take America's Deal," *New York Times*, December 17, 2013. Zebari's sentiments seem on target, at least according to a recent public opinion survey. A *Washington Post* poll conducted in December 2013 showed that 66 percent of Americans believe the war in Afghanistan was not worth fighting.

green sandbags and filled with well-armed guards. The structure was nearly identical to the one I remembered, but the grief and grim determination of the Northern Alliance fighters in the aftermath of Massoud's assassination no longer permeated the place.

As we rounded the corner, I saw the building that had been my first home in Afghanistan. It was an unusual shape for an Afghan building, an oval floor and roof sandwiched over a rectangle of living space. Eighteen round columns encircled the entire structure. But aside from needing a paint job, it was spare and very clean—unlike when we had occupied it. We'd packed it with more than a dozen staff reporters, producers, videographers, sound men, and engineers, all with their own equipment and kits. We'd filled the space with a clambering and chaotic urgency that contrasted sharply to the mopy, dejected Northern Alliance fighters.

Something else had changed: the front room of the house that had been Massoud's office, where he was killed, had been completely closed off when we were there in 2001. There had been a padlock on the door, and the windows had been boarded up with plywood. But now it was open.

I had looked at it daily, tracing with my fingertips the black phalanges that peaked from under the edges of the window coverings and locked door; they were the burn marks from the explosion that had killed Massoud. I once asked one of the fighters if I could go inside the room; he shook his head no and walked away.

This is how I described it in my journal at the time:

September 2001, the House of Massoud

We share a house with the Northern Alliance. No, actually more than that. We share with them the most sacred place in Khoja Bahauddin. This is where their leader, the Lion of Panjshir, was killed. This is the place General Ahmad Shah Massoud was killed, blown up by two assassins posing as television journalists. They had a bomb in their camera—it took out the "videographer," too. The "correspondent" was shot trying to run away. Samid told me that part.

He lives here as well, with a half dozen other soldiers. Samid was one of Massoud's bodyguards, out of town when it happened. He covers his face with his hands when he tells the story so I won't see him cry, but he has no tears left, only weariness. When he removes his hands, his face is as dry as Afghanistan.

Massoud fought against the Soviets when they invaded in 1979. Massoud fought against other muj when the Russians fled, and Massoud fought against the Taliban when they took power. He was killed by Al Qaeda, some believe, because he was the one warlord with enough skills to defeat the Taliban and oust Al Qaeda from its Afghan training grounds. He was a folk hero in many parts of Afghanistan. Now he's an icon. Nearly every vehicle here has his image plastered across the windshield. His house will become a shrine, they say, but for now, since we're paying for it, it's the Afghan Bureau of NBC News.

The three of us peered inside. It seemed that the house
of Massoud had indeed become a shrine. The once blackened walls were now covered with posters and photographs
of him as well as his quotes. The local police commander, a
man named Samiulla, met us at the door. He and twenty other
local police were charged with protecting the compound and
acting as guides for the "pilgrims" who came to visit. Even
though the rest of the building was nothing but empty rooms
and bare concrete walls, Samiulla said they got about thirty
visitors a month.

The place where Massoud had once lived still had a draw,
even for the national police who had escorted us to the place.
Many of the young officers posted only a mile or so away had
been only six or seven years old when Massoud was assassinated; they came and posed for photographs in the room with
the life-size poster of the man the Russians called the Lion of
Panjshir for his ferocity in battle.

As we walked around the building, each room brought
back new memories—the bathroom where a single toilet and
shower had served more than twenty people, the basement
bunk rooms that filled with water or sand, depending on
whether we had faced rain or windstorms that week.

Back then, I remembered, I woke up one morning to the
sound of sloshing water at the foot of my cot. I looked up to
see NBC engineer Paul Stimpson wearing his NBC protec-
tive suit—in this case, "NBC" stood for "nuclear, biological,
chemical," not our network—that each of us had in our survival kit in case of a chemical weapons attack. While there

was no sign of an attack, there was a steady downpour of rain, which had already flooded the basement and was now leaking into almost every other room in the building, including where we stored our most sensitive gear. For Stimpson, the NBC hazmat suit had simply provided the best way to stay dry, though the "chem couture" was a bit disconcerting for the rest of us. We scrambled to build makeshift water barriers and bailed out flooded rooms with plastic cups. Outside, we staked down our portable satellite dish and spread tarps across the rooftop to divert the rain. Finally, after battling the elements for hours, someone shouted that the rain was letting up.

"Yeah," producer Karl Bostic answered, "that's what Noah said."

On this day, there was nothing but sunshine, and I walked out back to the veranda and surveyed the verdant green fields and the kids playing on the banks of the Kokcha River near a concrete footbridge that looked very new. It seemed so pleasant—idyllic almost; it was hard to imagine there was still a war on. The same war.

4
THE GHOSTS OF KALAKATA

||||||||||||||

Destroyed and abandoned military hardware like this Russian tank
litters the Afghan landscape with the memories of wars past.

While walking through the Massoud house, my thoughts turned to a Radio France International journalist named Johanne Sutton. Just thirty-four years old, she had covered the conflicts in Kosovo and the Middle East and was one of just a handful of female journalists covering the war from inside northern Afghanistan.

In addition to being our home, the compound was also the de facto foreign ministry for the Northern Alliance, and as a result, a gathering place for dozens of journalists trying to get information on the fighting in the region. I remember seeing Johanne at the compound on the morning of Sunday, November 11, 2001. She smiled at me briefly as we passed each other on our way to the front lines. It was a sweet, shy smile, and I returned it warmly. It would be the first and last time I saw her alive.

That morning there was news that American air strikes and Northern Alliance fighters on horseback under the command of Abdul Rashid Dostum had pushed the Taliban out of the strategically important northern city of Mazar-e-Sharif, the fourth largest city in Afghanistan and the capital of Balkh Province.

Abdul Rashid Dostum was a legendary Uzbek warlord who seemed to change political allegiances as easily and casually as some people change their clothes. He had been both an enemy and an ally of Massoud. He had once fought on the side of the Soviets during their invasion and occupation and supported the communist government of Muhammad Najibullah* until 1992, but after the collapse of the Soviet Union, Dostum knew the Afghan communists wouldn't last and switched sides, partnering with Massoud against Najibullah.

In 1994, after fighting alongside Massoud to take Kabul and defend it against Pakistani-backed warlord Gulbuddin Hekmatyar, Dostum switched sides again, joining Hekmatyar's siege of Kabul. And when the Taliban captured Kabul, Dostum once again sided with Massoud, and then retreated with his sizeable army, reportedly as many as fifty thousand men, to his power center of gravity in Mazar-e-Sharif. Massoud and his forces then regrouped in his Tajik stronghold in the Panjshir Valley.

From 1996 to 1997, with thousands of troops still under his command, Dostum was at the peak of his power and able to maintain a nearly autonomous region from his base in Mazar-e-Sharif. He created an airline, printed his own currency, and, according to some accounts, created an environment favorable to women's rights. But in 1997, internal power struggles with some of his own lieutenants twice

---

* Dr. Mohammad Najibullah was the fourth and final president of the Soviet-backed Democratic Republic of Afghanistan from 1987 until 1992, when the mujahedin forces captured Kabul. Previously, as a member of the communist People's Democratic Party of Afghanistan, he had served as chief of the KHAD, the state intelligence agency and Afghan equivalent of the KGB, from which it received both direction and support. During Najibullah's tenure, the KHAD was accused of the widespread use of torture and the execution of political rivals. When the Taliban captured Kabul, they reportedly castrated Najibullah and dragged him behind a truck until he was dead. According to accounts reported on the BBC, his body was hung from a traffic light.

forced him into exile in Turkey. Dostum finally returned in 2001, when Massoud reportedly used CIA funds to fly him and his commanders back to Afghanistan to reconstitute their forces and open up a second front against the Taliban.

In early 2001, Massoud addressed the European Parliament in Brussels, warning that the Taliban and Al Qaeda had perverted Islam and that his intelligence sources had discovered that a large-scale attack against the United States was imminent. Six months later, he was dead and America was at war with Al Qaeda.

Though Dostum's penchant for switching sides made him suspect with some Afghans there was little doubt he was a proven warrior, bona fides enough for the CIA and special forces teams gathering in the north. Dostum and his men joined the fight against the Taliban with the support of Task Force Dagger, which included a group of U.S. Green Berets (Operational Detachment Alpha-595), air force combat air controllers, and the 160th Special Operations Aviation Regiment, all quickly assembled after the 9/11 attacks. On November 9, 2001, he, his men, and some of the Task Force Dagger Green Berets launched a series of charges on horseback, attacking Taliban lines in coordination with American laser-guided air strikes. The Taliban retreated, and Dostum took back control of Mazar-e-Sharif. The American Response Monument, also known as the Horse Soldier Statue, which is located across from Ground Zero in New York City, depicts a Green Beret on horseback and commemorates that action. "It's as if the Jetsons had met the Flintstones," special forces team member Ben Milo described that American-Afghan alliance in the early days of the war in the book *Horse Soldiers: The Extraordinary Story of a Band of U.S. Soldiers Who Rode to Victory in Afghanistan,* by Doug Stanton.

Dostum's success in retaking Mazar-e-Sharif inspired other Northern Alliance commanders based farther east, including Moammar Hassan, to begin their own advance. Another Uzbek warlord who had fought the Russians and whose family had wielded power in the region for generations, Hassan was a genial man who had studied economics at university and, unlike other commanders, seemed to enjoy media attention. Many of us, myself included, had stayed at his compound located on the fertile grounds of the orchards his family owned. We talked, laughed, and dined with him—and eventually asked when the offensive would begin. And now, it seemed, it would.

Nearly all the journalist were headed to the front lines, driving first to Dasht-e-Qala and then crossing the Kokcha River on horseback and riding the last few kilometers to the trenches dug into the hills of Kalakata, where the Taliban had been living in bunkers for more than a year.

Hassan had deployed his tanks along a wide swath on the ridge above the village of Chagatai facing the Kalakata hills. According to an account by Australian journalist Paul McGeough of the *Sydney Morning Herald*, the start of the attack was almost theatrical:

With a mix of bravura and contempt, he and his second in charge, Commander Amir Bashir, wandered openly in the line of Taliban fire. In the trenches we could hear bullets singing past our ears, but these two commanders refused to take cover.

Hassan held a two-way radio at arm's length, taking the pose of a Greek orator as he barked orders for the movement of men and machines. Then, with all the solemnity he could muster, he declared: "I order the men to start fighting."*

Together with a few colleagues, I headed to a Northern Alliance tank position on a hilltop known as Puze Pul-e-Khomri; a handful of others followed Hassan and Bashir to Chagatai Ridge. They included the Aussie, McGeough; my friend Levon, who had been born in Armenia but now lived in Canada and worked for the *Montreal Gazette*; a striking German reporter named Volker Handoik, whose curly blond hair fell past his shoulders and whose penchant for wearing a quilted green satin Afghan robe called a *chapan* made him stand out like some avenging angel from among the rest of us dusty, dreary war correspondents; and three other French reporters—Pierre Billaud, Véronique Reyberotte, and Johanne Sutton.

While we would all see battle that day, not all of us would survive. I barely escaped with my own life when a Taliban mortar shell exploded only 20 feet away; it injured a National

---

* Paul McGeough, et al. *Afghanistan at War: Australia's 9/11 Generation, Part 1*. "In the Heat of the Night." Sydney: Shortbooks (Interactive ebook curated by the journalists at the *Sydney Morning Herald* and *The Age*), March 9, 2002.

Geographic producer named Gary Scurka, who had been standing beside me.

From my journal:

November 2001 mortar attack

I am walking with my translator Shafiq. My skin feels flushed, and because I am wearing earplugs I can hear my breathing resonate through my skull. We are moving across the ridgeline now toward a Northern Alliance tank on a hilltop called Puze Pul-e-Khomri. This tank, a Russian T-55, has been firing into the Taliban-controlled valley. It is part of a Northern Alliance ground offensive following yesterday's capture of the strategic city of Mazar-e-Sharif. But the Taliban on this front line are firing back. They have tanks of their own. And mortars. And in the parlance of the military, they are currently "walking one in," firing and adjusting their 120-millimeter mortar to nail the Northern Alliance tank. We are doing everything you are taught not to do in hostile environment survival school. We are joining a firefight already in progress. We are advancing to a targeted position, just to get a better look.

According to a local Northern Alliance commander, the Taliban in the valley are some of the fiercest fighters in this war, made up mostly of Saudis, Chechens, and Pakistanis. Team bin Laden. But Northern Alliance commanders, I have learned, always say that. Their enemies are rarely just Afghans, but always the most highly trained Al Qaeda terrorists this side of the Amu Darya.

Regardless of their actual skill set, they are dropping some in our vicinity. From a bunker in the rear, we've timed their incoming mortar rounds. We've got between five and seven minutes to cross 500 yards. We hear the concussion of outgoing 81-millimeter mortars and machine gun fire all around, there's a bit of fear in every step, but the magic light of dusk has painted the mountain ridges burnt sienna and the trees below are awash in reds and yellows, and strangely, very strangely, I find myself thinking "what an absolutely beautiful fall day." That thought will soon be erased by a Taliban mortar that lands just 20 feet away from where we are standing.

Our timing is good. Shafiq and I make it across the 500 yards to the Northern Alliance tank position. We chat with the crew. Shoot some video. It grows quiet again—almost peaceful. Maybe, I think, this tank and mortar tennis match is over. In the meantime, National Geographic producer Gary Scurka, his shooter Neil Barrett, and USA Today writer Tim Friend use the lull to move up from the rear bunker to our position.

I videotape the tank commander, who is using the spotting scope I bought in Uzbekistan to spy on the Taliban below. An incoming 120-millimeter mortar makes a shrill whistling sound as it flies toward its target. It is a sound that seems so familiar from war movies that it is almost cliché—except when you hear it in person. Through my camera's viewfinder I can see the tank commander and his crew diving for the trenches. Before I can take cover, the round strikes the back end of hilltop so close to us that the concussion knocks me over and into the tank tread. Somehow I am still rolling. I turn and get the cloud of black smoke now drifting over us. Neil Barrett is standing intact, next to his tripod. Then I hear, "I'm hit. I'm hit and it's not in a good place."

I swing the camera around to see National Geographic producer Gary Scurka bleeding from his upper thigh. At that moment I faced a moral and logistical dilemma. I had to help him, but I also had to shoot the incident. He was, after all, only an arm's length away. This was the human face of the war, part of what had been missing in the news coverage so far—the aftermath of weapons release. But if his femoral artery was severed, Scurka would be dead in less than four minutes. I would try to do both—quickly. I film on, the gushing wound on his thigh, his hand covered in red trying to staunch the flow. I tilt up to the look of pain and disbelief on his face. But even in that moment, even in his shock—Scurka knew the value of what was happening to him.

"Shoot this," he groaned, "I'm bleeding."

So I do. For another ten seconds. Then I grab him with my left arm and while still filming with my right, we run to a trench 50 feet away. In the cover of the trench, I pull the Afghan scarf from his neck, wrap it around his thigh twice, pull tight, and tie it off in a square knot. I set my

camera down but leave it rolling. I want every frame. This
is what it looks like when bombs hit their targets, or just
miss them. I was here with a camera now, not yesterday
when ten Northern Alliance soldiers were killed near the
same position, not in a similar trench a mile away a few
hours later when three other journalist will be killed by
Taliban machine gun fire as they rode on top of Northern
Alliance armored personnel carriers.

Scurka will fully recover. He's the first American
wounded in Afghanistan by Taliban fire and a human face
who will help tell the story of the conflict. I think about
one of the dead journalists—a French girl who worked
for Radio France I met just that morning. She died in an
anonymous battle on an anonymous hill without a video
camera to capture it. And even though I knew her for only
five minutes, I will remember her shy smile—always.

I wouldn't learn what happened to Johanne Sutton and
the others until a day later, when my friend Levon told me
what took place on Chagatai Ridge. He said that after a
prolonged volley of shells, Hassan's second-in-command,
Amir Bashir, got a radio call from one of his commanders
saying that all five Taliban bunkers had been captured and
the area was clear—the enemy had been driven at least a
kilometer away. Levon said Bashir decided to inspect the
area and got into an armored personnel carrier, or APC,
even though the battle had lasted into the night and it was
already dark. Volker Handloik, who had stayed at Has-

san's compound the longest and had a good relationship with both the commander and his number two, asked if he could go along. Despite Bashir's warning that the area was heavily mined and that the Taliban could still be out there, Volker and then other journalists, including Levon, McGeough, and the three French reporters, all climbed on top of the APC, exposed and unprotected.

Levon said Bashir's APC moved toward the Taliban bunkers, careful to follow in the tracks of the other vehicles to avoid land mines. As they maneuvered around a large shell crater, they came under fire from about 30 meters away on their right. Levon told me there were at least five AK's and one light machine gun firing at them. They had rolled into an ambush.

He described the terrifying moments in detail in a dispatch he wrote for the *Gazette* on Monday, November 12, the day after the event—and also his thirty-second birthday.

As soon as the first shots were fired people started jumping from the armoured carrier.

Volker, who was sitting on the edge, appeared to be one of the first ones to jump. But he had been shot in the head and went into a death roll off the armoured carrier.

"Mines and unfamiliar territory, don't jump!" flashed in my mind.

Volker, in his green Uzbek coat rolling on the ground like a stuntman, was one of the last things I saw before the driver made a sharp left turn and started descending a steep hill. Those who had nothing to hold on to fell down. I was thrown in the air as we jolted violently and landed a metre away, flat on my back atop the armoured carrier, holding on to the cannon. Bullets started ricocheting off the armour; then I heard the familiar sound of the rocket propelled grenade and caught sight of an orange ball of fire moving fast in our direction. In the second it took the rocket to hit us I remember thinking: "If it's an anti-tank RPG, we're fried." The back doors of Russian armoured personnel carriers are hollow and serve as gas tanks; even a large caliber machine gun can turn the vehicle into a moving torch if it hits the doors. The carrier shook as the grenade hit us and I felt the explosion roll over me. Fortunately, it was an anti-personnel grenade and it didn't pierce the armour."[*]

Levon said the APC reversed directions and lurched forward, trying to get out of the kill zone. Other reporters may have jumped or been thrown off the vehicle as it headed for cover. Levon, who had once been a conscript in the Soviet army, relied on his former training: he remained calm under fire and made good decisions that saved his life.

"I grabbed the APC's gun turret and held on as it turned around and headed back to Northern Alliance territory," he told me back at the compound. "I'm just glad it didn't fire back at the Taliban, because my leg was right in front of the machine gun."

---

[*] Levon Sevunts, "We Were Under Fire," *The Gazette* (Montreal), November 12, 2001.

When they made it back to their own lines again, Volker Handloik, Pierre Billaud, and Johanne Sutton were all missing. Levon said Bashir sent out scouts to search for them. At about 9 p.m. he got a radio call from his men—one of the reporters had been found in the Taliban trenches, shot to death. It was Johanne Sutton. When they brought her back, Levon said the vehicle commander asked if he would hold on to her body to keep it from rolling off on the trip back to Khoja. He did. He described that slow, funereal procession for his paper this way:

> "Johanne's bullet-riddled body lay sprawled on the back of
> a Russian-made armoured personnel carrier, her dead eyes
> staring into the billions of stars in the Afghan sky. There
> was nothing I could do for her but to tie a piece of cloth
> around her head to close her half-open mouth and hold her
> lifeless hand for one last bumpy ride on Afghan roads."*

Handloik's and Billaud's bodies were found the next day. The three were the first foreign journalists to die in the Afghan conflict, but they would not be the last.

After talking with Levon, I made brief entry in my journal:

NOVEMBER 12, 2001—FRONT LINES?

It is the day after three European journalists were
killed here on northern Afghanistan's front lines. It is a
cruel day for this reason: the front line where they died

---

*Levon Sevunts,"We Were Under Fire," *The Gazette* (Montreal), November 12, 2001.

no longer exists. It is now three hours to the south. The
Taliban is on the run and Northern Alliance forces, which
recently controlled only 10 percent of the country, now con-
trol 80. If the journalists had waited one more day, just
one more day before climbing aboard Alliance armored
personnel carriers, there would not be three crude wooden
coffins in Khoja Bahauddin today.

But of course, they couldn't wait. They were journalists.
It's anathema to our very character to wait. But the price of
that impatience is sometimes very high. All these years later,
I wanted to again see the places where Johanne Sutton and
the others had lost their lives and where I, too, had come so
close to being killed. Matin made a call to one of his contacts,
a police commander in the nearby district of Khoja Ghar. He
knew the police commander in Chagatai, a man named Muhammad Ishaq, who had fought with the Northern Alliance
during that early offensive and remembered the deaths of our
three colleagues. He agreed to take us there.

Riding on motorcycles, Ishaq and his men escorted us first
to the trench lines where the mortar attack had occurred. We
parked our vehicles and began the long walk across several
acres of baked, red clay soil. It was late in the afternoon, an
hour or so from dusk, and the sun was slowly receding, the
harsh yellow reflection on the ground softening into a sooth-
ing rose color.

As we climbed a hill, one of Ishaq's men, dressed in khaki
fatigues and a red kaffiyeh piled loosely on top of his head,

showed us a small divot in the earth where a farmer had hit an old landmine with his plow, probably left by the Taliban years ago. He'd lost his foot, but he'd lived, said a local boy who had been following us as we walked. The mines, Red Kaffiyeh told us, were the only kind of violence left in Kalakata since the Taliban fled.

Once over the ridge, I saw the impressions of the old trenches snaking beneath the lip of the hillside like dry creek beds. I climbed inside and followed it as I had so many years ago. The trench led to a large pit, big enough and almost perfectly shaped to accommodate a tank. We were on Puze Pul-e-Khomri, the hilltop emplacement where the Northern Alliance tank had been during the mortar attack.

The years had packed the earth down as hard as concrete, and weeds grew around its edges. I closed my eyes and tried to imagine the moment of the mortar strike, its thunderous sound and the concussion that knocked my legs out from under me. It had been a monumental moment in my life, so I wondered why I didn't feel something equally powerful seeing it again.

But the site didn't make me swell with nostalgia. I had revisited that moment so many times in my mind over the years that I could easily have held on to it forever. What I really wanted to see was the place I hadn't been on that day, but still felt connected to: Chagatai Ridge.

Ishaq took us there next. We drove around several bends and down a steep hill, stopping next to a freshly plowed field. He pointed in the direction where the APC had crossed the field headed toward the Taliban bunkers. In my years of covering war I'd felt the fear of near-death experiences, the chilling emptiness of knowing that your life is likely going to end in a place so far away from the people and things you love that others may never know what happened to you.

I wondered if Johanne had felt that after she had jumped or fallen from the APC and been shot and then dragged back to the Taliban trench lines, her money and any other valuables stripped from her body as her lifeblood drained away. I hope not. I hope that she died quickly or was at least unconscious, existing in a place in her mind that was filled with happy moments, things that would trigger the shy smile that I had seen that morning before her death.

With the magic light of dusk, the Chagatai ridge of today began to feel distant in both time and geography from that earlier conflict. That so many of us had gathered here to remember Johanne Sutton, Pierre Billaud, and Volker Handloik made it somehow less lonely. There were no sounds of mortars or assault rifles, and all of the hills, as far as you could see, were covered in a golden crop of summer wheat, which people were harvesting with scythes, cutting small circular swaths, hands working across a clock face, just as they had for centuries.

A few days after the three journalists were killed in 2001, I returned to Chagatai ridge with some of my NBC colleagues. By the light of day, it was clear that the Northern Alliance had overrun the Taliban positions and was in full chase. We'd heard that the Taliban were fleeing toward Taloqan City and would perhaps regroup in Kunduz.

The bunkers they had left behind were too tempting for me to ignore. My colleagues warned me not to go inside the rabbit holes—that they could be booby-trapped—and they were right. But because I had survived the Taliban mortar, I felt invincible—the stupid invincibility that can get you killed. I climbed inside, and this is what I saw:

From my journal:

NOVEMBER 13, 2001, TALIBAN BUNKER

I am inside a Taliban bunker in the valley below Puze Pul-e-Khomri. It's an 8 x 10 room dug into the earth with a roof made of tree branches covered with sandbags. It's an unsettling realization that only two days earlier, men were shooting in my direction from this position. It's deep enough for me, at 6´1˝, to stand upright. As I shine my camera light around, the murkiness of this damp, dark place makes me think of the underwater video of the sunken Titanic. *A still life of common objects, as if the Taliban left with only moments to spare. There are matches and a candle on a tiny shelf cut into the clay. There's a fire pit in one corner and what looks like a small aluminum tripod in another—actually part of an RPG. I also see the bottom of a plastic water bottle. Inside, a sliver of soap and a filthy rag. A losing attempt at personal hygiene within this rabbit burrow, this dirty hole.*

Nearby is the carcass of a mouse. Skinned to the bone. A tiny snack, a mouthful of protein for men at war. But this is

the prize: a sheaf of notebook paper folded in half. It's cov-
ered with what looks like writing in two different languages.
My translator Shafiq tells me it is a homemade dictionary
of sorts. Urdu to Pashto. The language of Pakistan to the
language of Afghanistan's Pashtun people, many who sup-
port the Taliban since their dominant presence in the south,
near Kandahar, was the movement's spiritual and political
birthplace. It's anecdotal evidence of what Northern Alliance
commanders have been telling us: that many Taliban fight-
ers are actually foreigners—Pakistanis. But there is also a
larger picture here. Archaeology of war. Pompeii without the
volcano. Here, it says, is what men will endure when they
are locked in battle.

5
STICKS AND STONES

|||||||||||||

Uzbeks gather in Taloqan City to listen to their leaders speak shortly before violence broke out.

After ending our vigil on Chagatai Ridge, I ask Matin and Dost to head toward Taloqan City. I had gone there in 2001, following the Northern Alliance in their pursuit of the fleeing Taliban. When we'd arrived back then, the Taliban had just quit that city, and some of the residents were quick to celebrate their departure.

From my journal:

NOVEMBER 2001, TALOQAN CITY

We are in Taloqan, one of the latest places to be abandoned by the Taliban and first stop on our way to Kabul. Two local teenage boys greeted us in English as soon as we arrived. Now that the Taliban are gone they can listen to music again, they tell us, and the black turbans they were once forced to wear now lie heaped with other garbage. Young men play soccer in a park across the street. Now that the Taliban have fled, we are told, the teams can wear shorts again as part of their uniforms.

We'd camped out in an abandoned building in 2001. This time we stayed with one of Matin's family friends, a remarkable woman named Sammen Husini, who owned and operated a local radio station aimed at women listeners called Hamasada, which means "unity" in Dari, one of Afghanistan's two major languages. Husini and her husband were also connected to an old acquaintance of mine, former Northern Alliance commander General Moammar Hassan, in whose compound I had stayed in 2001. While the Uzbek warlord had played a critical role in helping to overthrow the Taliban, he'd now become involved in a growing rift with the Afghan national and provincial governments: ethnic Uzbeks felt that ethnic Tajiks, former allies in the fight against the Taliban, were monopolizing power at their expense. Husini set up a meeting with Hassan so we could discuss what this rift might mean for the future of Afghanistan. Could the former allies afford this kind of division when Afghanistan was still so far from being stable and secure?

With the exception of a few more wrinkles and a beard that had gone almost completely white, Moammar Hassan looked very much as he had twelve years earlier, his kind-eyed, genial nature still apparent. He shook my hand warmly upon entering Husini's guest room, where we had been waiting, and explained that while he was very busy that evening he wanted to make time for me since I was one of the journalists who had been there from the beginning.

"You've changed very little, Moammar Hassan," I said. He looked at me with my long hair and beard.

"You look very familiar to me as well," he said, being kind; I was certain he couldn't possibly remember me from among the swarm of journalists who passed through his compound.

He sat cross-legged on one of the pillows in the guest room, resting his hands on his knees—a meditative pose. My time with him was limited, so I jumped in quickly.

"Moammar Hassan, as a commander who's fought both the Soviets and the Taliban, what do you think will happen after 2014 if the U.S. withdraws all of its troops?"

"There will be a big problem," he said without hesitation. "People don't have trust in the government right now. In the twelve years the government was in power, they didn't attempt to get close to the people. They've failed the people.

"How has the government failed the people?" I asked.

"Corruption," Hassan continued. "All kinds of corruption. First, government officials are taking money from drug smugglers as bribes. Drug smugglers have strong links with officials at all levels of government. Second, there's corruption in the justice system. Judges and prosecutors take money from both those who are guilty and those who are not guilty— payments that keep them from being jailed. The justice system in Afghanistan doesn't work. The people are frustrated. And this is why in the western and southern provinces they go to the Taliban for justice and the application of Sharia law."

He was right, I knew. Corruption was endemic at nearly all levels of the Afghan government, with billions of dollars of U.S. and other foreign aid going largely unmonitored; it had likely done as much harm as good. Frustrated with the Afghan justice system, people were seeking redress for their grievances by other means, including the Taliban. It was just that kind of frustration that had brought the Taliban to power in 1996.

"Who's ultimately responsible, and what can be done?" I asked.

"Karzai," Hassan said, working his prayer beads with one hand. "Karzai is the first person responsible for all of this. If he did know about it, he needs to take responsibility. If he didn't know, he should have known. More than one hundred times I told him about this myself. He had all this opportunity to run the country. He had the resources and the support, but he also had people like [Marshal] Muhammad Fahim leading him in the wrong direction."

Muhammad Qasim Fahim* was Afghanistan's first vice president, an ethnic Tajik who had been Ahmad Shah Massoud's deputy and then succeeded him after he was assassinated. He was defense minister during the Afghan transitional government after the fall of the Taliban (thus the title of marshal) and was tapped by President Hamid Karzai to be first vice president during Karzai's 2009 reelection bid.

While Fahim helped shore up Tajik support for Karzai, a Pashtun, he had been a contentious choice from the start. He was neither charismatic nor photogenic—the very opposite of Massoud. Fahim was also alleged to have been involved in criminal activities, including kidnapping for ransom, smuggling, and other forms of corruption. His position as vice president, Hassan believed, had allowed him to advance his Tajik cronies (the Panjshiri Mafia, as they were sometimes called, since they, like Massoud, had come from the Panjshir

---

* Fahim died suddenly of a heart attack on Sunday March 9, 2014, just a month before the April presidential election. "It is with deep sadness that we learn of the passing away of Marshal Mohammad Qasim Fahim," Mr. Karzai's office said, declaring three days of national mourning. Matthew Rosenberg, "Warlord Who Tamped Conflicts as Afghan Vice President Dies," *New York Times*, March 9, 2014.

Valley) to positions of power in both the national and provincial governing bodies. Sometimes this came at the expense of other ethnic groups, like the Uzbeks, who, at just 9 percent of the population, didn't have much leverage to begin with. The most recent slight had come only a few weeks earlier, when the Takhar provincial police chief, an Uzbek, was sacked by the interior minister and replaced with a Tajik.

This had led to a weeklong protest by Uzbeks in Taloqan City, which, while peaceful so far, had the potential to turn violent. It was one of the reasons Moammar Hassan had come to town—to meet with other Uzbek leaders about the protest.

"Our main point is not to oppose the government of Karzai, but to rescue him," Hassan said, "but our rights must be recognized, too."

The ethnic and tribal divisions that have plagued Afghanistan have only ever been appeased temporarily—during fighting against the Soviets and the Taliban—but they've never been overcome.

"Before international troops leave Afghanistan, we need a free and transparent election. All parties should be invited to participate, even the Taliban," Hassan said.

This surprised me—the man had, after all, been so committed to toppling the Taliban just a dozen years ago. And in fact, thought he wanted elections to be held to engender a broader democracy, he had little faith that the Taliban shared his democratic goals.

"In order to be fair, the government has to invite the Taliban to take part in the elections. But people understand the

Taliban are not going to work on behalf of the country. They are only working for their own interest."

Perhaps things had changed in Afghanistan more profoundly than I had imagined. Here was a man who had been a part of the beginning of the offensive against the Taliban— uttering the dramatic command *"I order the men to start fighting,"* according to journalist Paul McGeough—now accepting their inclusion in the electoral process.

But with so much blood spilled already, I wondered whether that could ever actually occur. The Taliban were unlikely to agree to participate, and even former anti-Taliban allies, the Uzbeks and Tajiks, seemed headed toward a violent confrontation themselves in downtown Taloqan.

The next day I drove through downtown Taloqan City with Matin and Dost. It looked like an Afghan version of Occupy Wall Street. There were cops everywhere—at least four hundred of them; some were decked out in riot gear. There was even a cherry-red fire truck with a water cannon for crowd control, a gift from German International Security Assistance Force (ISAF) trainers. Streets were blocked off and Humvees with machine gun mounts were parked at strategic corners. More cops circled the city in the "official" vehicles of the Afghan National Police: green super-cab Ford pickup trucks, more "gifts" from the ISAF.

Ethnic Uzbeks had staged an ongoing, peaceful protest here, angry over what they believed was the lack of Uzbeks representation in both the provincial and national governments. Things had come to a head when the Takhar Province police chief, an Uzbek, was fired by the Afghan minister of the interior and replaced with one of his own cronies, a Tajik from Logar Province named Colonel Abdul Hanan Qataghni.

The contrast between the progress Afghanistan had made since 2001 and the challenges it still faced that morning was highlighted by the two stories competing for my attention: the progress toward women's rights, and the conflict between former allies.

Sammen Husini, at whose home we had spent the night, agreed to show me Hamasada, the radio station she had founded eight years earlier using German funding and her own determination. Her goal had been to break the isolation of so many Afghan women—some of whom felt like prisoners in their homes, unable, in some conservative areas, even to go to the market without being accompanied by a male relative. Her radio station gave them a sense of community and broadcast information about politics, health, and family issues. That women could listen to her radio station from inside their homes—where some were living nearly all of their lives— made the world bigger, accessible, and more interesting.

"I thought about how I should raise the voices of women. I think that the best way to reach them is through radio. Women are in the home, and they can listen without issues," Husini told me from her office and studio, purposely situated in a home in a residential neighborhood that did not stand out.

Husini said she had regularly received death threats from the local Taliban and others threatened by what she was doing. Her low profile confirmed that she took them seriously.

"We are afraid of them. They have real power, and they threaten us regularly," she said. Nonetheless, she was undeterred.

"By making people aware, they learn about their rights, and they can demand them. But they will face some obstacles and dangers," she said. "Radio helps to minimize those dangers, since they can listen in the safety of their own homes, or in their kitchens, where they have even more privacy."

The 300-watt Hamasada has an impressive scope and reach: it produces twenty hours of original programming each week and reaches just under a million listeners in the provinces of Takhar, Kunduz, and even distant Balochstan. While it airs some music and cultural programs, it's heavy on talk: *The Family Program*, which is aimed at both men and women, deals with family issues; *Roundtable* focuses on Afghan politics; and perhaps the most popular, *The Health Program*, is a call-in show during which a doctor answers women's health questions—an important resource in a place where many serious health issues are ignored because many can't afford to visit a doctor or are too afraid or ashamed to discuss their ailments.

The station, Husini told me, exists beyond the airwaves, sometimes breaking down barriers to seeking help.

"Women come to the station with their problems," she said. Which, she added, could be anything from domestic violence to health issues.

While we spoke, Matin called his contacts at the provincial police headquarters. Tension was continuing to build on the streets, and police prepared for what seemed an inevitable clash between the Uzbeks and Tajiks. I worried I might be missing a larger story—a breakdown in the anti-Taliban alliance.

Two of Hamasada's listeners, Najiba Haqqani and Homayra Sofezada, both teachers, came to the station at Sammen's request to tell me what the programs meant to them.

"When we are alone in our home and we are listening, we feel the entire community is with us," said Haqqani. "There are people I know whose families are upset about the radio. Husbands probably get upset, but it's helpful for us."

Sofezada nodded in agreement. "My whole family listens to this radio, and it motivates me to learn more."

Husini took me to a building in the back that houses the studio and control room. With two microphones set up on a long blue table around which six high-back chairs were arranged, the studio felt more like a formal dining room than a radio station, but perhaps that was the idea—to ensure the programs authentically reflected the lives of their listeners. The walls were painted colorfully in turquoise, pink, and red, and coated with a sound-absorbing material that had the look and consistency of sandpaper. Through a small window on one wall, you could see into the control room, where a twenty-year-old woman named Suwaba worked both a computer and the audio board to broadcast programs via a repeater tower located on a nearby mountaintop.

Dressed in a sharp business suit and wrapped in a headscarf, the diminutive Sammen Husini radiates a tireless drive that inspires devotion from her employees, who call her "Mom," and from her listeners, for whom she's unlocked the door to the home prisons in which so many of them are trapped.

Matin told me it was time to go. I posed for a picture with Husini and her staff, gave her a hug, and headed from one of Afghan's success stories to one of potential failure.

From Hamasada, we drove to Takhar Province's National Police headquarters. Matin knew the police spokesman, who got us a meeting with the new chief, Col. Hanan Qataghni, the man who had recently replaced the Uzbek chief.

While the Uzbek protests had been peaceful so far, we were told that some local shopkeepers were upset because the protests were keeping customers away and hurting their business. There were also rumors about a counterprotest where local Tajiks would confront the Uzbeks later that afternoon.

We were seated in Qataghni's office, a large room filled with burgundy-colored overstuffed leather chairs, glass tables, and fake flowers. Qataghni's dark wooden desk was positioned to one side of the room, but he sat across from us on one of the leather chairs. We had just sat down when one of his officers brought in four men handcuffed to one another. The men were all in their early to mid-thirties and each wore a *shalwar kameez* topped with a vest. They were beardless;

one had a headscarf hanging from one shoulder with the end clenched in his teeth. They looked defiant.

The officer told the colonel that the Uzbeks were trying to smuggle AK-47 rifles into the protest site. The colonel asked one of them a few questions, then nodded, and the men were taken away.

I asked the colonel how his men had discovered the guns.

"We use spies inside the protest to keep us aware of what's going on," he told me.

Not so different from any police force around the world, I thought.

"It's their right to protest," he said, "but we've mobilized our forces, and we'll be waiting for orders from the Interior Ministry for any further action."

A good sign, I thought: tolerating the concept of peaceful protest while policing its edges for sparks of violence. Maybe the $7 billion the U.S. had spent training the Afghan National Police (ANP) was beginning to pay off.

This would be one of the ANP's first big tests in a northern province: doing something more nuanced than fighting the Taliban. They would have to secure an area filled with lawful protestors expressing their dissent and protect both them and the community, all while keeping a lid on agitators from both sides pushing for violent confrontation. It would be a tricky operation for most police departments—even for those with much more practice. And there had been plenty of accusations—and evidence—against both of America's largest and most storied police departments, in Los Angeles and New York City, for brutality and heavy-handed tactics in their efforts to manage large, mostly peaceful demonstrations.

For the ANP, the stakes were high. Failure would likely mean the population in the area would continue to lose confidence in the police and the national government, something both northern warlords and the Taliban could capitalize on following the planned international withdrawal. And considering its history and reputation, the ANP's success was far from certain. Many regional experts saw them as one of the most corrupt institutions in Afghanistan. It is an unfortunate reality that three out of five Afghans regard the ANP—the de facto face of the national government for most Afghans—as corrupt, according to a 2011 survey conducted by the United Nations Development Programme.[*]

Of the ANP's roughly 157,000 personnel, more than 90 percent are illiterate, and an estimated 4 out of 10 police recruits tested positive for drugs.[†] And with only six weeks of training, some critics claim that the authority they're given merely makes the recruits more efficient at extorting those whom they are supposed to protect. But it's easier to understand their participation in such extracurricular activities after considering that theirs is one of the most dangerous jobs in the country. In late July 2013, Afghanistan's interior min-

---

[*] United Nations Development Programme, Police Perception Survey–2011, Afghan Center for Socio-Economic and Opinion Research (ACSOR) Surveys, Kabul, Langer Research Associates , 2011, UNDP-Afghanistan.

[†] Police Perception Survey–2011.

ister announced that a whopping 2,700 Afghan policemen had been killed or injured in the preceding four months.* And according to a report by the United States Institute of Peace, Afghan police officers are killed at three times the rate of Afghan National Army soldiers.

Still, Qataghani was steadfast in his claims that things were under control. "This is a completely Afghan operation," he told me. "We can take security into our own hands."

After we left the colonel's office, we walked down the street to meet with Haji Jamshed, one of the leaders of the Uzbek protest who also serves on Takhar's provincial council, part of the regional governance.

"We will try our best not to be violent," he said, "but if the government is violent against us, we will respond . . . with stones and sticks, not with bullets."

I spoke with him inside a small glass building located on the central downtown traffic circle that police used to monitor motorists. The Uzbeks had been occupying the building for a week, using it as a headquarters for organizing the protests.

I asked Haji Jamshed whether, as a member of the provincial council, he was concerned about the ability of the police to maintain order. If they failed, I asked, would it confirm the international community's worst fears about Afghanistan's inability to handle its own security or, even worse, embolden the Taliban to exploit the situation?

---

* Hamid Shalizi and Jessica Donati; "Afghan police deaths double as foreign troops withdraw," Reuters, September 2, 2013, http://www.reuters.com/article/2013/09/02/us-afghanistan-police-idUSBRE9810EP20130902.

"That's not up to us to decide," he said. "We simply want our rights." Our conversation was interrupted by his cell phone's ringtone. He answered, listening intently to the caller before hanging up and relaying the information to me: "It seems the government is organizing a counterprotest."

"How do you know that?" I asked.

"We have our informers inside," he said, smiling.

While Afghanistan's ethnic Uzbeks and Tajiks have historically been mistrustful of each other, they have at times been forced to put aside their differences to fight greater enemies. This was true during Soviet invasion in the 1980s, and more recently when they banded together against the Taliban. But while they share the common goal of ousting extremists from their country, twelve-plus years of constant battle have also deepened longstanding rifts between them.

A few hours later, I would see this rift turn violent in downtown Taloqan. Matin, Dost, and I were sitting in the Bahmani-mobile, parked on a street near police headquarters, when we saw groups of police vehicles speeding away from the downtown area. I asked Dost to follow them, which led us directly into the middle of the confrontation a half mile away.

I told Dost to remain in the car in case we needed to make a quick exit. Matin walked with me to where as many as five hundred men lined the street, taunting one another. The Tajiks stood on one side, with the majority of the police forces standing behind them in what appeared to be a display of support. Standing about 100 feet away were the

Uzbeks. A member of each group carried a large Afghan flag, but the Tajiks also hoisted a photograph of Marshal Fahim, Afghanistan's first vice president (to provide more balanced ethnic representation, there are two vice presidents) and the most prominent Tajik in the national government.

At first, only insults were hurled, but the atmosphere soon bristled with menace as young men gathered stones. One side was shouting things like "Kill all the Uzbeks," and the other responded with declarations like "This area is for Uzbeks, not Tajiks." Soon the first rock was thrown—I didn't see by whom—and both sides unleashed volleys of stones and debris.

As I waded in to shoot video and photographs, Matin told me to be careful. He had heard some men behind me say, "Look, there's a foreigner, hit him with some stones and they'll think it's coming from the other side." Fortunately, no one acted on the suggestion.

It wasn't long before members of the crowd removed their headscarves and fashioned them into homemade slingshots. A violent rhythm ensued: The Tajiks would advance with their flag as if they were storming the Bastille. Then they would be momentarily repelled as the Uzbeks charged ahead in the same fashion, stopping just short of crossing the invisible but mutually understood dividing line. The battle finally erupted when the Uzbeks grabbed hold of a Tajik man and beat him. The Tajiks responded by pelting the second story of a nearby house where a small group of Uzbeks had holed up to watch the fight.

Instead of using their new fire truck's water cannon or other tactically sound methods to disperse the increasingly agitated crowd, most of the police watched the brawl progress from behind the Tajik line and did nothing to prevent its escalation. During lulls in the fighting, a dozen officers would approach the mob and impotently attempt to separate the groups by chiding them as if they were school kids fighting on the playground.

We watched the debacle unfold until dusk, when it seemed to be winding down, so we left. But a few hours later we learned that shortly after our departure, the protestors had taken out their guns and begun shooting. By the time the mob had dispersed, three people lay dead in the street and fifty-two others had been wounded.

Even more depressing, the incident served as yet another example of how the billions of dollars invested in staffing, tactical training, and nonlethal weaponry for the ANP had been wasted. And I wondered if the situation were even more troublesome than it appeared: had the phone call that the Uzbek leader Haji Jamshed received earlier alerted him to something sinister? He had mentioned that the government was organizing a counterprotest. Had the ANP had forgotten their training on purpose—or perhaps even instigated the violence?

The police denied the allegations of complicity, but their inaction, especially when things turned violent, could itself be considered criminal. It raised a key question the international community has been trying to answer for years: would Afghan security forces be capable of keeping the peace when

there were no longer any American or NATO troops around
to provide support? If the results of this Uzbek-versus-Tajik
confrontation were any indication, the answer, at least in
Takhar Province, was clearly no.

But who or what was to blame? Was it poor pay, bad training, an endemic culture of corruption? Or was it simply impossible to assemble an efficacious national police force in the
world's tenth-poorest nation in less than a decade, in the middle
of a war? Whatever the answer, the national police had once
again neither earned nor inspired any respect—certainly not
from those whom it had failed to protect that day; the injured
on both sides, the friends and relatives of those killed, but also
the larger community likely puzzled that its internationally
trained and funded police couldn't even stop a street brawl.

That evening, we drove to Matin's hometown of Kunduz
City, where we planned to overnight. I was eager to see it;
I'd been there only during a fleeting nighttime stopover years
earlier while I was chasing the Northern Alliance chasing the
Taliban.

Kunduz is unusual for a northern province. Unlike Takhar,
its neighbor to the east, which is made up mainly of Uzbeks
and Tajiks, nearly half of the residents of Kunduz are Pashtun,
many of whom migrated to the region in the 1800s. (Matin's
own family was Pashtun.)

I was intrigued by stories that the Taliban had once again
been gaining a foothold in the area, so much so that Ameri-

can commanders were worried about a disruption in the vital NATO supply line that ran into the country from Tajikistan.

A Taliban resurgence in Kunduz wasn't hard to explain. A myriad of militias in the province, some directly and some loosely affiliated with the Taliban, provided an ongoing feeder source for insurgent activities. The groups included the infamous Haqqani Network, the Islamic Movement of Uzbekistan (IMU), and former Massoud foe Gulbuddin Hekmatyar and his Hizb-i-Islami group.

But before this recent resurgence in late November 2001, Kunduz had also been the site of two of the darkest and most troubling incidents of the war. They occurred when Taliban and Al Qaeda fighters, retreating from Taloqan and Mazar-e-Sharif, were in desperate straits, surrounded by Northern Alliance troops. They either had to surrender or risk being massacred. As it turned out, they were massacred after surrendering.

On the outskirts of the city as many as three thousand Taliban fighters surrendered to the forces of Gen. Abdul Rashid Dostum (of the now legendary Task Force Dagger horseback charge). The prisoners were separated; between three hundred to five hundred of them, those suspected of being foreign fighters, were transported to a nineteenth-century fortress known as Qala-i-Jangi that Dostum had used as his headquarters in Mazar-i-Sharif.* The rest were to be sent to

---

* The CIA questioned the captive fighters sent to the old fortress and became particularly interested in a "Sulayman al-Faris" who turned out to be the man who would become known as the "American Taliban," John Walker Lindh. The interviews were interrupted by a bloody

Shibarghan, a prison about one hundred miles away, run by Dostum's forces. According to witnesses quoted in the *New York Times** and *Newsweek*,[†] the Taliban prisoners destined for Shibarghan were forced into metal shipping containers with little room and no food or water. Hundreds or even thousands of the Taliban prisoners reportedly died from suffocation or dehydration en route. There were even allegations that some of Dostum's men fired into some of the containers.

The bodies were reportedly buried in the desert in a mass grave outside Shibarghan. Dostum has denied his forces purposely killed any Taliban, claiming that only two hundred had died on the way to the prison, and claimed they'd died of disease and combat injuries. Early calls for a thorough investigation were thwarted by the Bush administration, according to a 2009 article in the *New York Times*,[‡] which cites Dostum's connection to U.S. Special Forces and also implies that he, like so many anti-Taliban warlords, was on the CIA's payroll. While the issue of the Talib deaths in the shipping container may have haunted Dostum's past, it doesn't seem to be thwarting his political future. Dostum was chosen by Afghan presidential candidate Ashraf Ghani

---

prisoner uprising which started on November 25 and was finally suppressed on December 1, 2001. By the time it was over, more than eighty prisoners were dead, along with some of their guards as well as the first American casualty of the war, CIA officer Johnny "Mike" Spann.

* Carlotta Gall with Mark Landler, "A Nation Challenged: The Captives; Prison Packed with Taliban Raises Concern," *New York Times*, January 5, 2002.

† John Barry, "The Death Convoy of Afghanistan," *Newsweek*, August 25, 2002, updated March 13, 2012.

‡ James Risen, "U.S. Inaction Seen after Taliban POWs Died," *New York Times*, July 10, 2009.

to be his chief running mate and the ticket took second place in the April 5, 2014, election. That gained them a spot in a June 4 runoff election against former foreign minister Dr. Abdullah Abdullah. (After the runoff, Abdullah accused President Hamid Karzai of ballot stuffing in favor of Ghani. As of this writing, the runoff candidates have agreed to a complete recount of all the runoff ballots.) If successful in the runoff, the notorious warlord could become the second most powerful man in Afghanistan.

But while the Kunduz containers story is dark, another event, if true, is a grotesque geopolitical absurdity built atop so many lies and betrayals that it prompted the United States to knowingly help its own enemies escape from the city during the early days of the war.

In addition to the thousands of Taliban fighters who had already surrendered to Dostum in Kunduz in 2001, thousands more were trapped in the city. Trapped with them were their Al Qaeda comrades, as well as Pakistani military and intelligence advisors and volunteers. Many had been in Afghanistan prior to 9/11, helping the Taliban in their fight against the Northern Alliance. While the Afghan Taliban might expect some lenient surrender terms from their countrymen, the foreigners, especially the Pakistanis, would likely be dealt with more harshly.

This, according to different media accounts about the incident, put Pakistan's president, Pervez Musharraf, in an uncomfortable position. Musharraf had seized power in a military coup in 1999, and his hold on the presidency was shaky, especially after he came out in support of America's military actions in Afghanistan; his own military—including Inter-Services Intelligence (ISI), Pakistan's spy agency—had been supporting the Taliban for years.

The capture or death of so many Pakistani soldiers and spies in Kunduz might have been enough to bring down the Musharraf government. With the Afghan war already going full tilt, it was a scenario the Bush administration reportedly did not believe it could afford. The Americans purportedly struck a deal that allowed Pakistan to land two army cargo planes, pick up their men, and fly them back to Pakistan.

But then, of course, it all went to shit. In an article in the *New Yorker* aptly titled "The Getaway," veteran journalist Seymour Hersh, who also broke the story of the Mai Lai massacre in Vietnam, wrote:

American intelligence officials and high-ranking military officers said that Pakistanis were indeed flown to safety in a series of nighttime airlifts that were approved by the Bush administration. The Americans also said that what was supposed to be a limited evacuation apparently slipped out of control, and, as an unintended consequence, an unknown number of Taliban and Al Qaeda fighters managed to join in the exodus. "Dirt got through the screen," a senior intelligence official told me. Last week, Secretary of Defense Rumsfeld did not respond to a request for comment.*

---

* Seymour M Hersh, "The Getaway," *New Yorker*, January 28, 2002.

In a column on MSNBC.com, journalist Michael Moran wrote, "calls by MSNBC.com and NBC News to U.S. military and intelligence officials shed no light on the evacuation reports, though they clearly were a hot topic of conversation. 'Oh, you mean "Operation Evil Airlift"?' one military source joked."*

The Pakistan and the U.S. governments both denied the airlift had taken place, but the end result, according to those who pieced it together through military sources, eyewitness accounts, Indian military intelligence reports, and other sources, was that not a few, but possibly thousands of Taliban and Al Qaeda fighters, in addition to Pakistani military and intelligence personnel, were whisked away to Pakistan, able to return to Afghanistan to fight and kill Afghans as well as the soldiers of the country that had just helped set them free.

I heard a rumor about the story when I arrived in Kunduz, in 2001, but thought it too preposterous to be true. Now it seems perfectly clear: the decision to enlist Pakistan as a close ally in the Afghan war is one of the reasons it is still going on.

But perhaps the most shortsighted covert gambit the U.S. had made in Afghanistan—and the one with the direst consequences—was made following the Russian invasion in 1979. The United States had again been relying heavily on Pakistan and its ISI spy agency to aid the Afghan mujahedin resistance to the Soviets.

---

* Micahel Moran, "The Airlift of Evil: Why did we let Pakistan pull 'volunteers' out of Kunduz?", MSNBC.com, November 29, 2001, http://www.nbcnews.com/id/3340165/ns/world_news-brave_new_world/t/airlift-evil/#.U6kAP42SxDJ.

That led the CIA to provide the lion's share of weapons and funding to two of the ISI's favorite mujahedin leaders, Jalaluddin Haqqani and Gulbuddin Hekmatyar, founders of the Haqqani Network and Hizb-i-Islami, organizations affiliated with the Taliban and Al Qaeda that have been among the most active, and in Haqqani's case, the most effective armed militias opposing U.S. efforts in Afghanistan to this day.

As the leader of the Mujahedin Army from 1980 to 1992, Jalaluddin Haqqani recruited foreigners to help fight the Soviets, including Saudi national Osama bin Laden. Some experts also believe that Haqqani was key in helping bin Laden escape from Tora Bora to Pakistan in 2001, since his forces operated, and continue to operate, on both sides of the border, finding safe haven in North Waziristan, Pakistan's tribal areas that form the country's border with southeastern Afghanistan.

While Haqqani is reportedly a member of the Taliban's ruling council, or Quetta Shura, experts believe the organization maintains its own leadership and fighters and conducts independent operations. Haqqani's son Siraj is now leader of the Haqqani Network. According to the Institute for the Study of War (ISW), a Washington, DC, think tank, he is more extreme than his father, maintains a closer relationship with Al Qaeda and other foreign extremists in Pakistan, and has been a willing proxy in Pakistan's ongoing conflict with its archenemy India by attacking the sites of Indian investments in Afghanistan.

In a brief on the Haqqani Network, ISW analysts wrote:

The Pakistani army has consistently refused to launch a military operation in North Waziristan despite the presence of Al Qaeda senior leadership. Elements within the Pakistani security establishment continue to view the Haqqani Network as a useful ally and proxy force to represent their interests in Afghanistan. To this end, Haqqani forces have repeatedly targeted Indian infrastructure and construction projects in Afghanistan.*

Gulbuddin Hekmatyar's Hizb-i-Islami has also wreaked havoc across Afghanistan, but the well-publicized double-crossings of its leader, who, in his early years was pro-Soviet, then fought against them, and later regularly joined and broke alliances with other warlords as it suited him, have diminished some of its current influence. Like Abdul Rashid Dostum, Hekmatyar was once a pro-Soviet militant and member of the communist People's Democratic Party of Afghanistan (PDPA), but he evolved early on into an Islamic extremist whose followers have been accused of throwing acid in the faces of unveiled women and who himself was arrested for the alleged murder of a fellow student while studying at Kabul University. Hekmatyar founded Hizb-i-Islami in 1977, and with the aid of the Pakistani ISI and the CIA took it into the fight against the Soviets in 1979.

---

* Jeffrey A. Dressler, "Afghanistan Report #6: The Haqqani Network from Pakistan to Afghanistan" (Washington, DC: The Institute for the Study of War, October 2002).

But while he received as much as $600 million in aid from the U.S., according to author Peter Bergen's *Holy War, Inc.: Inside the Secret World of Osama bin Laden*, "Hekmatyar's party had the dubious distinction of never winning a significant battle during the war, training a variety of militant Islamists from around the world, killing significant numbers of mujahedin from other parties, and taking a virulently anti-Western line."[*]

When Afghanistan's communist government fell in 1992, Hekmatyar's Hizb-i-Islami was also accused of being the primary instigator of the battle between Afghan warlords that led to the deaths of fifty thousand civilians; Heymatyar's group was singled out for intentionally shelling civilian areas. When the Taliban wrested power from competing warlords and took control of the country in 1996, Hekmatyar fled. But after the U.S. invasion in 2001, he voiced support for the Taliban insurgency and has reportedly reconstituted a military force.

However, the ISW reports[†]that in since 2004, as many as 150 of Hekmatyar's former commanders laid down their arms and formed a new political party called Hizb-i-Islami Afghanistan (HIA), which supports the presidency of Hamid Karzai. Hekmatyar declared in an interview that those who have joined the Afghan political process are no longer part

---

[*] Peter L. Bergen, *Holy War, Inc: Inside the Secret World of Osama bin Laden* (New York: Free Press, 2001).

[†] The Institute for the Study of War, "HIZB-I-ISLAMI GULBUDDIN (HIG)," Washington, DC:, http://www.understandingwar.org/hizb-i-islami-gulbuddin-hig.

of his organization, now called Hizb-i-Islami Gulbuddin, or HIG.

Karzai has made overtures to Hekmatyar, hinting at a cabinet position for him, but so far he's resisted. The U.S. government still designates him as a "global terrorist," and American and Afghan military commanders still consider HIG a component of the Taliban threat.

In Kunduz, Matin had an office in a small compound where he worked with other local journalists. A German NGO had wired the place with a communications satellite dish, and the journalists had high-speed Internet access that was likely the best in the country. He thought it would be a good place to lie low until nightfall. At the office, I wrote my story, selected some pictures, and edited some video for a web post on Vice.com about the Taloqan street fighting I had just witnessed. It was dark by the time I uploaded everything. We drove to Matin's home and parked inside the gates so onlookers wouldn't see us.

Simply by having a foreigner stay at his house, Matin was inviting an attack by the Taliban and putting himself and his family at risk for kidnapping and other violence. I had protested: staying with him would be too dangerous. But he'd insisted. Afghan's do not take hospitality lightly.

I was dirty and exhausted from the day's events and just wanted to clean up and go to sleep, but part of what had been missing from my previous reporting about Afghanistan was the rhythm of workaday family life. I had focused so much on war that my audience had almost no context—how most Afghans actually live.

Matin's family overwhelmed me with kindness. Running water is a luxury in most Afghan homes. Matin's house had indoor plumbing, but it wasn't working. So his brothers brought up a large bucket and a plastic cup to the bathroom so that I could "shower."

As I squatted on the tile floor and dumped cups of water over my head, the electricity went off for a few minutes— something Afghans endure daily. I paused for a moment in the darkness to remember where I was and to appreciate both the generosity and courage that surrounded me. My experience of these hardships was, after all, a choice—I was free to leave at any time. When I was finished cleaning up as best I could, I pulled on my dirty clothes—I had no clean ones left—and went downstairs.

In the guest room, Matin's family rolled out the *dastarkhwan* and then covered it with delicious food—pilaw, bread, vegetables, a lemony noodle soup called *osh*, and a thick yogurt drink called *doogh*.

After the plates were cleared, we went to sleep in the same room, on paisley-covered mattresses under the steady buzz of a ceiling fan on turned up as high as it would go. In the morning, we slipped out early to avoid nosy neighbors and began our trip to meet an infamous Turkman warlord named Nabi Gechi.

6

THE WARLORD AND
THE TALIBAN

||||||||||||

Northern Afghan warlord Nabi Gechi flanked by bodyguards at one of his eighteen military outposts throughout the Qal-i-Zal district in Kunduz Province.

Nabi Gechi's men looked like pirates. Not skinny Somali pirates, but the kind you find illustrated in a Howard Pyle book or on a ship in the middle of the seventeenth century, wrapped in dark turbans, flashing hard steel and cold stares.

They were a microcosm of Afghan society—Turkmen, Hazara, Uzbek, Tajik. They were men who'd fought alongside Gechi for years—some had even fought against him. All of them earned and continued to earn their living in blood. To lead killers like that you need to be a killer yourself—the best killer of them all—and the men you lead must believe that you are difficult, if not impossible, to kill. It was obvious that Nabi Gechi's men believed this. If they didn't, at least one among them might have tried to collect the price on his head.

"There's a $500,000 reward to kill Nabi," said Mullah Jilani, a former Taliban soldier turned Gechi lieutenant. "The Taliban are very afraid of him."

Two years ago, when Jilani had been with the Taliban, he'd wanted to kill Nabi Gechi. And shortly after Gechi was hired to provide security for his home district of Qal-e-Zal in northern Afghanistan's Kunduz Province, Jilani said he did, in fact, set out with more than two hundred of his Taliban comrades to assassinate him.

Instead, Gechi routed them. According to Jilani's explanation, Gechi executed a flanking maneuver that seemed straight out of Sun Tzu's *The Art of War,* corralling most of the Taliban in one of the wooden stalls in the village market. Then, using his favorite weapon, the Russian GP-34 rifle-mounted 40-mm grenade launcher, he killed the Taliban commander.

"After that," said Jilani, "we called off the attack and left the village."

When Gechi defeated the Taliban during a second assassination attempt, Mullah Jilani arranged a meeting with the warlord.

"I told him, 'I don't want to fight you anymore. There's no benefit for either of us,' " Jilani told me. Then he switched sides and began fighting with Gechi against the Taliban.

Gechi's reputation as the fiercest Taliban killer in the north has only grown since his return to the district. In early July 2013, he directed an attack against a house in northern Afghanistan filled with Taliban. After his men surrounded the house, Gechi, again using a rifle-mounted grenade launcher, personally unleashing a hell storm that seemed extreme even for Afghanistan. Each grenade had a lethal blast radius of 18 feet, and Gechi fired not just a few, not a dozen, not 50 or even 75. Gechi alone fired 123 grenades at the house. They were meant to be lobbed in a long arc at a target hundreds of meters away, but Haji Muhammad, Gechi's son-in-law and bodyguard, said the commander fired them like they were bullets—straight at his target.

I had come here to meet this warlord, who until recently had been on the Americans' payroll in their effort to roll back the Taliban resurgence in the region. Although feared by most, Gechi was also revered by many in the Qal-e-Zal District as their protector and enforcer—a thoughtful, soft-spoken local boy who carried a big grenade launcher.

He made his name not with talk but by plying Afghan's national trade: warcraft. He'd distinguished himself in the past as a lieutenant with some of the biggest and bloodiest names in Afghanistan's warlord business, including Gulbuddin Hekmatyar and Abdul Rashid Dostum.

So it was surprising when, in 2009, Gechi gave up the fight to start a successful fish and kebab restaurant in Mazar-e-Sharif. But two years later, in 2011, the local elders asked him to come back to Qal-e-Zal and provide security for them in a place overrun with Taliban. The district was also overwhelmed by a massive drug problem: almost half of its population—nearly fifteen thousand people—were addicted to hashish, opium, and other drugs. That number included many children, whose mothers, who worked long hours weaving carpets, fed their children sedatives so they could work undisturbed.

Gechi did return. He reconstituted his loyal followers as a standing militia of three hundred, setting up eighteen command checkpoints around the district that shut down Taliban operations there.

Malika Gharebyr, the head of women's affairs for the district, told me that the Taliban had harassed her every time she went outside her house. "Nabi brought security here," she told me when I visited her home a day after leaving Gechi's compound. "It's much better now."

Gechi also provided the protection that allowed the government to destroy poppy fields in the area.

"Without Nabi, we wouldn't have been able to eradicate the fields in Qal-e-Zal, said Abdul Bashir Morshid, the head of the Department of Counter-Narcotics in Kunduz Province, from his office in Kunduz City.

The American military initially liked what Gechi was doing so much that they sent in Special Forces soldiers to train, arm, and pay his men as part of a controversial program called CIP, or Critical Infrastructure Police. These were irregular units set up mostly in northern Afghanistan, sometimes even comprised of former Taliban. It was the perpetuation of an American counterinsurgency tactic used in Iraq: find a way to badge certain types of militia men—those not wed to a specific ideology—arm them, pay them, and train them. And hopefully, next time they'll be shooting for your side. The Sons of Iraq program in Al Anbar Province, also a CIP, seemed to work—as long as the money continued to flow.

In Afghanistan, the CIP were given yellow armbands but no uniforms and were co-opted, at least part-time, to fight the Taliban. But many of the CIP units, taking advantage of their guns and badges, began to freelance, shaking down the local communities for food, fuel, and whatever else they wanted.

Similar allegations surfaced against Gechi's militia. While each militia member was paid about $200 a month from a NATO discretionary fund, Gechi's group was accused of "taxing" the locals for security, taking payments in bags of wheat and chicken or other foodstuffs to eat or sell on the market.

The CIP program was created by the Americans, reportedly without the knowledge or consent of President Hamid Karzai, who ordered it dismantled in 2012. Karzai feared that irregular forces with no official or financial connection to the national government might one day pose a threat to it.

Eventually, the American money dried up and the CIP program dissolved—but Gechi's militia did not. With a security tax made up of foodstuffs regularly delivered to his compound and checkpoints in the district, the militia has been able to stay in business. And while he's been a proven asset in the fight against the Taliban, Gechi has evolved into what Karzai had feared most: a battle-tested, off-the-books warlord with no formal allegiance to the Afghan government.

While trying to solve one problem covertly, the U.S. military had inadvertently helped extend the most popular Afghan franchise: warlord-ism, an institution in which he with the most guns wins. But Qal-e-Zal's elders, who showed up by the dozens to meet with me at Gechi's compound when I arrived with Matin and Dost, told me they needed Gechi for security. They said Karzai should either turn Gechi's militia into a full-time, government-paid local police force, or send in another of their own. Until then, they would welcome the security Gechi's militia provided, even if they had to pay for it, though they admitted not everyone in the community was happy with the taxes.

"The people asked me to come here and provide security," Gechi said to me. "I'm happy to serve them, and if I've done anything wrong, I should be in a court, and let them speak out against me for my crimes."

Gechi walked us around a few of his strongholds, high-walled compounds with watchtowers where his men kept a lookout for approaching Taliban. Inside the compounds were dozens of bags of summer wheat. When I asked Gechi if these were taxes paid by the locals, he nodded.

"Yes, it is both food that the soldiers can eat or that can be sold to buy supplies."

It was clear he didn't want to dwell on the topic, and I wasn't keen on pushing the issue. While we met with the village elders, Gechi played the silent, humble servant, letting everyone else speak on his behalf. When he did speak, his voice was so soft you had to lean in to hear him. And while his face betrayed nothing, I sensed a quiet malevolence that he could summon at any moment.

This was in part because I knew some stories about him, and I also felt it again later at the broad, muddy Kunduz River, where he took us for a swim at dusk.

Our driver, Dost Muhammad, who seemed willing to try anything, stripped down to his underwear and jumped in first. Then, like kids on summer break, Gechi and I did the same and plunged into the coffee-brown water, whose current was so strong you had to swim full force to avoid being swept downstream.

The beautiful light of dusk turned everything a dusty, rose color, and as I swam I recalled a similar moment during another war, when I'd videotaped Kurdish Peshmerga fighters doing backflips off a bridge into a stream filled with anti-tank mines outside the city of Kirkuk in northern Iraq.

Matin took photographs of us as we climbed out onto the muddy bank and dove back in. Momentarily, it didn't matter that men with guns were watching over us; it seemed simple pleasures could be found anywhere in the world, no matter how odd the situation.

But when we clambered out a final time to take a group photograph, Gechi pushed down hard on my shoulder and threw his leg in front of mine, ready to toss me to the ground. I was surprised by his aggressiveness and wondered if I'd done something to piss him off, or if he was just having some fun. I looked over to Matin, who held the camera with an alarmed look on his face; Dost and Gechi's men were laughing hard.

I'm not a bad wrestler, but I couldn't see a good way out of the predicament. If I made a real effort and won, he'd lose face in front of his men, especially problematic since we were scheduled to stay at Gechi's compound that night. But if he legitimately took me down—or worse, if I let him—he'd likely lose respect for me, and there were still a lot of questions I wanted to ask him without being unduly deferential.

I chose an Afghan standoff. I held him at a distance, smiled, and tried to maintain equilibrium, without provoking him. After a few minutes of this he grew bored with me and broke off from the grapple. I took a deep breath of relief and posited that if the Taliban here had used the same technique with him, more of them might still be alive. Maybe this was exactly what Mullah Jilani had figured out and that's why he wasn't buried with his former comrades.

After we dressed, Gechi asked if we'd like to see how he and his men captured Taliban fighters when they used the river to smuggle supplies. I nodded enthusiastically. Gechi directed two of his men to board a flat-bottomed boat nearby and cover their faces with their scarves so they looked like Taliban. A boy then poled them out to the middle of the river, where the current wasn't as strong.

When they were in position, Gechi's men on shore pointed and shouted as if they had discovered the Taliban trying to slip by them on the boat. Gechi squatted on his haunches and used his AK-47 with the mounted grenade launcher to casually fire a grenade in a high arc over the boat and hundreds of yards up river. For almost forty seconds, nothing happened.

"That looks like a dud," I said.

But then we saw a thin spout of water splash high into the distance, and then the low, thundering sound of the explosion sped toward us, loud enough to set off the alarm on Dost's car.

"Spoke too soon," I said. "Is the commander going to have some fish for dinner tonight?" I joked. But as with the grenade, there was a sound delay—just long enough for Matin to translate—and then Nabi Gechi and his men laughed.

The boy poled the boat back into shore. The "Taliban" had their hands raised in surrender. Luckily for them, I thought, Gechi had decided to fire only one grenade.

Back at his compound that evening, Nabi Gechi was a gracious host, giving us appetizers of fresh watermelon, nuts, raisins, and tea and then feting us with a big dinner of pilaw, heavy flat bread, yogurt, and, oddly, Mountain Dew. Besides his two lieutenants, one of whom was the ex-Taliban Mullah Jillani, we were his only guests. Gechi chatted with us in between taking phone calls, which came in one after another for hours.

Gechi told us that he had seven daughters and four sons from three wives. (Islam allowed four wives, if a man could afford to take care of them all equally.) This seemed standard practice for warlords of means like himself, who exuded power, wealth, and virility, not just through their firepower but also through the size of their families.

One of his sons, a precocious five-year-old named Atiq, joined us in the guest room and became interested in the strange-looking foreigner in his father's house. I wrote his name in English on my notepad and told him to copy it exactly the same way. He wrote it instead in Dari. I guess something got lost in the translation.

His father called him over and told him something that sent him scurrying to a back room. When he returned, he was struggling to carry Nabi Gechi's battered and dirty AK-47 rifle with the GP-34 grenade launcher. It was obvious Gechi didn't fetishize his gun like many fighters did. To him it wasn't a showpiece, like those shiny, toy-like gangster guns pimped out with pearl handles and plated in gold, nickel, or silver that had been brandished by dead former dictators like Iraq's Saddam Hussein and Libya's Muammar Gaddafi. Gechi's rifle was not a garish tool for conveying wealth and power but a practical tool for killing, with a simple, fold-down metal stock and a wood fore-end covered with age-darkened gashes and scars.

The boy brought the rifle to his father, who adjusted the strap and then hung it over his son's shoulders. Atiq's eyes became huge and seemed like they were rolling around his head like the eyes of some crazy cartoon cat. He struggled to keep the weapon pointed up and at an imaginary enemy.

The rifle was on safe and Atiq kept his fingers off the trigger, but there was a thirty-round clip locked in place, and it was hard to stop staring at it, imagining the boy sliding the lever down, pulling the trigger, and then pogo-sticking the muzzle in an accidental death dance around the room.

I took a few pictures of him in the hopes of ending the show-and-tell portion of the evening's entertainment a little more quickly. Matin, Dost, and I all let out a little sigh when Atiq took the AK back to where it hung in the back room.

A little later, Gechi's tea boy connected a camcorder to a television in the room. We saw the images of the aftermath of his most recent victory over the Taliban, their bodies blackened, peppered with shrapnel, and stiff. There were close-ups of the entry and exit points of their wounds and of the body parts they'd lost to one of Gechi's grenades. Toward the end of the video, they were piled onto the back of a pickup like cord wood and presented as a gift at the Afghan National Police headquarters. At the press conference the next day, also recorded, the police chief called Gechi a hero. I looked over to see his reaction. He was already asleep and snoring, sprawled out on the floor like a bearskin rug. Just a few minutes before, his son-in-law and bodyguard, Haji Muhammad, had been walking on his back in an effort to massage out the knots in his burly frame. It must've worked.

After we watched the video of Nabi Gechi's bloody Taliban slaughter, I wondered what his ex-Taliban lieutenant, Mullah Jilani, had been thinking while watching those images.

"Yes, I chose the right way," Jilani said when Matin and I later asked him about the gory video. "I could have been one of those bodies." He continued. "If I had met you a few years ago I would've killed you. Killing is the first option, because we [the Taliban] were really angry with the foreigners. We would use a Kalashnikov to kill you. And we would be very happy, because it's really good for us to kill a foreigner."

While I was the only foreigner in the room, Matin would not have been spared, Mullah Jilani assured us.

"Because you are working with him," Jilani said to Matin, "you would be killed as well; you are the same."

But Jilani said it wasn't only his respect for Gechi's fighting prowess that prompted his battlefield conversion. He said he also had a revelation of sorts. After he developed kidney stones, the pain was so bad he eventually went to a German military hospital, part of NATO's Provincial Reconstruction

Team (PRT) in the region. Jilani said the staff treated him with such kindness that he began to think what the Taliban had been telling him about the foreigners was just propaganda.

"I found them to be really good people. They were helping me a lot, and everything was free. They weren't just in Afghanistan to kill people, but to help others. I was blind to that."

While that finally convinced him to break ranks with the Taliban, there were a lot of other things that troubled him about the organization.

"The Taliban is really from Pakistan; they came here to destroy our country. That is clear to everyone," said Jilani. "In the beginning, I thought it was jihad against international troops, but I found out we were fighting for Pakistani interests—we were getting orders from Pakistan. Most of the leaders are not religious; they want to come to Afghanistan and tax the locals during the time of the harvest and take the money back to Pakistan. There is no jihad," Jilani said.

"Our leaders were in Pakistan in nice houses spending a lot of money on themselves—good food, good clothes—but they're asking us to go to Afghanistan to fight on the front line. They were giving us 500 Pakistani rupees for a week (about US$5). You cannot eat for a day on that," he said. "It was a really hard time when I was with the Taliban. During the day we were fighting and at night we had to be careful because we were afraid of the night operations [NATO Special Forces]. We changed our positions several times a night."

I asked Jilani about Taliban tactics and how they were organized.

"At the beginning of an operation we would pray, and then the commander would divide us into small groups of about ten men called a *delgai*. In each *delgai* there was one fighter with an RPG [rocket-propelled grenade] launcher and one fighter with a [Russian] PK machine gun. The rest would be armed with Kalashnikovs. Each *delgai* had a commander. We used two kinds of attacks, either encircling our enemy or an ambush which starts with the RPG and PK."

Jilani said bomb-makers and suicide bombers were different from regular Taliban fighters.

"I never had any real contact with those who made the [roadside] bombs. They wore camouflage uniforms, sometimes the same as the ANA [Afghan National Army]. These people were separate from us, not Afghans—either Uzbeks, Chechens, Al Qaeda. I also never saw a suicide bomber, but I believe they were the same people. I heard our leaders talk about them."

If more Taliban had experienced the foreign medical care and technology that Jilani had, I wondered, would they have switched sides too? Or was its promise enough to at least get regular Afghans to reconsider their support for the Taliban?

Embedded with American troops in southern Afghanistan in 2010, I'd watched American military surgeons in a remote field hospital work on a thirteen-year-old Afghan farm boy named Habibullah, whose arms had been severed in a threshing machine. They not only kept him alive but also, miraculously, reattached both arms, a difficult surgical feat even under the best conditions, let alone in a combat zone. He became a living testament that American technology could save lives just as skillfully as it could take them.

Even so, that would unlikely be enough to convince the Afghans, especially those in rural areas, to accept all the other things the Americans and other foreigners brought with them. This included the concepts of women's rights and freedom of expression that often offended conservative sensibilities—things they likely believed were incompatible with Islam.

No matter how many hospitals with twenty-first-century life-saving medical care were built in Afghanistan, many Afghans would continue to see foreigners as would-be conquerors and an assault on Islam. That mindset, I knew, wouldn't disappear with a single kidney stone procedure or even a miracle like Habibullah's arms. Perhaps it never would. But at least it had with some, like Mullah Jilani.

While everyone else was preparing to sleep, Jilani watched Matin use his computer to Skype with a colleague. He had never seen anything like it and was awed by the technology and Matin's mastery of it.

"This takes education," Jilani said to Matin. "All the educated youth like you are good for our country. I am an uneducated person, so why should I kill you?" Not so much a question as a reminder to himself.

After a peaceful night's sleep and a quick breakfast of bread, cheese, and coffee, Nabi Gechi took us down a small stairway that led to a dark enclosure under his compound.

The cramped room, lit by a single overhead bulb hanging from a wire, was filled with three different-size spinning wheels connected to each other by drive belts similar to those used in car engines. But what force was powering them? Gechi must've been reading my thoughts because he ushered me over to an exit through a hole in the wall on the other side of the room. The sound of rushing water was too loud to speak over. Attached to a wall outside the compound was a large wooden paddlewheel turning swiftly to the rushing current of a man-made waterway that Gechi had diverted from the Kunduz River.

Nabi Gechi's talents, it seemed, went far beyond handling a grenade launcher. The man I had seen only through the prism of his Taliban-killing prowess had also constructed a small hydroelectric plant that generated a continuous power supply for him and many of the local businesses. When I asked him how he was able to put together such a complex engineering system, he said he looked at other working models, read schematics, scavenged the materials, and then simply built it. If he were able to do it on a bigger scale, to get permission from the government to divert more of the river, he added, he could generate enough power for the entire district. I looked at him as he inspected the machinery and felt a bit ashamed of myself. Like so many foreigners in Afghanistan, I had failed to see beneath the surface. At the river, I had been quick to sense Nabi Gechi's quiet malevolence, which might really have been only been playful energy, while overlooking his genius completely. The strong current of the Kunduz River in which we had both swum was just a workout for me, but it was a source of power for him. While I stroked against it for fun, he had harnessed its energy underneath his own home.

My failure of imagination, I thought, came from a Western arrogance that characterized the Afghan people as an impediment to the development and stability of their own country, rather than the solution to it. Nabi Gechi was indeed a spectacular instrument of war, but also, at times, effective in creating instruments of peace. If he could hang up his grenade launcher and devote all his energy to projects like these, I wondered what he might be capable of creating. But the truth was Nabi Gechi would probably be dead in a year. While hard to kill, he was also a very tempting target.

Warlords have a short shelf life in Afghanistan.

7
KURASH

||||||||||||

Akram Uddin referees a *kurash* practice match at the Kunduz Central Club.

After we left Qal-e-Zal and returned to Kunduz, Matin, Dost, and I talked about why so much foreign coverage of Afghanistan focused only on the war. While undeniably the most important ongoing story, that myopic vision created a one-dimensional picture of the nation, which was so much more than the sum of its war stories. Matin agreed and made a phone call to longtime friend, and within the hour we were driving to a large, renovated warehouse on the edge of Kunduz City.

The space was Spartan and clean, filled only with a wall-to-wall beige wrestling mat with a red bull's-eye in the center and a single red circle surrounding it. On the mat, twenty-four young athletes, most dressed in a grubby gi tied with a colored belt that signified the need to improvise rather than the skill level achieved by its wearer, were already training, using the only equipment available—their own bodies.

They took turns carrying each other on their shoulders, jumping over and crawling under each other, and most impressively, lining up as many as four colleagues in a row and launching themselves like flying squirrels over their backs. It was both exciting and exhausting to watch. It was also encouraging to see this many young men of military age not pointing guns at each other, but cooperating in training for perhaps the one thing on which most Afghans, whether

Tajik, Uzbek, Hazara, or Pashtun, could agree: kurash. Even the Taliban liked kurash.

According to the sport's Asian confederation, it originated in what is now Uzbekistan in about 1500 BCE. Kurash could be considered mixed martial arts, as it combines elements of both upright wrestling and judo. Since opponents cannot grapple below the waist or wrestle on the ground, kurash moves at a very fast pace. The goal is to put your opponent on the mat. When a competitor's knee touches the floor, the action is stopped and they begin again from a standing position.

Kurash is so popular that even amateur matches can draw thousands of spectators (male only—women not allowed), who will often bet on the outcomes. In Kunduz, it was local money, not an NGO, that had paid to transform this building into a gymnasium.

Matin and Dost introduce me to Muhammad Anwar, the director of the Kunduz Central Club, which runs recreation centers all across Kunduz and has two thousand members. Dost and Anwar embraced warmly.

"He used to be my coach," Dost told me in English and then interpreted for Anwar, who nodded and replied in Dari.

"Dost Muhammad was very good at kurash at one time, but now he is too old," he said. This made us all laugh.

With his long beard, traditional white skullcap, or kufi, and *shalwar kameez*, Anwar looked more like an imam rather than an athletic director. But the jobs may not have been so different: he considered the boys' spiritual well-being part of his responsibilities.

"It keeps them from doing bad things," said Anwar. "They come here and they make their bodies healthy, and it helps keep them away from drugs and other troubles."

It's also a chance to briefly escape the dangers and everyday problems of living in a nation that has been at war for decades.

Akram Uddin, a twenty-nine-year-old tree trunk of a man wearing a blue gi tied with a black belt, told me he'd started training at this club thirteen years ago, when he was sixteen. He got so good that by the time he was twenty-two he was invited to compete in a tournament in Macau; it was a chance to show both his countrymen and the world that Afghanistan was not defined only by war. There were lights and crowds and music and a magnificent ring. Uddin entered it, carrying the hopes of so many Afghans. Although he lost, he was not defeated, and emerged inspired.

"When I saw how hard all of the other athletes trained, how good they were and what it looked like when their flags were raised up when they got their medals, I said to myself, I will do that for Afghanistan."

And so he did. Uddin went home and trained hard enough to compete in twenty different countries throughout Asia and Europe. A few years ago he went on to become a top champion in the Asia Confederation.

Kurash had reportedly been considered as a sport for the 2020 Tokyo Olympic Games, but it didn't make the shortlist and most likely never will—even Greco-Roman wrestling, long an Olympic staple, is on shaky ground (it was dropped from the Tokyo Games but re-added after an outcry).

Still, Akram Uddin would have been thirty-six by then, way past his prime for an athlete in a combat sport. He insists he could've been ready, but he'll have to settle for making Afghanistan proud on slightly smaller stages.

The other club members practice their moves, gracefully shifting their weight, using the physics of energy, gravity, and motion to throw each other down to the mat. Akram Uddin refereed a few practice matches between heavy, medium, and lightweight fighters. Each showed an intensity and skill level rivaling that of any mixed martial arts club in the world. The warrior spirit, I knew, was not in short supply in Afghanistan. Fortunately, when these young men fight each other, no one ends up dead.

I climbed on top of one of the hand-over-hand bars bolted to the ceiling and took a group photograph of the participants arranged on the outer red circle of the mat surrounding Anwar, who stood on the bull's-eye. They were sweaty and proud, happy to be recognized, even momentarily, for something—anything—other than their war.

Our northern journey completed, we left them and got on the road to Kabul.

8

HINDU KUSH

||||||||||||||

Trucks backed up at the entrance to the Soviet-built Salang
Tunnel, which cuts through the Hindu Kush, the mountain range dividing northern and southern Afghanistan.

In 2001, with the Taliban in full retreat, my NBC colleagues and I packed up everything in Khoja Bahaudin and headed toward the geographic feature that divides Afghanistan in half, north from south: the legendary mountain range known as the Hindu Kush. We would be on a steady incline until we reached the Salang Tunnel, built by the Soviets in 1964. Once through the tunnel, we'd be on our way to Kabul—or so we hoped.

This is an excerpt from my journal:

NOVEMBER 2001, THE ROAD TO KABUL

We are lost—in a minefield. We are on the road to Kabul, where one-fifth of all the landmines in the world are planted. A journey of less than 200 miles, it will take us five days. This is just the beginning. It does not bode well. We were supposed to be in a convoy with other journalists. Safety in numbers. But it dissolved before we left Khoja Bahaudin, and now we are alone: just our two Toyota pickups, a Russian jeep, and a minefield. We took the wrong road.

That is not true. There is no road. Not one that I can see. Just some tire tracks in the sand. Sometimes the tracks disappear. That's what happened here. Now we have two choices: forward or reverse. My translator Shafiq and I inspect the ground in front of our lead truck. We see

*them, faintly—tread marks. They lead back to the road
we missed. The one that will not explode. Forward. We
go forward, driving very carefully in the tread marks of
some guardian angel that passed this way not so long ago.
Kabul has fallen.*

*It's Ramadan, a month of fasting and prayer for Mus-
lims. During this time they do not eat between sunup
and sundown, breaking their fast only when the last
light of day has disappeared. It is now dark, and we
are in the middle of a mountain pass. Our drivers stop
their vehicles to munch on crackers and sip juice. We sit
and wait.*

*Actually, we can use the break. We have been
driving since 3 a.m. The roads have alternated between camel paths of dust that have coated us inside
and out to kidney-busting stalactite trails. I laugh,
thinking about those sport utility vehicle TV ads back
in the States that sell the concept of seeing the back-
country without getting a case of hemorrhoids. If they
only knew. For three days now we have driven through
minefields, over tire-shredding rocks, across waist-
deep rivers, and climbed nearly-vertical berms, all
without incident—until now.*

*On the Khawak Pass over the legendary snow-topped
mountain range known as the Hindu Kush, I can see
our jeep. It is on its side. Jim Maceda, Jim Bruton, and
a Voice of America Reporter named Iris are climbing*

*out over the top as we pull up behind them. Maceda has
banged his knee and the driver his head, but otherwise
they are in good shape. We're not so sure about the jeep.
They tipped over while making a turn around a very
steep bend in the road. We tie a rope around the top front
axle of the overturned jeep and use the pickup to pull it
back onto its wheels. Surprisingly, it starts up without
hesitation. The driver's-side mirror and door, however,
are toast.*

*I switch Maceda and Iris to my truck. Bruton and I
ride in the jeep. Like a thirsty horse that cannot pass a
stream, we must stop at every water source to refill the
leaking radiator. For the rest of the journey, we rarely top
30 kilometers per hour. We will reach Kabul two days
later with no brakes, no clutch, limping past 20-foot-deep
craters and the Swiss cheese remains of outlying buildings,
all destroyed by American bombs. On the left, before we
enter the city, is Farqah 16, formerly a major Taliban
military base, now just acres of twisted rebar and scorched
earth.*

While in 2001 that trip took five days, the journey from
the north to Kabul in 2013 normally takes only six to eight
hours. The roads are good and mostly safe, at least while
there's daylight. But in Afghanistan, there is no such thing
as a trouble-free operation. Our problems began as soon as
we hit the incline. Something was wrong with the Bahmani-

mobile. The engine seemed to be losing compression. Even when Dost had the gas pedal floored, the Corolla barely limped forward.

It was not a good time for this to happen. Just like the tail end of the 2001 trip after the jeep flipped and we had to stop to refill the radiator, we now had to stop every ten minutes to let the car cool down, even though the engine didn't seem to be overheating. What was the problem, I wondered. Bad gas? I would soon ask the same question of myself after we made an ill-advised purchase from a roadside vendor.

At the beginning of the drive, we had stopped to buy several bottles of *doogh*. I had drunk it both at the Dasht-e-Qala police chief's house and at Matin's with no problem, so I wasn't wary of what we had purchased, especially since it was in a labeled plastic bottle with a sealed cap, or so I thought. I was so thirsty I drank two of them back-to-back. It was not a wise move. I learned later that many of the drinks sold along that route are homebrews made with unfiltered river water and other questionable ingredients. Within a half hour, the potion had me curled up in a fetal position. I like to pride myself on my cast-iron traveler's stomach, hard-earned from time in the trenches. After suffering for two weeks with a case of dysentery while covering a story in Mexico years ago, my body seemed impervious to all manner of bugs and bacteria in food and drink around the world. The *doogh*, however, had done me in.

Right before we were about to enter the Salang Tunnel I told Dost to pull over. We were at 11,000 feet and the mountains were rugged, ancient, majestic, with a layer of ice frosting their highest peaks, just as I remembered them from the first time I had made this passage. But I had little time to bask in their splendor. I pushed away from the road and clambered behind a crumbling wall next to a beautiful mountain stream.

What was next to the wall was not at all beautiful. It seemed that others had been here before me, and I had to be careful where I tread. I found a spot to squat between two boulders. I thought I might shit out most of my major organs. I felt like a cold, mangy dog.

I limped back to the car, climbed into the backseat, and collapsed. As we approached Salang Tunnel, I knew the passage would take all of my strength and willpower. It was an engineering marvel when the Russians built it in the sixties, but it had taken a beaten since. As many as a thousand Soviet troops were killed in it during a fire in 1982. The badly lit, poorly ventilated mile-and-a-half-long tunnel still caused a few deaths from carbon monoxide poisoning every year when black diesel exhaust from nonstop truck traffic turns the Salang as dark as an abandoned mineshaft.

As the tunnel burrowed through the Kush, I could feel the uninvited river amoeba burrowing further into my lower intestines. The Bahmani-mobile seemed to be struggling as well, pushing forward in fits and starts, losing power and then regaining it in the blackness of the tunnel, taillights in front of us and headlights behind us. I prayed to the gods of bad gas that neither the Bahmani nor I would falter irreversibly. We did not want to be stalled blocking this major commercial passage, nor did I want to have to exit the vehicle and drop drawers as a sideshow for bored travelers.

Finally, after what seemed like an endless plunge into blackness but in reality a twenty-minute drive, we literally saw the light at the end of the tunnel. We had made it from north to south. I learned later that our passage had been easier than anticipated because the U.S. Army Corp of Engineers had just completed a nearly $20 million renovation of the tunnel in preparation for their 2014 withdrawal. While the Americans and NATO preferred to use more direct routes through Pakistan for moving supplies in and out of Afghanistan, they wanted a secure, reliable backup plan in case something went wrong in their dealings with Pakistan—as they very well might.

American drone strikes against Al Qaeda and Haqqani Network leaders inside Pakistan's tribal areas had stirred violent protests, and the Pakistani government had shut down all NATO trucking for more than six months in November 2011, after a U.S. airstrike killed twenty-four Pakistani troops.

While the troubles with the Bahmani-mobile and my lower GI tract made the trip less than the nostalgic passage I had hoped for, we had made it, and I was tempted to offer something in sacrifice—Dost maybe? Instead, nearly delirious, I passed out again until Kabul.

SHADOW AND LIGHT SOURCE BOTH

How does a part of the world leave the world?
How does wetness leave water? Don't try to
Put out a fire by throwing on more fire! Don't
wash a wound with blood. No no matter how fast
you run, your shadow keeps up. Sometimes it's
in front! Only full overhead sun diminishes
your shadow. But that shadow has been serving
you. What hurts you, blesses you. Darkness is
your candle. Your boundaries are your quest.
I could explain this, but it will break the
glass cover on your heart, and there's no
fixing that. You must have shadow and light
sources both. Listen, and lay your head under
the tree of awe. When from that tree feathers
and wings sprout on you, be quieter than
a dove. Don't open your mouth for even a *coo*.[*]

* "Shadow and Light Source Both," from *The Soul of Rumi: A New Collection of Ecstatic Poems*, translation by Coleman Barks (Harper One, 2001).

PART II
KABUL

A very rare sight: an Afghan couple hold hands while walking through down-town Kabul. (Image captured through our car's windshield.)

9
YESTERDAY, TODAY, AND TOMORROW

||||||||||||||

Shadow of anti-Taliban militiaman.

Dost drove to the apartment he shares with his second wife in a nice part of west Kabul near the parliament building. It was dark by the time we arrived. We unloaded our gear from the trunk and took it into the ground-floor apartment, trying not to wake the neighbors. He led me to the guest room, and I staggered toward one of mattresses against the wall, plopped down, and curled up into a ball. Fuck *doogh*, I thought, and fell asleep. It was an inauspicious return.

By the next morning, with most of the *doogh* out of my system, I woke up feeling much better. In another room, filled with couches and a large television screen, Dost spread out the *dastarkhwan* on the floor and placed dishes of boiled eggs, meats, cheese, fresh, warm bread, and steaming chai.

My stomach was still queasy, but I knew that eating would help me regain some strength. I was also very dehydrated and drank nearly a full liter of water.

"This one belongs to you," Dost said, pointing at the one hard-boiled egg left on the plate. I shook my head. It was typical Afghan hospitality—unrelenting concern and deference for guests, a willingness to drop any all tasks and responsibilities, to forgo any personal needs or desires in order to ensure a visitor's comfort. It's an authentic, deeply embedded Afghan trait that I've encountered throughout the country. It's also one that requires guests to be cautious to avoid stripping their hosts of their most valued possessions. If you make the mistake of telling your host you like his ring, he'll pluck it from his finger and give it to you immediately, despite its being a gift from his now dead father. (I made just that mistake on my second trip to Afghanistan.)

Dost had invited me to stay at his apartment while I was in town. I was grateful, because as a freelancer, I paid all of my own expenses. (Back when I worked at NBC, we would actually carry briefcases of cash to keep a war zone bureau operating.) While Kabul was a more progressive and cosmopolitan city than Kunduz, and its people used to seeing foreign faces on the streets, staying with Dost still posed risks for all of us.

When I raised the issue, he shrugged it off and loaded a DVD into the player next to the television. He wanted to show me some public service announcements (PSAs) made by the government in which he appeared. In the most memorable, he played an Afghan man paid by terrorists to plant a bomb. In the PSA, Dost carries multiple sticks of dynamite tied in a bundle with an alarm clock timer under his clothes. It reminded me of the kind of bomb Wile E. Coyote used against his nemesis, the Road Runner.

Dost's character plants the bomb under the cart of a food vendor on a busy Kabul street, then slips away down an alley. He hears the bomb explode and knows he's been successful. But a little later, after he returns home, he gets a phone call— his wife was killed by a street bomb earlier in the day. There's a smash-cut close-up to a look of horror on his face when he realizes he's killed his own wife. The slate after, Dost told me, reinforced the message with something surprisingly direct

like "Don't take money from foreigners to plant bombs."
Well, why risk losing the message to subtlety, I thought. I
slapped Dost's shoulder—an attaboy.

Sitting in his home, comfortably full and sipping hot chai,
I thought about my first experiences of people's homes in
Kabul after we had arrived from the north. There had been
bombs involved then, too. The comfort of a home in Afghanistan, it seemed, could be very fleeting.

An excerpt from my journal:

NOVEMBER 2001—HOUSE BOMB

*Our colleagues have rented a house for us in Kabul.
It has running water and wood-burning stoves for heat.
After five days on the road wearing the same clothes, we
are giddy with the thought of a hot shower and some rest.
Everyone sleeps peacefully that night, never knowing that
there is a hole in the roof, a hole that leads inside a locked
pantry adjacent to our bedrooms. When NBC's de facto
Kabul bureau chief, Babak Behnam, inspects the roof the
next day, he sees the hole and calls the landlord to come
to the house and unlock the pantry. The landlord does so
reluctantly. We soon understand why.*

*After the padlock is removed, Babak pushes the door
open and its shadow sweeps across the thing that caused
the hole—a five-hundred-pound American bomb that had
pierced the roof weeks earlier and now stands, at a jaunty
angle, nose buried in the concrete floor, unexploded. We
are too stunned to run and instead simply stare at the gray*

rocket ship—shaped bomb with its fins ass-up. We back away slowly.

A few hours later a bomb disposal squad has removed the ordnance, and fortunately, our trust in the proprietor is the only real casualty. We moved to the Hotel Intercontinental, a defensible perch on top of a hill overlooking the city.

A neighborhood in Kabul. Wednesday morning, October 17, 2001. Abdul Basar is coming home from the market when he hears the explosion. He runs toward the sound. He arrives to find the west side of his apartment building peeled away like an orange. It is the side in which he lives. Then on the ground, a sight no father should have to endure. Under a pile of glass, rubble, and broken furniture, his five-year-old daughter. Her name was Nazalla. Killed by an American bomb. A dumb bomb (meaning it had no internal targeting mechanism). It was a bomb that missed its target, a Taliban military communications complex called Base 52, by only a block. In this nation where, for the last twenty-two years, bombs have fallen more indiscriminately and more frequently than raindrops, that is very close. Very close for being dropped from 30,000 feet. But not close enough for Abdul.

"She liked apples and pomegranates," he tells me, holding up her photograph, "only fruit, she would eat only fruit." She is a tiny girl wearing a light-blue dress.

*A girl with eyes as big as planets, beautiful brown, new-
born planets. She never knew what hit her. Never thought
she would die. This way. This young. Abdul looks at her
picture lovingly. She would crawl into my bed at night
when she was afraid of the dark. Abdul says he does not
blame Americans—he knows it was a mistake. Still, he
cries every night when he thinks of her.*

Through his work for the *New York Times*, Matin had made
a friend and source out of one of the most powerful men in
Kabul: Gen. Ayub Salangi. At the time he was chief of the
Afghan National Police (ANP) in the capital, but he would
soon be named deputy minister of the interior for security.
Salangi was a Tajik, a friend and former commander under
Ahmad Shah Massoud, and now, in Kabul, part of the so-
called Panjshiri Mafia, men from the Panjshir Valley all at
one time connected to Massoud.

While we waited to see him at a reception area in an outer
office of the ANP's Kabul headquarters, we talked with one
of his aides, a young guy named Nasir, who sat behind a desk
that was completely empty, without even a telephone.

Nasir looked enthused. He was learning English from
some American police trainers based at the headquarters and
was happy to try it out on me.

"Where are you from?" he asked me in English.

"The U.S., originally. California, when I last lived there,"
I said.

"I love America," he said, "I love Hollywood."

"Have you been?" I asked him.

"No, but I want to go. It looks so nice in the movies," he said with an endearing enthusiasm that I had heard on many trips abroad, from Iran to Sri Lanka.

"What kind of movies do you like?" I asked.

"Oh I love the movies with John Wayne," he said without hesitation.

I nodded. It was hard to disagree. John Wayne was the shit.

Then a yell came from down the hallway. Nasir stood up and gestured for us to follow one of his colleagues: Salangi was almost ready for us. We were ushered into a large, dark office with black leather chairs against both wall. On one wall was a giant street map of Kabul covered in plastic, with hundreds of pushpins in different colors. Salangi was not there yet, so Matin and I sat next to each other on the left.

Within a few minutes, the same door through which we'd entered burst open. It was the Kabul police chief followed by a gray-haired uniformed officer carrying a sheaf of papers. Salangi wore a gray suit, white shirt, and burgundy tie, but with his linebacker build, close-cropped black hair, and facial scruff, he still looked like the guerrilla leader he had once been when fighting with Massoud against the Russians and the Taliban. After Matin introduced us, I asked Salangi about his time with Massoud.

It was a sure-fire way to break the ice, I knew, and Salangi smiled widely. He pressed a red button that rang a bell, and another one of his aides came running into the room. Salangi said a few words to him and the man left, returning shortly with a photograph of Salangi and some other fighters in the Panjshir Valley standing around Massoud. Salangi was reportedly one of Massoud's favorite young commanders and is standing closest to him in the picture. In a story Salangi likes to tell, Massoud, while attending Salangi's wedding years ago, took the groom aside and made him promise that this would be his first and last marriage, that like Massoud himself, he would take only one wife. Salangi said he promised his friend, and to this day has kept his word.

While we talked, Salangi continued to press the red button, and each time his aide came back with new papers or information. He pressed it every few seconds, it seemed, running the man back and forth like a badminton shuttlecock.

After Massoud's assassination and the U.S. decision to retaliate against Al Qaeda following 9/11, Salangi had been one of the first of Massoud's men to meet with the CIA in order to devise a way for the Northern Alliance to coordinate with the CIA and U.S. Special Forces on the ground. Salangi's relationship with the CIA was said to be so close that his house in the tony Sher Pur neighborhood of Kabul (locals refer to it disparagingly as "Sher Chur" which means "to steal something and run," which many believe the residents there have done)—a mansion with a faux Greek column and a large fountain—was actually purchased with money given to him by the spy agency. The same was suspected of many other

Afghan government officials reportedly living well above their meager government salaries. But if the rumors were true, that relationship seemed to have soured, as today Salangi was one of the CIA's harshest critics.

"Yes, there has been progress in Afghanistan over the last twelve years," Salangi said, answering my question about whether Afghans felt they still had something worth fighting for, "but also a lot of mistakes. The Americans didn't examine the situation in Afghanistan very carefully. If they had, they would've gone to the place where the Taliban originated."

"Pakistan," I asked?

Salangi raised his eyebrows to indicate *of course—where else?**

"They found Osama bin Laden in Pakistan," he said. "Then the Americans realized what was going on."

I was about to interject that the U.S. drones had actually been bombing North Waziristan, the tribal areas of Pakistan, for years, when Salangi waved me off for a moment to focus on another document his aide had just given him.

Matin spoke to him in Dari, and he replied, still writing.

"He just rewrote a press release for an appearance he's making on national TV tonight," Matin told me.

---

* Longtime *New York Times* correspondent in Afghanistan Carlotta Gall agreed with Salangi's assertion, even releasing a book in April 2014 in which the main premise was that Pakistan's Inter-Services Intelligence agency (ISI) has been working against American interests in Afghanistan from the beginning, even protecting and hiding Osama Bin Laden. It's titled *The Wrong Enemy: America in Afghanistan, 2001–2014*, implying that Pakistan was the right one.

Salangi looked up for a moment, smiled, and then continued.

"The CIA should admit two things," he said. "First, they
were too weak to understand what Pakistan was doing, and
second, they ignored that the ISI [Inter-Services Intelligence,
Pakistan's spy agency] was helping the Taliban. The CIA
should apologize to the Afghan people, who have been given
the wrong information for years. You have to make good
policy through good intelligence."

"It think Pakistan's meddling in Afghanistan has been
obvious for years," I replied, "but I've just been in Kabul a
single day and several people have told me already that Iran
has also been busy trying to win influence in Afghanistan."

Iran's efforts in Afghanistan, I'd researched, had utilized
both the front and back doors of diplomacy. As an international
donor, it had pledged $500 million in aid and funded various in-
frastructure projects, including a road linking the western city of
Herat to Iran's eastern border. But in 2010, President Karzai also
admitted that Iran had several times given as much as $1 million
in cash to his chief of staff, sometimes simply stuffed into bags,
for what has been called "official presidential expenses."

But Iran may simply have been copying the United States.
In a December 2013 article, the *Daily Beast** reported that
Karzai's top aide, Said Jawad, had been on two different U.S.
Agency for International Development (USAID) contract

---

* Eli Lake and Josh Rogin, "Why the U.S. Paid Karzai's Top Aide," *The Daily Beast*,
  December 28, 2013.

payrolls in 2002 and 2003, drawing a combined salary of more than $100,000 a year. U.S. officials defended the practice as necessary for encouraging Western-educated Afghans and technocrats to return to their homeland to rebuild the government.

But also suspect in Iran's back-door efforts to gain influence was Khatam al-Nabyeen Islamic University in western Kabul. The $17 million madrassa, or religious school, opened in 2006, and was built by Grand Ayatollah Mohseni, a seventy-five-year-old Afghan cleric and former mujahedin leader with close ties to Iran. Critics say Mosheni got the money from Tehran. He claims it was all his.

Regardless, Iran's efforts seemed to be paying off; while President Karzai ignored U.S. pressure to sign the Bilateral Security Agreement (BSA) that would extend some American military presence in Afghanistan beyond 2014, he did sign a long-term cooperation pact with Iranian president Hassan Rouhani during a December 2013 trip to Tehran.

"When we were fighting the Taliban," Salangi said, "Iran supported the Northern Alliance a lot—they were very helpful to us. But currently, Iran is not happy with the U.S. involvement in Afghanistan. Now our country has become a playground where the two power players wrestle. I just want the Iranian government to take their issues with the United States elsewhere, and not put us in the middle."

I moved him away from the geopolitical and back to a bite-size view of the conflict. In the past few months, Kabul had been besieged by a series of suicide bombings that were undermining the belief that the one place the government *did* maintain control was the capital. Most of the targets had been police stations and many of the victims cops. Salangi tried to remain sanguine about the situation.

"People are suffering, but if the Taliban is going to target important places, I'd prefer they attack military bases rather than civilians," he said, "The last attack lasted only three hours before Afghan soldiers and police beat them back. In the past, the attacks could be as long at seventeen hours. It shows the police and army are loyal and love their country."

Salangi also said that Afghan intelligence agencies had prevented many more suicide bombings than had actually taken place. Still, he conceded, they were dealing with a formidable enemy.

"Americans, with all the technology they have, is nothing compared with the Taliban's research in suicide bombing."

"What about the other crime in Kabul and the rest of Afghanistan?" I asked. "As the head of the police here, you're directing almost all your resources and time to fighting the Taliban. How can you also enforce the law?"

For the first time, Salangi put down his pen and stopped pushing the red button and looked directly at me.

"This is imposed on us," he said. "We must fight the Taliban, and every day we lose five to ten police. *Every day*. It is pretty clear what the job of the police is. Until we eliminate terrorism, we can't enforce the law."

I wondered about the cumulative effects of putting the entire nation's criminal justice system on hold for more than a decade. While the police were busy fighting a war, justice had become another one of its casualties. If Afghans could not expect the fair application of law and order from their government, it seemed natural for them to look to other sources to provide it.

We were invited to dinner at the house of one of Matin's colleagues, an Afghan journalist named Bilal Sarwary who works for the BBC in Kabul.

"Bilal is a really, really nice person," Matin told me before dinner, "but he looks a little like a Taliban commander," he joked.

When we arrive at Bilal's house in the Qala-e-Fathullah neighborhood of Kabul, an area filled with high-rent NGO and expat compounds, I saw what Matin meant. Bilal is thick, barrel-chested, and balding, with a full, black beard. But he had a broad, warm smile and, as I would soon find out, a very dry sense of humor. He had been an exchange student in America in New Hampshire, the "live free or die" state. He said he loved the people and the culture, and his time abroad had contributed to his easygoing nature.

The gathering was just what you'd expect from a collection of witty, well-informed, cynical journalists around a dinner table in a warzone. It was the Afghanistan version of Dorothy Parker's Algonquin Roundtable. Matin, Bilal, and I were joined by one of Bilal's BBC colleagues, a savagely funny man named Mahfuouz Zubaide; a local producer

named Massoud Popalzai, who had just left the BBC to join
CNN; and New Zealander Jacob Bryant, an award-winning
cinematographer filming a documentary.

I was the newest foreigner at the table; Bilal took the opportunity tell me a joke:

> *"An Afghan man sees a foreigner carrying a notepad
> and camera walking in an area of Kabul called Chicken
> Street. With genuine hospitality, the Afghan welcomes the
> foreigner,"* said Bilal.

> *"What brings you to Afghanistan,"* the local asks, noting
> the camera and notepad.

> *"I'm writing a book,"* the man replied.

> *"Ah, good for you—what's the book about?"*

> *"It's about Afghanistan."*

> *"I see,"* said the Afghan, stroking his beard, *"and when
> did you arrive?"*

> *"Yesterday,"* said the foreigner.

> *"Ah, and how much time will you spend in my country?"*

"Just today," the foreigner said, glancing at his wrist-watch.

Now the Afghan was puzzled. *"So when will you depart,"* he asked?

"Tomorrow," the foreigner shrugged.

"I'm not sure I understand," the Afghan said, *"so what will be the title of this book?"*

"Well," the foreigner said confidently, *"it's called Afghanistan: Yesterday, Today, and Tomorrow."*

We all laughed, but we knew how close to the truth it was. At times I was afraid of being that man. I'd learned during my years in Afghanistan that it was too easy to get it wrong, to witness something and then make sweeping—incorrect—conclusions about its meaning. The myth and magic of Afghanistan was so fierce that we who wrote about it were often distracted from digging the plough in deeply enough to understand the country's volatile ethnic mix, its legendary subterfuge, the anachronisms and historical complexities.

We might think we're somehow playing the "Great Game,"* while it was actually playing us. The truth was

---

* A term referring to the British-Russian rivalry for dominance in Central Asia, which

that Afghanistan could easily swallow us whole and shit us out. We would believe we'd had an epiphany while Afghanistan went on pretty much as before—maybe even with new immunities against whatever it was we thought we had to offer by telling its story. Most of these men around the table weren't parachute journalists like me. They lived here, knew the story better than most, and wouldn't, or couldn't, leave when it was over—and for them it never would be.

"What do you think will happen in 2014 after the Americans withdraw" I asked Bilal, "if they withdraw completely?"

He thought about it while taking a draw on one of his small cigars and then exhaling.

"There will be some troubles of course, some adjustments. But I think everything is going to be all right. For the first time, Afghans have something to lose," he said. "I don't think they'll let that happen."

---

lasted throughout much of the nineteenth century. It's attributed to Arthur Conolly, a British intelligence officer, but was popularized by writer Rudyard Kipling in his 1901 novel *Kim*.

10
FIXERS

||||||||||||

Dost (my driver), Matin (my interpreter), and I in the guest
room of northern police chief Imam Muhammed.

Foreign correspondents often encourage or do little to diminish the myth that we're intrepid, globetrotting sleuths going it alone in the pursuit of truth. But in reality, we are so dependent on our hired local help that we're more or less useless on our own. Without necessary language skills and cultural knowledge, parachute journalists, as we are often known because we visit a location briefly rather than living there, are like big babies who must constantly be fed and sheltered and pointed in the right direction to get anything done at all. In my own case, it was Matin's contacts that led us to Nabi Gechi, Mullah Jilani, Salangi, and nearly everyone else I'd met with and interviewed on my trip thus far.

In the news media, we call people like Matin "fixers," a term so loaded it can seem complimentary and pejorative at the same time. To foreign correspondents, a fixer is someone who interprets the local language and "fixes" the problems the correspondent must overcome—everything from rebel groups and the government to the political and actual landmines that inhibit their ability to report a story. The fixer is the ultimate enabler and often the very prism through which correspondents view the nation they're covering. Any access a foreign correspondent gets, any big interviews, any scoops can likely be attributed to a good fixer (who is often a journalist, too), who helps him understand the language and culture and identify the dangers, the players, the trends.

While sometimes a prestigious, well-paying position, especially in war zones, being a fixer can also be the worst job in show business—especially in Afghanistan. While fixers do much of the phone calling, the begging for interviews, the bribing and backroom dealing , they usually get little of the credit, and much of the blame. And their lives are often more at risk than those of their foreign colleagues. Of the twenty-five journalists who have been killed in Afghanistan since the beginning of the American war, nine have been native Afghans, and six of those were actually working for foreign news organizations when they were killed. Most recently murdered (as of this writing) was Sardar Ahmad, a man widely respected in both the Afghan and western media circles. Ahmad worked for Agence France-Presse but had also started a company called Pressistan, which trained Afghan journalists and provided reporting services to outside clients. On March 20, 2014, Ahmad had gone with his wife and three young children to the upscale Serena Hotel in Kabul when Taliban gunmen stormed in, killing Ahmad, his wife, and two of his children with pistols they had smuggled in in their socks. Ahmad's youngest, a two-year-old named Abu Zar, survived despite being shot in the head three times. By the time the incident ended, nine people had died, including the four attackers.*

Ian Olds, a friend of mine and filmmaker, made a critically acclaimed documentary about the perils of being an

---

* Rod Nordland and Habib Zahori, "Killing of Afghan Journalist and Family Members Stuns Media Peers," *New York Times*, March 26, 2014.

Afghan interpreter for a foreign correspondent: *Fixer: The Taking of Ajmal Naqshbandi*. It's the story of a well-respected twenty-four-year-old Afghan journalist who, while working as a fixer, set up an interview with the Taliban for Italian journalist Daniele Mastrogiacomo in April 2007. But the interview went very wrong. Their driver was beheaded, and the Taliban took Mastrogiacomo and Naqshbandi captive. International and local efforts resulted in Mastrogiacomo being freed, but Naqshbandi was left behind and eventually killed.

In 2009, British commandos rescued *New York Times* correspondent Stephen Farrell from the Taliban, but his fixer, Sultan Munadi, was killed during the operation. And fixers often lead perilous lives even after the foreign correspondents have gone home. By working with Western media or even in the ranks of their own national press corps, fixers are often seen as spies and collaborators and continue to be targets.

My fixer and colleague Matin Sarfraz was no exception. Unable to work under his own byline for the *New York Times*, he had to ply his craft anonymously—or risk being killed. Working closely with me also put him in danger.

While I had worked with many Afghan colleagues over the years, one has accompanied me on nearly every trip I've made to Afghanistan, including my first in 2001. His name is Haroon Khadim, and we remained close from the very first story we had reported together, a feature on Marjan, the lion at the Kabul Zoo. Since Matin was from the north and didn't know Kabul well, we decided he'd hand me off to Haroon in

Kabul; Haroon would shepherd me through the second and third parts of my journey.

Haroon was a child of Afghanistan's endless conflicts. He was born in Kabul, the middle son in a family of four girls and three boys. His mother was Pashtun and his father Tajik. His parents weren't educated. His mother was a homemaker and his father drove a taxi, but he never made much money, Haroon said, since he spent most of his time picking up civilians wounded during the fighting between warlords in the early nineties and taking them to the hospital for free.

After school, Haroon worked a pushcart selling *ferni*, an Afghan pudding his mother made from milk, sugar, and corn flour to help the family survive.

"I remember the rockets would explode night and day," he told me. "We didn't have electricity for years, but we were still safe for a while. Then one of our neighborhood friends, a boy named Mahmood, was killed."

But despite all the chaos that surrounded him, Haroon discovered he had a gift for languages, especially English. He found a Persian-to-English dictionary and practiced translating old newspapers that were used to wrap fruit in the marketplace. He asked his father to enroll him for a semester at one of the local English schools, and within just a few months he won a scholarship that paid for the following two years of his studies. He became so proficient in English that after he graduated the school hired him to teach there. But by that time, the fight for power among competing warlords and the Taliban had left the capital in flaming ruins.

During the civil war Haroon and his family went to Pe-
shawar, Pakistan, for six months. But then finally, in 1996,
the Taliban took Kabul.

"When the Taliban came to power, we were happy," he
said, "because at least the fighting had stopped. So we moved
back to our house in Kabul. But then the Taliban put my
father in jail because he looked like he was from Panjshir,"
Massoud's stronghold in northern Afghanistan.

Haroon began teaching again, eventually opening his own
school across from the Intercontinental Hotel, where some of
the Taliban's top leadership stayed. He was summoned to the
hotel for a meeting with them, and shortly thereafter began
teaching them English.

"I grew a beard and wore a *shalwar kameez* to teach them,"
he said. "I would travel to the Ministry of Foreign Affairs to
give them lessons. I saw how they were to my father in jail, so
I treated them like children. I would make them stand up and
say very simple, elementary sentences, and they made a lot of
mistakes and I would correct them harshly. They seemed to
like it," he laughed.

Haroon used his earnings from teaching to support his
family, and eventually, with savings and the money from the
sale of some of the family's possessions, he was able to raise
$1 million afghanis, about $700 at the time, and used it to buy
his father's way out of jail.

Teaching twelve hours a day, six days a week, took its
toll, and in 1999 Haroon took a job as an interpreter with
the United Nations World Food Program (WFP), earning a

small but steady paycheck of $105 per month. In 2000, he left the WFP and took a job for $200 per month as a radio operator at the International Committee for the Red Cross. When the fighting broke out again in 2001 and the Taliban regime collapsed, his best friend Hakim, who with his cousin Shafiq had been working for us at our NBC bureau in the north, told Haroon he should try to get a job with NBC in Kabul at our newly relocated bureau at the Intercontinental Hotel. The bureau chief, Babak Behnam, hired him for $600 a week.

Paying those kind of war wages drew the scorn and ire of all the NGOs in Afghanistan, which couldn't afford to pay interpreters even the going rate of US$100 per day, and Haroon, with his vast vocabulary and nearly perfect diction, was one of the best. Although he had never before worked as a journalist, he instinctively understood our business—that the real story, especially in Afghanistan, was always beneath the surface. In 2001, we began working together to tell a deeper, more nuanced story of Afghanistan, and we've continued that partnership until this day.

11
LIONS

||||||||||||||

Bronze statue of Marjan the lion at the entrance to the Kabul Zoo.

When the Taliban regime fell in December 2001, I rushed to Kabul from northern Afghanistan with a handful of other journalists to report on its demise. We had not expected the fighting to end so soon.

We scurried across the capital, gathering stories about the Taliban's defeat and retreat, and the return of normalcy. Women could once again be seen outside their homes, music heard on street corners; tales of repression, oppression, and executions filled our notepads and videocassettes.

But the story that captured the imagination of my American news audience had little to do with all that. It was a story rife with symbolism, a story about an enduring lion in the Kabul Zoo. And since Haroon had not been with us in the north, it was also the first opportunity we had to work together.

The piece I wrote for the MSNBC website started like this:

Though his roar is more of a yawn these days, it was not so long ago when this lion, Marjan, used to be the king of Kabul's urban jungle. A mujahedin fighter who had survived combat with the Soviet Red Army was not so lucky, when he jumped into the lion's den to tease the beast. Marjan promptly ate him.

"The next day," says zookeeper Sheraq Omar, "the man's angry brother threw a hand grenade into the cage.

When Marjan pounced on it, thinking it was food, he lost one eye and 95 percent of his sight in the other."[*]

For many Americans, Marjan the lion became an entry point to their understanding of a larger story. It was a narrative of war, hardship, and survival presented through a battle-scarred symbol of the Afghan people, their outlast-them-all, last-cat-standing, grenade-munching, muj-eating Marjan.

Marjan had been a gift from Germany in the late 1960s, during the more peaceful time of the Afghan monarchy. The king's son, Prince Nader, was put in charge of the zoo, since its creation was considered an important rung on the ladder of the nation's ascent to modernity.

But the onslaught of war brought hardships for Marjan and even worse for many of the other animals. While they had survived the Soviet invasion, the zoo ended up on the front lines of Afghanistan's civil war in 1992. The animals that didn't die of starvation ended up on the dinner plates of hungry fighters. A sadistic mujahedin fighter reportedly killed an elephant with an RPG.

When the Taliban came to power, they initially shored up the zoo, rebuilding its outer walls, but as time passed and money became scarce for the pariah regime, there were calls to shut the zoo down. But the tenacious zookeeper, Sheraq Omar, fought back. He told me then that he went to the faculty of Islamic studies at the University of Kabul and had

---

[*] Kevin Sites, "Kabul's Lion Still King of the Beasts." MSNBC.com, November 23, 2001.

them write down every animal reference in the Koran connected to the prophet Muhammad.

"I collected them all and presented them to the Ministry of Justice," said Omar back in 2001.

Faced with evidence that the Prophet himself may have kept pets, the Taliban allowed Omar to keep the zoo open. But when the Taliban regime finally fell, the zoo also teetered on collapse. The buildings had been bombed, the staff had not been paid for months, food for the animals was running out, and their cages were not prepared for the winter. The 450 species of animals, reptiles, and fish once housed there had dwindled to only about a dozen. One of those who had survived was Marjan.

I remember entering the gates back then, seeing the decimated grounds and the malnourished animals. There was an Afghan bear pacing his cage, his muzzle red, raw, and swollen. Zoo officials said that Taliban soldiers would tease the bear by holding out food and then smack him on the nose with sticks when he reached for it. It was a desperate time for both the zoo and the city, but through all of it. Marjan the lion remained alive; he had endured it all: the Russian invasion, the civil war, the grenade, and even the Taliban. He had even outlived Afghanistan's other lion, Ahmad Shah Massoud, the Lion of the Panjshir.

When Haroon and I pulled our car inside the zoo's gates in the summer of 2013, I could see immediately that a lot had changed. The buildings had been repaired and refurbished. The grounds were clean, and a large fountain shot water high in the air. As we walked around the grounds, we watched people strolling past the cages. There were foxes and pigs, and even a pen with two polar bears. The place looked sparse but clean—almost modern.

We met with Aziz Gul Saqib, the zoo's director for the previous nine years. Dressed in a tailored suit and designer glasses, Saqib looked more like a businessman than a zoo official, an indication of the zoo's value to the capital as a cultural institution and a symbol of normalcy amid the unending conflict. He filled us in on what had taken place since last I'd been there.

Inspired by the stories of the indomitable spirits of both the former zookeeper Sheraq Omar and Marjan the lion, the North Carolina Zoo came to the rescue following the Taliban's ouster in 2001. They began a fundraising campaign, initially hoping to raise $30,000. With the help of donations worldwide, they eventually raised more than $300,000.

Saqib said they also sent over experts to help with animal care in the critical months after the Taliban's defeat, when many of the animals were on the brink of death. Additionally, they assisted with staff education and helped create a business plan for the zoo.

It was a lifeline that has allowed the Kabul Zoo to survive and even thrive in the years since. While the institution is still modest by the standards of most big-city zoos, Saqib claims they are back up to 100 species of animals and had more than 650,000 visitors in 2012, making the zoo not just one of the most popular attractions in Kabul, but profitable as well: "That same year, the zoo grossed

15,000 million afghanis (roughly US\$264,000) against 7.5 million afghanis (nearly US\$132,000) in costs, according to Saqib.

With those kinds of numbers (they have not been independently verified), the zoo is one of the most efficient government-run entities in Afghanistan. To solidify these gains, Saqib has joined professional organizations that can help in its evolution, like the South Asian Zoo Association, which provides vital certifications for worldwide standards of professionalism. With the help of outside donors, he's installed a zoo-wide security system with dozens of cameras and audio speakers directed at the enclosures and recorded messages reminding guests not to feed or tease the animals—a big problem in the past. A new education program reached thirty thousand students last year, teaching them about endangered species and conservation through special multimedia presentations in a renovated auditorium.

The Kabul Zoo now reflects the stated values of most modern zoos worldwide: preservation, conservation, and education. But beyond the education and exhibits, the zoo has provided another benefit for Afghans: after decades of turmoil, it has become a peaceful escape from the war's fears and worries that still play out just beyond its walls. Here families can enjoy picnics and young sweethearts can walk and talk together, free momentarily from prying eyes and wagging tongues. While the Taliban's Ministry of Virtue and Vice has disappeared, Afghanistan is not a place where unmarried men and women can be alone together. The zoo, at least, gives them the opportunity to meet one another without repercussion.

Things seem to be going so well at the zoo that the mayor of Kabul, Muhammad Yunus Nawandish, a diminutive, highly popular figure with boundless energy and on a perpetual, citywide building spree, wants to make the zoo five times larger and fill it with more exotic animals.

But experts, including one of the Kabul Zoo's biggest supporters, David Jones, director of the North Carolina Zoo, feel the expansion would be unsustainable, especially in light of Afghanistan's uncertain political future.

Whatever happens, one zoo fixture will be missing: Marjan the lion died in 2002, having survived three decades of war and upheaval. Marjan is buried in a lush flower garden at the rear of the zoo, but a bronze statue of the cat, another gift of the North Carolina Zoo, greets visitors at the entrance; many pet the statue or pose for photographs beside it. (Just a day after Marjan died, China donated two new African lions to the zoo, male and female, but zoo director Saqib said the male died of cancer in 2012 and the female isn't the tourist draw that Marjan had been.)

As I looked at the statue of the lion, a beautiful piece made by Texan sculptor Bob Coffee, I realized that reality will always fall short of the myth of Marjan, the same way it had with Afghanistan's other lion, Ahmad Shah Massoud, the Lion of Panjshir. They were both symbols of the nation: photographs of Massoud are hung in nearly every public building in Afghanistan next to those of President Hamid Karzai. And while they both inspired others while they were alive, the potency of their legend has grown in death.

One year from now, I wondered, when American troops have been partially or completely withdrawn and Afghan security forces left in charge, will the mere symbols of Afghanistan's lions be inspiration enough?

12
UNINTENDED
CONSEQUENCES

||||||||||||||

A dust storm outside Kabul turns everything into a rose-colored haze.

A few days after I arrived in Kabul, Haroon invited me to his house for dinner with a group of his friends, all young, educated Afghans whose lives, like his own, had changed drastically after the U.S. involvement in Afghanistan began in 2001.

I was still staying at Dost's apartment, so I asked both him and Matin to join me. Matin was heading back to Kunduz the next day to be with his family, and I thought contact with Haroon's network could be helpful to him since he'd expressed an interest in moving to Kabul .

We drove the Bahmani-mobile to Haroon's neighborhood and parked in front of a small convenience shop. There were billboards on top of the building, ads for a local gymnasium featuring photos of monstrously muscled and ripped guys juxtaposed with Hollywood action heroes like Bruce Willis and Sylvester Stallone.

I called Haroon, and within a few minutes his younger brother met us and got into the car. Haroon's father had died a few years earlier, so he became the de facto patriarch, bringing his brother and mother to live in his house with his wife and three daughters, aged eight, six, and one. The brother directed us to the house. We drove through a large metal gate and parked behind the cinderblock walls that surrounded it. Though it was already dark, I ducked down in the backseat to avoid being seen by Haroon's neighbors, just as I had at Ma-

tin's house in Kunduz. It was risky for most Afghans to entertain foreigners at their homes even in Kabul, and Haroon and
his family were already being threatened.

In 2012, Haroon had received a scholarship from the
Public-Private Partnership for Justice Reform in Afghanistan, founded by former secretary of state Condoleezza Rice.
He went to Hofstra University on Long Island, in New York
State, to study for a master's in law. He told me that while he
was in the U.S., his wife and brothers received phone calls
from someone who said Haroon was away being trained by
the Americans and British to be a spy, and that he, his wife,
and his children would all be killed.

"We'll send them to hell," Haroon said, echoing the caller's words to his family. "It literally made me sick. I wanted
to come home. But I couldn't."

The phone calls stopped when he did return home, but he
made an effort to reestablish himself in the neighborhood,
attending his local mosque regularly and publicly meeting
with the imam. He finally felt that things had gotten back to
normal, so I didn't want to do anything to jeopardize his family's safety.

Haroon's house was a large, sturdy brick building that he
had built with the money he had made working at NBC from
2001 to 2003. The basement, where we gathered, seemed
more an American male's ideal man cave than an Afghan
home. There was a ping-pong table to the left of the entrance,
an office area with a computer printer near the back, and next
to that a sitting area with a fireplace. Against the wall on the

right side was a whole gym's worth of free weights, pulley-operated exercise machines, and boxing gear, including a heavy bag and speed bag.

"Does some of that look familiar?" Haroon asked me when he saw me eyeballing the exercise equipment.

"Very," I said.

"It should. It's the stuff we had at the NBC house until they closed the bureau there."

When the security situation seemed to stabilize in early 2002, NBC moved its bureau out of the Intercontinental Hotel to a house in the pricey Wazir Akbar Khan neighborhood, home to foreign embassies, expats, and key post-Taliban Afghan leaders and influencers. We worked, ate, and slept in the walled compound, doing our television live shots from the roof. It still wasn't completely safe for us to go outside to exercise, and we were going stir crazy from spending so much time there. So we bought almost everything in a nearby sporting goods store—rusty weight plates, iron bars, an old bench press, punching bags—and set up a gym in the yard. When the bureau closed, no one else had enough space for the equipment, so Haroon took it home and turned it into his own private gym. I was envious.

Haroon introduced us to five friends whom I'd never met and surprised me with two old mutual friends who had also been fixers for NBC. One was Haroon's best friend, Hakim, a Tajik from the Panjshir who had been one of the first interpreters hired by NBC. With his light skin, sandy hair, and green eyes, Hakim looked even less Afghan than me. Haroon often joked with him, telling others that Hakim was a Russian who had stayed behind after the invasion and converted to Islam.

Hakim was a quiet man, watching everything going on around him with just a hint of a smile on his face while puffing on an endless supply of Korean Esse cigarettes. When he did speak, his voice was deep and resonant. Maybe Haroon's joke had planted the thought in my head, but when Hakim spoke English, he did sound like a Russian to me, rolling his *r*'s and hitting his final consonants hard. He and his cousin Shafiq had been with me through some of my craziest moments in my early days in the north and also later, when I traveled to Jalalabad and Tora Bora following the Taliban as they retreated across the border to Pakistan.

The other was a man named Ahmad who, like Haroon, had joined us in Kabul, a sweet and garrulous guy who was forever telling stories first in Dari, then to English and back, weaving both the foreigners and the Afghans who worked with us into the joke. He was deeply curious about everything in the West, asking questions about our lives and families, even probing into relationships with wives and girlfriends and happily sharing his own intimate secrets. He was and has remained guileless, and I love that about him.

I gave them both bear hugs and then worked my way around the room, chatting and soaking up the laughter and buzz. Most had benefited in some way from the Americans' presence in Afghanistan and were cautiously optimistic about the future.

Twenty-six-year-old Munib Zuhoori had been washing cars and selling fruit on the street before a series of foreign aid scholarships allowed him to finish high school, go to college, and then on to law school. He now worked for the Informal Justice System, a project of the United States Agency for International Development (USAID). He said he wouldn't have had the same opportunities under the old regime.

"There's been a lot of change in all aspects of life here," he told me. "Under the Taliban, it was a gloomy time. Since the change, six million students are going to school, including girls. Now there are more than thirty state-run universities in the country."

Rohullah Azizi, an assistant law professor at the American University of Afghanistan, agreed.

"Before 2001, when the question 'What do you want to be in the future?' came up, everyone said 'shopkeeper.' There were no other opportunities," he told me. "But in 2001, there were so many positive changes—now you had other opportunities. You could choose to do other things."

Another Afghan lawyer at the gathering, who didn't want to be identified, was more circumspect about the changes in Afghanistan.

"The collapse of the Taliban regime was applauded by 99 percent of the people. They were a foreign force, they oppressed people, and killed people," he said. "Their fall was a blessing. The last twelve years were good, but there were mistakes, and some things were promised that weren't delivered. I've worked in USAID projects where only 2 percent of the money is being spent on projects—most of the budgets are spent on capacity-building* studies, not actual factories or facilities."

Of the dozen men in the room, all—save Matin and me—had worked for the U.S. government in some capacity, and most had done project work for USAID. Thanks to massive investment by the United States (an estimated $600 billion to date), most Afghans could find work in one of two areas: If you were illiterate or uneducated, you could join the Afghan National Army, the Afghan National Police, or any of the other half dozen public or hundreds of private security armies that emerged after 2001. If you had secondary education or some college, you could work in the civilian sector—the Afghan government, international assistance organizations, or their local NGO clients. Almost anyone in Afghanistan who had set foot in a university classroom had fed at the USAID trough at some point in the last twelve years.

USAID has spent an estimated $17 billion in projects in Afghanistan since 2002. Nearly $4 billion has been spent on infrastructure like buildings, roads, energy and water facilities, schools, and hospitals, as well as training and maintenance. The rest has been spread out evenly among other sectors—agriculture, economic development, democracy and gover-

---

* A term often used by NGOs and others involved in global development, "capacity building" refers to understanding the obstacles and pathways to achieving sustainable progress.

nance, stabilization, health, education, and programs that support each of these sectors, according to USAID spokesman Kevin O'Loughlin, whom I met with at the USAID offices at the American Embassy in Kabul later in my trip.

The biggest investment, $3.5 billion, came in 2010. Some critics say the large infusion of funds was an effort to shore up sagging support for the government, which the Afghan public viewed as corrupt and impotent, incapable of providing even the most basic protection or services outside Kabul. O'Loughlin said that since 2010, investment has leveled off to $1.8 billion annually, and there are no new major infrastructure projects in the pipeline. USAID's current focus is working with the Afghan government to support the operations and maintenance of the existing projects, according to O'Loughlin.

For Afghans working on USAID projects, it was a solid, if not permanent, paycheck, a way to support their families. But to many, including the Office of the Special Inspector General for Afghanistan Reconstruction (SIGAR), the projects often seemed only to make Afghan warlords richer. In 2008, Congress created SIGAR to look into allegations of massive mismanagement, corruption, and fraud, and to provide ongoing spending oversight to American rebuilding and reconstruction projects in Afghanistan. Since that time, SIGAR's inspector general, John Sopko, has become one of the harshest critics of USAID projects in Afghanistan. His office pumps out press releases almost daily, highlighting USAID's shortcoming and failures.[*]

---

[*] Matthew Rosenberg and Azam Ahmed, "U.S. Aid to Afghans Flows on Despite Warn-

When I asked USAID's O'Loughlin about SIGAR's relentless criticism, he shook his head ruefully. "They really just don't understand what we're trying to do here."

And despite good intentions, USAID often seemed to be a hostage to the very government it was attempting to support. In one of SIGAR's largest spending audits, it discovered allegations that the Afghan government had levied $1 billion in fraudulent taxes against contractors working on American reconstruction projects—costs ultimately passed on to American taxpayers.

After NBC, Haroon had worked as a logistician for a USAID project from 2003 to 2006, where he saw such corruption firsthand.

"By 2006, I felt like the corruption was getting worse every day," Haroon told me. "The warlords were becoming more powerful. They were getting all the contracts from international firms, but nothing was getting done, buildings weren't getting built, roads weren't getting paved. Finally, my boss convinced me I should go to law school as a backup plan."

And so he did, working during the day managing forty people, and going to school at night. He also married—against his family's wishes—a woman who is not only a Shia

---

ings of Misuse," *New York Times*, January 30, 2014." In a report released on January 30, 2014, SIGAR criticized USAID for funding Afghan government operations despite its auditors' claims that none of the sixteen Afghan ministries could guarantee the funds would not be stolen or wasted. Inspector General Sopko called the practice "the biggest gamble with taxpayer money that USAID has ever made." The criticism is likely to further deteriorate the relationship between the U.S. and Afghan governments.

Muslim (Haroon is Sunni) but who had also been forced, under the Taliban, to end her formal education at the fifth grade.

"I was in love. It's what I wanted," he explained. "I had to teach her to read and write."

But despite the marriage and law school, his anxiety and anger about the direction in which Afghanistan was being taken increased. I saw him during a reporting trip in 2006, when the violence wracking the country seemed to increase each day—as did the number of civilian casualties. Human Rights Watch estimated that 929 civilians were killed that year, 699 in insurgent actions and 230 in NATO operations.[*]

Working with him then, I noticed a simmering bitterness filling the void of dissipating hope.

"I called that your Taliban Period," I joked with him at the party. "When you were unhappy about everything."

He laughed, but it was true, and like so many other Afghans who believed their country would finally emerge from the darkness of decades of war, he felt betrayed—by the U.S., its NATO allies, and by the corrupt government they helped create and then propped up with endless amounts of unmonitored money.

"But my anger was an uneducated anger," he told me, "My education and my wife helped me to get over it, eventually."

---

[*] Human Rights Watch, "Afghanistan: Civilian Deaths from Airstrikes: Airstrikes Cause Public Backlash, Undermine Protection Efforts." September 9, 2008. http://www.hrw.org/news/2008/09/07/afghanistan-civilian-deaths-airstrikes.

Haroon also embraced a mystical form of Islam called Sufism, which he credits with helping to transform his outlook. Sufism encourages a pathway to the truth through meditation and ritual prayer known as *dhikr*, which can include continual repetition of the word "Allah."

"My God is a God of love, not of anger," he said. "Those people that believe in killing are perverting the Holy Koran. They're uneducated."

But his transformation from angry young man to lawyer, husband, father, and Sufi had not erased his fear or his concerns about his country. One of the stipulations of his scholarship was that he return to Afghanistan and attempt to use his skills to help in the judicial reform process. And while he'd returned willingly, he believed his options to promote change are limited.

"I can work for the government," he said, "but if I take a job in the judicial system, I'll be expected to take bribes like everyone else. Or I can work for private companies controlled by the warlords, where the corruption is even worse."

Haroon, I realized, like most of his friends in the room, had both benefited from USAID programs and been marginalized by them. He was able to earn enough money to support his family and attend law school, but all the while he and his friends had worked on impermanent USAID projects and remained outside the government. They helped build infrastructure and encourage investment in other sectors, but when the work was over, they would find themselves without a job, without any real influence on the future of Afghanistan.

In an email, I asked USAID's O'Loughlin about my theory that USAID may be unintentionally disenfranchising those it had hoped to empower, which he shared with USAID/Afghanistan's deputy mission director, Carolyn (Teddy) Bryan. This was her response:

> USAID aims to support a wide variety of leaders and "change agents" to help their countries along their development path. In contexts where there is a dearth of experienced leaders, those few go back and forth between the private sector and the public sector. Change not only happens from within, but often is spurred from outside government. Furthermore, where the "real power" to create change lies is a matter of political science and sociological debate.

After dinner we sat on the floor and Ahmad pulled out a harmonium, a traditional keyboard instrument that looks a little like an accordion, originally from India but also popular in Afghanistan. In his typical guileless style, he committed fully to a song about unrequited love, singing and playing with all that was inside him, as if nothing else in the world mattered. And for those few moments, as I looked around at all the faces, nothing else did.

We had to leave Haroon's house early in the evening because we had another appointment at 9 p.m. Bilal from the BBC had set up an informal interview with one of his close contacts, Mirwais Yasini, first deputy speaker of Afghanistan's Wolesi Jirga, its parliament's lower house. He is a key power broker in Afghan politics and one of the most vocal critics of the Karzai government.

Yasini was a flip and funny straight-talker, smart enough to take you apart in five different languages if he wanted to. One of his early claims to fame was that he was the key fixer for former CBS News anchor Dan Rather and succeeded in smuggling him from Pakistan across the border into Afghanistan in 1980 to report for *60 Minutes* on the Russian invasion. To blend in, Rather wore traditional Afghan clothing, including baggy pants, a *shalwar kameez*, and a *pakool*, the woolen cap favored by Massoud. *Washington Post* television critic Tom Shales dubbed him "Gunga Dan" after seeing him report from Afghanistan wearing local clothes. But Rather's ballsy move earned begrudging admiration from critics and colleagues alike, and he and Yasini became lifelong friends after.

Yasini was from Nangarhar Province in eastern Afghanistan, near the Pakistan border. He, like so many others in the national government, had fought both the Russians and the Taliban, and had reaped positions of power for his efforts.

He had become the minister of finance after the fall of the Taliban and was later named director general of counter-narcotics, but disagreements with Karzai led him to run for president in the 2009 election, which he lost. He'd used his position as deputy speaker to pointedly criticize Karzai's administration ever since.

Bilal, Matin, and I waited for Yasini at his home. He arrived about twenty minutes after we did. It was a warm summer evening, so we sat in his backyard, talking and eating mangos. Yasini lay flat on a lounge chair, complaining about back pain and smoking skinny Korean Esse cigarettes. He was bald, a little thick around the middle, with dark, deep-set eyes and a salt-and-pepper beard. His wit was knife-blade sharp. From the research I had done, I knew that we were the same age, both born in 1962.

"You know, after 9/11, one of my cousins was working in a restaurant in London and he was taking a cab home from work one night," Yasini said, reeling us in. "The cab driver looked at him in the rearview mirror and asked him where he was from. My cousin, because of the recent events in the news, got nervous and didn't want to say he was from Afghanistan, so he looked back at the driver's reflection and said, 'I am from Spain.' So wouldn't you know, the cab driver begins prattling to him in Spanish. My cousin, of course, didn't understand a word of it. So the cab driver switches back to English and says, 'I thought you said you were from Spain?' My cousin, not knowing what do said, 'I am from a very small part of Spain in India.'" Yasini and the rest of us broke out into laughter.

"A small part of Spain in India," he repeats, still laughing. "Half-literacy is our problem here. That's the problem."

"Mr. Speaker, can I bum a cigarette off you?" I asked, mirroring his casual manner.

He gave me his pack with five cigarettes left and told me to keep them. I knew our time was limited and now that we were all comfortable, I jumped into my questioning.

"What's going to happen in Afghanistan after 2014?" I asked.

He paused for a moment. "I hope you understand some of this is on the record and some of it is off," he said. I didn't respond, already writing notes.

"We will be disrupted," he said. "There will be issues. The leadership is fragile. The corruption is rooted deeply in society. Democracy is fragile. Afghanistan lost a golden opportunity to build a system and institutions. The current leadership didn't focus on the national agenda. Most of those around [Karzai] were focused on their personal wealth, and you can't buy the loyalty of people with money."

I said nothing, wanting him to go on.

"The mistake was made from the very beginning: not creating an inclusive government. The Northern Alliance was given too many government positions."

"A government dominated by warlords?" I asked, understanding that many Afghans considered the Northern Alliance to have been a coalition of warlords.

He ignored the question and continued his train of thought.

"No one paid attention to governance, no one paid attention to international cooperation," he said. "Where are the dams, where are the economic opportunities? People have gone back to a poppy economy."

"Will you run for president again in 2014?" I asked. "And if so, what would you do differently?"

Yasini paused, took a long drag from his cigarette, and exhaled.

"If we can have a good election, transparent, inclusive, on time . . . yes," he said. "But if it's like the election in 2009, no."

"How would you be different?" I pressed.

"I would not be above the constitution; I would not be above the national interests. I'm living in a global village. There's good government and responsible government that's not selected by wheeling and dealing."

"How would you and your administration rise above the corruption?" I asked. "You yourself said it runs deep here."

He seemed weary, or perhaps because of his back pain, his answers were almost dismissive.

"If I'm not corrupt, my brothers are not corrupt," Yasini replied, "Positions would be distributed by merit, not by ethnic makeup."

"What about stability and economic growth?" I asked, "Many critics say the national government is simply Kabul's City Hall. That its influence doesn't extend past the capital."

"We need to look at connecting the regional area by railroad and then focus on income generation. Next would be extending our water resources, agriculture development, and then the mines and minerals."

Yasini seemed to grow bored with talking about his plans, as if he had done it so many times already he'd tired of hearing himself speak. He changed the subject a few times, told some more jokes, and then finally came back to me with an explanation that could have been mistaken for a long sigh.

"I'm trying to be optimistic here, but it doesn't always work. There's no leadership. There's a volunteer army made up of shopkeepers and cab drivers from Kabul rather than professional soldiers. Without some kind of national unity . . ." He trailed off.

"I don't know." He paused again. "I would like *not* to leave my country. I'd like to die here."

I wondered if Afghanistan could slide into that abyss again, whether people like Yasini would pack up and go into self-imposed exile again, leaving behind the warlords and the Taliban to slug it out over the remains of another failed state—one that, in the mid-nineties, had allowed Al Qaeda to set up shop and eventually launch the attacks on the United States that started this war.

In 2001, I saw the remains of one of the Al Qaeda camps after it had been obliterated by American airstrikes. It was depressing to imagine that history repeating itself.

From my journal:

DECEMBER 2001, AL QAEDA CAMP

This morning we headed to a village called Reshkhor, about an hour south of Kabul, said to have been the location of one of the largest Al Qaeda terrorist training bases in the country. American B-52s bombed it for a week straight. It is a field of rubble and twisted rebar. Building

*facades turned to Swiss cheese, making holey shadows on
the ground, Russian T-55 tanks flashed-cooked in their
tracks.* [Jim] *Avila does an on-camera standup in the 15-
foot crater left by a 500-pound American bomb.* [Later,
colleagues who see the video all say the same thing:
"Good to see U.S. tax dollars at work."]

*Muhammad Yahia, the Northern Alliance soldier who
serves as both guard and tour guide at Reshkhor, takes
us to what's left of a thatch of connected buildings about
a mile from the base's entrance. He tells us to watch our
step, and then points out exposed land mines amid the
chunks of wood and concrete. He takes us to a room that,
he says, was the Al Qaeda library. There are papers and
books scattered everywhere. I pick up a cover with the title
"Special Forces Operations." It has a photograph of a
British commando on the front, but the face is scribbled
out with pen. Avila picks up a chemistry manual. There is
also a pair of black rubber gloves under the debris.*

*These are clues for the investigatively challenged. In-
spector Clouseau could crack this case. It is all so obvious
that we wonder if the evidence has been planted. A U.S.
black bag op, scattering terrorism's accouterments after
the air raids, knowing we would find them and make the
Taliban-Al Qaeda terrorism link indisputable. But in a
country of perpetual chaos, conspiracies are tough to hatch
and there's no word from local villagers that any other
Americans, besides journalists, have actually been on the
ground here. Muhammad tells us there is one other place*

*that we should see. We follow him up a dirt road that
leads to a bunker in the hillside.*

*From sophomore science I remember this: potential
energy is stored energy, the energy equivalent of basket-
ball's sixth man—on the bench when the game starts but
the first one buzzed in to play. Kinetic energy is the energy
of something in motion. As we walk past the door of the
bunker, what we see is a bit hard to comprehend. Piles and
piles of potential energy. Pandora's box—filled with ammunition. Islands of misfit ordinance. If we slip, trip, or
drop, say, the camera, all of it could be quickly converted
to the kinetic kind of energy.*

*At this moment, I am walking on a carpet of copper,
my boots chinkling through thousands of live Kalashnikov rounds. To the left, an open wooden crate filled with
TS-50s—in military circles, they call them Chinese toe-
poppers—landmines with just enough explosives to take off
your foot. Engineered, diabolically, not to kill, but to maim,
so your comrades must shoulder their weapons while they
try to carry you to safety. They are plastic and paperweight-
small, with little pressure triggers on the top. They are
benign-looking, almost cute. If you were a child you would
want to stack them up like blocks. Adults here plant them like
seeds. But this is just the beginning. In another corner, stacks
of discus-shaped anti-tank mines. A colleague from the Voice
of America saw a man and his donkey step on one of these
on the road outside Khodja Bahaudin. She told me when the
parts finally landed she couldn't tell man from beast.*

In the back of the room are hundreds of cylinders stacked from floor to ceiling. They are loaded with rocket-propelled grenades, as ubiquitous as dust here. To the right, sinister-looking rockets with fins, and against the east wall, a stack of Claymore anti-personnel mines. They are printed with these words in English: "Front towards enemy." I think that anyone truly needing instructions like these will eventually blow himself or herself up anyway. The room is frightening, but at the same time deadly fascinating. I know the destructive power that surrounds me—have seen it firsthand, the history and potential of these weapons to wreak havoc and heartache, to permanently make people and families and villages less than whole forever.

Despite this, I am intrigued by it all. It is perhaps that hardwired male desire to see things explode. I don't want anyone hurt, but Lord help me—I do want to reach down into the pile of hand grenades, pull the pin, and toss it into an open field. Just to see what happens. I am able to control the impulse. On my way out of the room, in a corner behind the door, I see something less lethal—stacks of old Russian helmets. A few of them have messages scribbled across them with a black marker. They are written in Pashto. I pick one up and show my translator, Ahmed. His eyes widen as he reads: "It says, 'This is the Jihad of the Taliban.'" I nod with approval and then tuck it under the backseat of the van. Later, I will take it to America to remind me of the deadly potential energy here.

In a nearby village, I see a man with crutches moving around on one leg. I ask him what happened. He points to a field and pantomimes an erupting explosion. When we are finally finished, ready to leave, Muhammad, the soldier guard/guide, asks us to contact the de-mining unit of the United Nations.

"They should know about this," he says. "Villagers are coming in and taking things from here."

13
UNDER THE BRIDGE

||||||||||||||

Heroin addicts and other drug users gather by the hundreds under the Pul-e-Sokhta Bridge in West Kabul.

I thought about what Deputy Speaker Mirwais Yasini said to me about Afghanistan's return to a "poppy economy." It was only half true: poppy had never really disappeared from the Afghan economy.

For most of their five-year reign in Afghanistan, the Taliban permitted poppy farming and benefited from the lucrative opium trade it enabled. Only in July 2000, four years after taking power, did Taliban leader Mullah Muhammad Omar decide to outlaw poppy cultivation. And through the use of forced eradication and severe punishments, he created one of the most successful anti-drug campaigns in history, resulting in a 99 percent reduction in growing areas under Taliban control, a reduction that, according to some records, amounted to three-fourths of the world's heroin supply at the time.* It's rumored, however, that the Taliban and many others benefited from the brief worldwide price hike the shortage created by stockpiling dried opium during the ban. When the Taliban were deposed, poppy growing and opium production went back into high gear and have increased nearly every year since.

Afghanistan is the largest producer of opium poppies, the raw material from which heroin is made. Recently, the United

---

* Graham Farrella and John Thorneb, "Where have all the flowers gone?: evaluation of the Taliban crackdown against opium poppy cultivation in Afghanistan," International Journal of Drug Policy 16 (2005) 81–91. http://reformdrugpolicy.com/wp-content/uploads/2011/09/AfghanTalibanOpium.pdf.

Nations Office on Drugs and Crime (UNODC) reported it has also become one of largest cannabis growers and as a result, the world's biggest producer of hashish. More troubling, Afghans have now become leading consumers of their own drugs.

According to the UNODC 2009 survey "Drug Use in Afghanistan," nearly one million Afghans between the ages of fifteen and sixty-four are addicted to drugs. The report states that at 8 percent of the population, this rate is twice the global average. The survey shows an increase of 53 percent in the number of opium users, from 150,000 to 230,000, and a leap of 140 percent in the number of heroin users, from 50,000 to 140,000, compared to a similar survey conducted in 2005.[*]

This enormous drug problem, some experts believe, may present a greater long-term threat to the stability of the country than the war. But I knew I wouldn't be able to understand that impact from numbers and stats alone. I wanted to see it in the faces of the Afghans suffering from addiction. So I asked Haroon to take me to one of most notorious drug hangouts in all of Afghanistan, the Pul-e-Sokhta Bridge in West Kabul.

We might as well have kicked over a rock or tree stump. The gray objects below scurried from side to side like insects, some crawling over others who lay motionless, others covering themselves with garbage bags, scraps of fabric, or

---

[*] Drug Use in Afghanistan: 2009 Survey, Executive Summary. United National Office on Drugs and Crime. https://www.unodc.org/documents/data-and-analysis/Studies/Afghan-Drug-Survey-2009-Executive-Summary-web.pdf

cardboard—anything to hide them from the sunlight and from the eyes of others. Haroon and I watched from the street above for a few minutes, and I nearly threw up from the stench, filth, and collective misery below.

Hundreds of drug addicts had gathered in the perpetual darkness under this bridge to shoot up, buy and sell drugs, or nod off after using. Raw sewage flowed openly under the bridge, and garbage covered nearly every inch of ground.

In one spot we saw a group of men, syringes in hand, injecting each other, the heroin addicts' version of a circle jerk. In another, a young guy, wrapped in his headscarf, lay on the bank, legs crossed, hands in pockets, in a narco-doze that might have appeared bucolic if it weren't for the river of shit, piss, and toxic sludge flowing next to him.

We climbed down a dirt path next to the bridge and stepped cautiously around this hellish perimeter, concerned that every footfall could bring us in contact with a dirty needle or some other long, slow death sentence.

Almost immediately after I took a few photographs, one of the addicts ran at me, shouting, "What is he doing here? Why is he taking pictures?" Haroon intercepted him and tried to calm him down, and also gave me a look that said, "We need to get out of here. Quickly."

The man followed us as we climbed back up the bank. At the top, he grabbed my arm and reached for the camera. I pulled the camera back, pushed him away, and raised my fist in a warning for him to back down. Then another man patted the guy on the shoulder and told him to calm down, and that we were "guests."

"If they're guests, why does he have his fist raised like that," the man asked?

The man who had helped us out, a twenty-three-year-old named Hasibullah, sent the other guy back down under the bridge and walked us away from the path and back onto the street. Haroon knew that I still wanted to talk to some of the addicts and told Hasibullah to follow us back to the car and get inside. It was a smart move that gave us the privacy to talk and some protection from another attack by other addicts who might be unhappy with us for shooting photos and picking at the scabs of their desperation just for a news story.

Inside the car, Hasibullah agreed to tell us about life under the bridge, but denied that he was a drug addict himself.

"It's hell down here. We sleep in the dirt and shit. Everyone is always fighting, but once they inject they just fall asleep, fall down, and forget where they are. When someone dies, the government comes and gets the body, and they hold it for the family to pick it up. There are doctor's assistants down there, university graduates, soldiers—they lost people in the war, have family issues, economic problems, or too much money. They started having fun, and now can't stop."

He told us that the addicts smoked heroin as well as shooting it up, using foil, sometimes from the inside of cigarette packs, to put the heroin on; then they would light it up and suck in the smoke using straws from juice boxes.

While the UNODC claims there are a million drug-addicted Afghans, the number is actually much higher, since the annual UN Opium Survey doesn't include women or children. A whopping 50 percent of Afghanistan's opium-using parents admit to giving the drug to their children.* UN officials blame the addiction problem in Afghanistan on three things: 1) decades of war-related trauma; 2) the unlimited availability of cheap narcotics; and 3) limited access to treatment.

As we talked to Hasibullah, another guy who called himself Shir Shaw lumbered up to the driver's side window. He said he wanted to talk about life under the bridge, too, but he smelled so bad we decided not to let him into the car.

Through the window, told us he'd been doing heroin for a year. He'd smoked hashish while in the Afghan army and eventually added heroin to it. He said he'd deserted the army and now steals, begs, or works rounding up passengers to fill up taxis to earn the equivalent of a couple of dollars a day, with which he buys four ampules of heroin. He said he spends his days shooting up and his nights hustling for money.

Users like Shir Shaw have ensured those who cultivate and sell the drug a steady income. Poppies can thrive in even the poorest soil, and Afghan farmers can make up to $10,000 a year per hectare of raw opium. By comparison, they earn

---

* "UN: Drug Addiction Growing at 'Alarming' Rate in Afghanistan," Voice of America. June 20, 2010. http://www.voanews.com/content/un-report-finds-afghan-drug-addiction-is-twice-global-average-96796459/120038.html.

about $120 per hectare of wheat. Nearly 900 tons of opium and 375 tons of heroin are exported from Afghanistan every year, according to the UNODC Opium Survey. And an estimated 1,500 to 3,500 tons of hashish is also produced from cannabis grown there.

Despite the $541 million the U.S. Agency for International Development spent from 2009 to 2012 to help Afghan farmers develop financially viable alternatives to growing poppy, addiction to the profits from the crop seems to be harder to kick than addiction to the drug it produces. And the billions more that have been spent on eradication and interdiction efforts (the US spent $782 million in 2005 alone)[*] have had little impact.

Opium cultivation has also helped fund Afghanistan's never-ending war. The UNODC estimates that the Taliban may have earned as much as $700 million from the poppy crop in 2011 alone, and despite billions spent by the international community on counter-narcotics programs, widespread corruption within the Afghan government has severely undercut efforts to reduce cultivation and trafficking. Even the president's own brother, Ahmed Wali Karzai, was linked to the drug trade, allegations he denied before being shot to death in July 2012 by one of his own militia commanders.

---

[*] U.S. State Department, Bureau of International Narcotics and Law Enforcement Affairs U.S. Counternarcotics Strategy for Afghanistan, Archive, Compiled by the Coordinator for Counternarcotics and Justice Reform in Afghanistan, Ambassador Thomas A. Schweich, U.S. Department of State, 2009. http://2001-2009.state.gov/p/inl/rls/rpt/90561.htm.

Without a more holistic approach to the problem that includes more treatment centers and a crackdown on drug-related corruption, Afghanistan's seemingly infinite fields of poppy will continue to fuel the war and strangle what little hope the country might have left.

Nowhere was this more evident than in my conversations with Shir Shaw and Hasibullah. When we finished talking, they asked us for money, as I expected. Instead, we gave them bags of juicy red plums—far from what they were craving, but easier on my conscience. I watched as they sulked away, disappointed, and headed back under the bridge. The smell of their resignation lingered.

14

WALL OF BONES

||||||||||||||

Kabul municipal district chief Al Haj Aq Masoomi leading the climb along
Afghanistan's "Great Wall."

While that place under the Pul-e-Sokhta Bridge reeked of hopelessness, there is a place in Kabul where you can follow a trail of history out of the city and into a peaceful, if impermanent, escape into a dark, fantastic Afghan legend.

At the foot of the eastern slope of the Shir Darwaza ("gate of the lions") mountains, there's an old citadel known as Bala Hissar, an ancient seat of power in Afghanistan. The first fortress is said to have been built there in the fifth century CE or even earlier; the more recent was built at the end of the nineteenth century, when its predecessor was destroyed by the British at the end of the Second Anglo-Afghan War.

But the ancient citadel walls, 3 to 6 feet thick and possibly more than 1,500 years old, extend in crumbling bits and pieces from the fortress, soaring beyond the ridgeline to towering heights above the city—in some places, as high as 20 feet.

While most of Kabul's city walls built in the last twelve years are ugly concrete slabs snapped into place like giant LEGOs around government ministries and other important buildings, this ancient wall has the worn, red-rock patina of the pyramids—and a similar macabre allure.

Historical facts about the wall are difficult to come by, but legend has it that it was a project of King Zamburak Shaw in the sixth century, built to keep out Arab invaders. Zamburak is said to have forced all of his male subjects to work on the wall; those who refused or became too sick to continue were killed on the spot and their bones encased within the wall. But Zamburak met with poetic justice: During a visit to the site, he was attacked and killed by angry workers, who then buried his bones within the walls along with those of all his victims. Or so the story goes.

In all the trips I've made to Afghanistan, I'd never seen the wall close up, but Dost Muhammad, through his television program contacts, knew a perfect guide. His name was Al Haj Aq Masoomi, and he was Kabul's municipal district chief, the city's overseer for building and construction projects.

Masoomi made the three-hour hike nearly every Friday, his day off, along with his pal and boss, Kabul mayor Muhammad Younas Nawandish. They visited a copse of fruit trees they had planted a few years back as a symbol of peace. Masoomi had even had an elaborate pipeline constructed on the mountain to make sure the trees were properly irrigated.

We met Masoomi at his office near the base of the mountains. He had a kind face, with a close-cropped white beard and the ruddy complexion of a man who spends most of his time outdoors. He was dressed in a loose gray shirt and slacks—his municipal uniform—and was swapping his sandals for some white sneakers when we arrived.

The climb was steep, winding around rock faces, tapering into narrow cliffs, and zigzagging around hundreds of gravity-defying homes built on angles as sharp as 40 degrees. The people who lived in them were squatters from other provinces, escaping the war, poverty, or both. But while they built with great skill, nearly all of them built without permission. While this illegal construction was under Masoomi's jurisdiction, it had been going on so long that it had become an accepted reality of life in a nation with bigger problems to deal with. In fact, many of the families waved warmly to the municipal chief, and he stopped to chat briefly with some during our climb.

Along the way, we also met children hauling heavy yellow water containers and green propane tanks, which they'd fetched at the base of the mountain and had to carry back to their homes. Climbing twice a day for these living essentials was the price of free housing. The other, apparently, was a lack of sanitation; open sewage and garbage filled the channels in between homes.

After forty minutes on the trail, it became clear that Masoomi, who ran up the shale remnants of a portion of the wall, was part mountain goat.

We paused at an impressive section about an hour from the bottom. The edges had been rounded by a thousand-plus years of wind and weather but still stood high despite pockmarks from artillery rounds fired during the civil war from 1992 to 1996, when warlords battled one another for control of the city. On the very ridge where we stood, the Hizb-i-Islami forces of Pakistani-aligned warlord Gulbuddin Hekmatyar faced off against the forces of Ahmad Shah Massoud.

To the north of us was the city center; its noise, traffic, and palpable collective anxiety caused by weekly suicide bombings were imperceptible here. Below to the west were the Babur Gardens and the Kabul Zoo; behind us to the southwest, the massive Shohada-ye Salehin cemetery. And despite both the legend and the actual history of the wall, it felt serene where we stood, a remote, peaceful place bathed in a quiet beauty perceptible only from this height.

There Masoomi finished the story of the wall's construction, with the towering wall to his back and a shrill wind threading through its gaps.

"These walls," he said, "were built from the blood of people." I nodded yes, having heard the legend. But he had more to offer.

"Three months ago, bones were found within the walls. They've been taken away and sent for scientific evaluation."

I was surprised by his revelation. If examined and accurately dated, the bones could help to turn the dark legend of the wall into an irresistible fact. In a nation not torn apart by decades of war, the find would make the wall a major tourist attraction. But tourists or no, Masoomi was clearly happy to revel in the wall's ancient, violent history while hoping a modern peace would take root—perhaps beginning with the copse of fruit trees he had planted at the top of Kabul's wall of bones.

15

MORE THAN WAR

||||||||||||||

An NGO called Skateistan provides Afghan boys and girls an escape from the war that surrounds them: skateboarding.

For foreign correspondents, the expectations of editors and audiences can be a powerful incentive to reinforce rather than unmask national stereotypes. A testament to this truth is how little we know about Afghanistan beyond the war, the Taliban, and the blue burka—even twelve years later.

Even in the most riven conflict zones, there is life beyond war, and Afghanistan is no exception. On my most recent visit, I saw that life had not only resumed, it had evolved in unexpected ways, both because of the foreign intervention and in spite of it. In Kabul, a burgeoning contemporary art scene and the introduction of skateboarding are just two such examples.

Art can reflect the soul of a nation, and that has been especially true for Afghanistan, whose geography along the Silk Road trading route between East and West ensured a steady stream of varied artistic, cultural, and religious influences creating a cultural heritage both diverse and unique. But the perpetual cycle of war has destroyed or dispersed many of these artworks, and for the past three decades it has been nearly impossible for artists to express themselves at all.

Following the Russian invasion in 1979, Afghan art floundered amid the stifling social realism of the Soviets; the civil war from 1992 to 1996 nearly destroyed the capital and supplanted creative endeavors with the effort to survive. But perhaps the darkest period for Afghan art was during the rule of the Taliban, whose fundamentalist interpretation of the Koran forbid the portrayal of living things, and any drawing, painting, or sculpture depicting animals or humans was considered blasphemy. The Taliban, in effect, declared war on art, seizing paintings, books, and music from homes and burning them in the streets. And in March 2001, the Taliban dynamited the giant statues of Buddha that had stood in Bamiyan since the seventh century BCE, their most outrageous assault on culture and history. Despite all of this, art has not only survived in Afghanistan, an art scene has reemerged, albeit on a small scale, becoming a creative and provocative force in Kabul.

Painter and video artist Rahraw Omarzad deserves much of the credit. Omarzad was a student of fine arts at Kabul University but fled to Pakistan during the reign of the Taliban. While there, he started an art magazine for Afghans, keeping the country's creative flame alive despite an unfolding diaspora.

"There was nothing for Afghan artists during that time, no way to share our work with others," he told me when Haroon and I visited him at his office and gallery on a Saturday afternoon.

When the Taliban government was forced from power, Omarzad returned to Kabul and continued publishing his magazine. With the help of several international organizations, including the Open Society and Women of the World foundations, he also opened the Afghan Center for Contemporary Art and the Women's Art Center.

"This is a place where we can teach each other new skills and reflect on our country," said Omarzad. Students come to the center to work on their art as well as to show it.

Omarzad took us to the gallery space in the back of his building, a high-ceilinged, loft-like structure with a gravel floor and egg cartons paneling the walls. Inside were more than a dozen engaging works from a recent exhibit titled *Balloons*. Among the works were balloons dressed as burka-clad women, balloons surrounded by barbed wired, and even a skeleton holding deflated balloons titled "The Balloon Seller."

"The balloons in this exhibit are the symbol of empty promises," he explained.

While the Center offered Afghan artists a chance to work in a relatively secure environment and even create art that spoke against government corruption and betrayals, Omarzad was cautious, knowing that the threat to free speech might never dissipate completely. This became clear from his reaction after I took a picture of an Afghan flag drooping on the ground from a broken staff. He rushed to adjust it so it no longer touched the floor. The flag was not part of some anti-government exhibit, he explained—the aluminum staff had recently snapped.

"Freedom of expression has some limitations all over the world. You cannot find any country that has full freedom of expression, and Afghanistan also has some limitations and borders," said Omarzad. "Working as an artist here is a risk, but you have to accept that risk. Without accepting the risk, you cannot be a responsible artist."

In the aftermath of the Taliban's war on art, those risks are being embraced, and while the canvas is small, Omarzad feels Kabul's contemporary arts movement will reflect the promises—both real and hollow—of a new Afghanistan.

Not so far away from Omarzad's gallery, Fareed Wahidi was tearing it up at Skateistan, Kabul's indoor skateboarding park. Wearing a green T-shirt, jeans, and black sneakers, the sixteen-year-old Afghan looked like he had been born on a deck. He plunged down a steep ramp and caught serious air on the other side. Until two years ago he'd never seen a real skateboard; now he made it look like part of his body.

"After I skated the first time," he said, "I dreamt about it at night."

A middle child out of six brothers and three sisters, skating was the thing that was his, a space he didn't have to share but owned outright, and he launched himself into it over and over. This was a place where muscle memory was king, where the endless repetition of tricks eventually transcended from banged knees and bruised elbows to jaw-dropping acrobatics. This simple thing, a chance to defy the laws of gravity, even briefly, also allowed him to defy the grim realities of his own life: a dead father (whom he didn't want to talk about), and the conflict and poverty that makes up the twenty-three hours of the day when he's not flying off ramps.

Skateistan, like many successes in Afghanistan, was the product of accidental good intentions. In 2007, an Australian skater named Oliver Percovich came to visit Afghan-istan with his girlfriend, a former aid worker. He brought three of his skateboards, and the minute he put them down to ride he was surrounded by throngs of curious kids. Some of them seemed to be naturals, and Percovich gave them the boards so they could practice. This gave him the idea to bring more boards to Afghanistan to start a school and build a skate park indoors so girls could also partici-pate.

Percovich mobilized friends, raised money, talked to the media. The story was irresistible—girls pulling on helmets over headscarves and boys tugging up kneepads over their baggy *shalwar kameez*, all of them taking their first Bambi-legged rides and grinning from ear to ear. Skateistan would be a refuge for kids in the midst of deadly conflict. Skate-boarding in a war zone? It was genius, as is the logo: a silhou-ette of a skater doing a kick flip off an AK-47 and snapping its muzzle.

Two years later, Skateistan Kabul was complete: an indoor skate park and educational facility of more than 54,000 square feet. It is filled with ramps and jumps and even pipes for grinding. There more than 1,200 members, many of them working street kids, some with disabilities, almost half of them girls, come to ride.

But Percovich preaches that Skateistan is also a way to empower kids by giving them a chance to learn as well as to skate. There are classrooms where young Afghans can de-velop leadership skills, explore art and multimedia, or just talk to other kids about their lives and the war's impact on them. And it seems to be working.

Shams Razi was one of the first to gravitate to Skateistan. He worked his was up from being a volunteer fixer and translator to the manager of all of Skateistan's Afghan operations. He's since left for an opportunity to study computer science in Australia.

The Kabul manager, a twenty-year old named Hamdullah, walked around with me as I shot video and snapped pictures of a boys' intermediate class. The dozen skaters working the ramps were at different skill levels; some were just getting the hang of it, others clearly on their way to mastery.

The operation was clearly well run. When I arrived at the park unannounced, my credentials were checked, and Hamdullah made phone calls to his supervisors to determine whether I should be let in. Protecting the kids, even from the media, was paramount. I was impressed, and I smiled at the irony: skateboarders, who didn't always have the best reputation for civic responsibility in the West, seemed to be running one of the better-organized and more effective NGOs in Afghanistan.

The skate park in Kabul was built on space donated by the Afghan Olympic Committee and is near the Olympic Stadium, where the Taliban had staged public executions. Skateistan has since opened up another location in Mazar-e-Sharif and also has two locations in Cambodia.

I shot video of a skater launching off the lip of a ramp; in this place, it seemed, with enough speed and thrust, a kid on a board could fly high enough to transcend the past.

Later, reviewing my notes, photos, and video from Skateistan, I was reminded of a story I had reported in 2001 about kids at a Kabul orphanage. I'd kicked around a soccer ball with them. I wonder how they might've thrived in a place like Skateistan.

From my journal:

DECEMBER 2001: ORPHANS

This is how it works: there are two wires jammed into the socket openings in the wall. Follow the wires. They wrap a couple of times around a steel bed frame, across the floor, and finally thread the grooves carved into a brick sitting on other bricks in the middle of the room. The wired brick is glowing. On this chilly night in December, this is where the orphans warm their hands—huddled around this glowing brick. They are not sad or whining or feeling sorry for themselves. They are laughing, campfire faces flushed in red—happy for this one thing, this small warm thing.

It seems like a cruel thing to do, but I can justify it: it's part of the story, part of the tragic story of Afghanistan. "Fazel," I say, and my interpreter translates, "when you think of your parents—when you think of your life before, what is it that you remember fondly. What thoughts make you smile to yourself?"

It is indeed a painful question for a boy whose parents were killed during the vicious civil strife between 1992 and 1996. Feuding Afghan warlords trying to carve up sepa-

rate fiefdoms. Fazel Allah came home from school to find
his house destroyed by a rocket attack, his parents dead
inside. To this day, he still doesn't know who is responsible, probably never will. He has been at this orphanage
nearly half his life now, seven years. He is fifteen. His
brother, Shukre, has been here since he was three. We are
sitting on the steps of the dormitory where the orphans
live, five hundred boys at this site near central Kabul.
Fazel rubs his face but does not cry as he struggles with
the images of the past.

"I remember," he says slowly, "sitting down for
dinner, eating my mother's pilaw." He pauses. "She made
very good pilaw."

He says that he and his brother often go to bed hungry
at the orphanage, at least two or three nights each week.
When they do eat, it is usually mostly starches—rice
and beans, or potatoes. When I see the dining hall, I am
struck at how much it looks like a scene from the movie
Oliver. A dark room with long wooden tables. Boys use
their bare hands to shovel steaming rice into their mouths
from scuffed aluminum bowls.

There's a line waiting near a window where a server
scoops up beans from a giant pot and slops them into
outstretched dishes as the boys file by. I am waiting for
a barefoot waif to walk up hesitantly and say the words,
"Please sir, can I have some more?" There is steam,
patches of light and dirty faces, clanking of bowls and
scraping of chairs. It is so moody, so sensually rich that it

is almost a chiaroscuro, a Renaissance painting of Afghan poverty. Fazel stands in the doorway, watching it all. Now that he is a young man, he is fasting during the Muslim holy month of Ramadan—almost redundant in a place like this.

There is a vocational school on the orphanage grounds. It teaches carpentry, tailoring, shoemaking, and carpet weaving. Although well intentioned, I'm sure, it seems to me like the perfect feeder pool for child-labor sweat- shops—or it would be, if they only had some supplies. Inside the woodshop there are a few hammers and saws but nothing to use them on. No wood, no nails, no nothing. Kids here enthusiastically hammer on tables and saw the air, a vaudeville skit, a slapstick show, another small absurdity in a world ripped from Salvador Dalí's sketch- pad rejects.

In Fazel's room there is the electric brick. Right now it has a tin bucket sitting on top. A whiff of steam on the water's surface. Though the contraption calls to mind a Chilean torture chamber during the Pinochet era, it actually seems to work. The boys will have hot water to wash with tonight. Good thing, too—a little personal hygiene goes a long way in keeping away lice and scabies in a place where the boys have only one set of clothes—the ones on their backs. Fazel's clothes are already threadbare, going into the winter months. He points to his sneakers, which are disintegrating around the seams. I ask him if he has any other clothes. He laughs, and then lifts up his mattress to show me the sum total of all his worldly possessions. Under the mattress are a black cotton vest and a toothbrush. He has one more thing. A book of Farsi poetry. When he reads it, he says, he disappears from this place.

16
WOMEN

||||||||||||

Not all Afghan women remain shrouded in burkas, especially in Kabul.

Dost was clearly taking a risk by letting me stay at his apartment. But it took nearly a week before that risk became real danger. As a freelancer working in the tight-money Internet era, staying with a friend while on assignment has become a necessity. Unlike my NBC and CNN days, when all expenses were covered, I had to front everything for my assignments and hope to recoup the expenses—not when I was done reporting, but after the story had actually been written and submitted.

Even for newbies with no families to support or mortgages to pay, it was tough. But for guys who had been around long enough to be spoiled by the good old days at the networks, this was a cruel new world—if one that sometimes pushed us to do our job better. Instead of being segregated into journo and NGO hotel ghettos, we had to immerse ourselves in the story, eating, sleeping, and living not just *like* the people we covered but also often *with* them.

The cross-cultural exposure was a gift for us, but not always for our hosts. I had settled into a nice routine with Dost and his second wife, Reyhana. While we were sharing a small space, it was three days before I actually met her. Because of the social dictates of conservative Islam, especially in Afghanistan, adult women rarely, if ever, interact with male strangers, even in their own homes; they stay in the kitchen while the male head of household entertains other men in a designated guest room. In fact, Reyhana was the only wife of any of my Afghan friends whom I had ever met.

One morning after breakfast, when Dost would usually go to his television station and Haroon and I would go out to cover stories, Dost told me he had to take a trip outside of Kabul for a few days. He was somewhat evasive, even a little sheepish when he said it. But I knew what that meant: I had to go. There was no way I could stay in his apartment with his wife while he was away; that would be problematic even in less conservative societies. What I didn't know was that some of his neighbors had seen me coming and going from his place and confronted him. Dost was too proud to tell me.

Haroon had a contact at the Safi Landmark Hotel, located inside the Kabul City Centre Tower, an upscale mall. It's a Western-style hotel with a full gym and a coffee shop and shisha bar on the roof, which is crowded nearly every night with Kabul's new upper class, who enjoy long drags of fruity tobacco smoldering atop meter-high shisha pipes. The Safi Landmark was managed by Indians and catered to foreign journalists and businessmen, and features huge blast doors, armed security, and X-ray machines at both the front and side entrances. When I got to my tiny but comfortable room, I noticed there were no windows and that the walls were so thick the place seemed soundproof as well as bombproof. I had gone from fully immersed in Afghan society to hermetically sealed away from it. It was a very safe place but also very distant from the world I wanted to cover. But I was short on cash and it was affordable and took credit cards. This would be home for now.

I hadn't been able to reach Dost by telephone so I called Matin in Kunduz, and he told me the news: Dost's landlord had asked him to move out; he had seen me in the apartment, which was on the ground floor, and confronted Dost about it. Dost, being Dost, was unapologetic, and the landlord gave him the boot.

"But don't worry, Kevin," Matin told me over the phone. "Dost is fine. He said he found a better place that is bigger and costs $100 less. So he's okay."

I still felt terrible about the situation I had put him in. Even after twelve years of a highly visible foreign presence, Afghan society was still suspicious of foreigners and their intentions. Simply by being a guest for a few nights, I had cost Dost and Reyanna their apartment. I tried to make myself feel better by rationalizing that it could've been worse: being evicted was better than being dead.

On a wall across the street from Raharan Omarzad's Afghan Center for Contemporary Art was something I hadn't seen much in my years in Afghanistan: graffiti. Along with some nondescript tagging in Dari and English, someone had painted the image of a skeleton wrapped in a long, flowing blue burka. No words accompanied it, and I wondered what the artist had meant. Was it the death of the burka? Or perhaps the burka itself was a metaphorical, anonymous death for those who wore it.

It reminded me of something I'd seen on my way home from the orphanage years ago. . . .

  From my journal:

DECEMBER 2001, KABUL

I am bone tired and discouraged. Then I see it. Fleeting glimpse to the right. Outside the van window. A tiny, no, infinitesimal sign of hope. Beneath a burka I see the feet of a woman wearing sandals—and she has painted toenails. They are deep purple. Majestic, beautiful, colorful toenails. In a country draped in despair, this is the light seeping from under the doorway. This is the sign, at least for me, that all is not lost. Though she is a blue ghost, though she is covered from head to toe, though she sees the world through a curtain of lace—she has proud feet. Uncovered and moving forward. They are ignoring the dust, grime, and garbage of this Kabul street. Moving past the past.

But perhaps I've imbued them with too much significance. Projected onto them unrealistic meaning and metaphor. Made them iconic when actually they are just toes. Pretty toes. But toes that can set off landmines with every step.

I hated the blue burka then and still do. Some female Afghan activists deride such a reaction as typically Western: the real problem for women, they point out, is not a bolt of blue fabric but forced child marriages and domestic violence. Nevertheless, the idea that women have to be shrouded like ghosts to avoid tempting men seems ridiculous to me.

I understand the modesty of conservative Islam but not the blinding, smothering oppression of the burka. It has unfortunately become a symbol of Afghanistan over the last seventeen years. But it has not always been. In the 1970s, most women in Kabul went without covering their heads, and some even wore miniskirts. Islamic conservatism returned to Kabul during the civil war, and with the Taliban's rise to power in 1996, fundamentalism and the burka became the new law of the land.

In 2001, even after the Taliban fled the capital, most women continued to wear burkas in Kabul; five and half years of fear did not go away overnight. But now, on my return, it seemed that as many as half the women chose to wear only the hijab, or headscarf: their faces remained uncovered, more like Teheran than Kabul. I had even seen stories about a decline in burka manufacturing and sales in Kabul as younger women more and more often chose not to wear them. However, the same stories reported that sales in rural areas, especially in regions from which foreign troops were withdrawing, were actually steady or increasing, possibly in preparation for a return of the Taliban.

During the Taliban's reign, toadies from the Committee for the Propagation of Virtue and the Prevention of Vice took to the streets daily, beating women who dared to show their ankles or wrists and men whose beards were too short.

By 1998, the Taliban had driven women off the streets completely, even forcing households to blacken their windows so
women couldn't be seen from outside. They weren't allowed
to go to school or to work, except in health care, and then
only to treat other women. In essence, the Taliban had tried
to make Afghan women disappear from everywhere but the
home.

So burkas or no, I was curious about what else had
changed for women in Afghanistan in the previous twelve
years. Haroon introduced me to a young woman name Farzana Nawabi, whose life was a dramatic example of the progress women have made since the Taliban were driven from
power. Nawabi had just begun her studies in dentistry at
Kabul University when the Taliban took control of the capital
in September 1996.

"There was an announcement in the newspapers that
women couldn't leave the house to go to school or work anymore," she said from her dental office above a busy street in
Kabul. "I was shocked, and I was crying. I thought I had no
future."

For the next five years she stayed at home, watching television via an illegal satellite dish concealed on the roof of
the house she shared with mother, brother, two sisters, and
father—a retired Afghan Army officer.

"I also studied English and cooked. But I had nothing to
look forward to."

She kept a diary in which she recorded the battles and
progress of the Northern Alliance. She also wrote about her

anger and frustration. Her dreams of becoming a dentist were fading with each passing year. She suffered from depression and insomnia.

In mid-November 2001, her brother came into the house with news.

"My brother came back from the bakery. He said there are no Taliban in the streets—they're all gone. Only Northern Alliance. I turned on the BBC and saw Jon Simpson walking down the street, reporting."

Nawabi didn't waste much time celebrating; she rechanneled five years of frustration into her life's goal.

"I was the first female student to register for classes at Kabul University," she said. But she had plenty of catching up to do. "When I returned to school, my male colleagues were already doctors. I felt that I had lost a lot of time, but I was still happy to be back."

Dr. Farzana Nawabi graduated from dental school in 2009 and now works part-time at a teaching hospital. She also runs her own private practice. The majority of her patients are female; those too poor to pay she treats for free. Haroon and I sat in the small waiting room in her office. Her modest practice had no receptionist or hygienist but was providing an essential service, evidenced by the number of women lining up outside her door.

But she also wants to cement the gains women had made in her field since the fall of the Taliban. To do so, she founded the Afghan Dental Association, through which Afghan dentists can share their knowledge about treat-

ments and business, and encourage new practitioners—
especially women.

When I ask Nawabi if she would read me something from
the diary that she kept, she smiled and shook her head.

"I burned it," she said. "Too many bad memories." She
wanted to live in the present, not the past.

But while she's afraid of what could happen to her life again
if the Taliban return to power, she's betting they won't; she
believes there are many people who think like her—people
who have too much to lose.

"I don't think they'll be back," she said. We Afghans are
fed up with those people."

There's little doubt that women have made significant
gains in the last dozen years, with millions of girls now going
to school and many others in the army, police, and government agencies. And women now make up 28 percent of Afghanistan's parliament.* Perhaps most significantly, in 2009
President Hamid Karzai enacted by decree the Law on the
Elimination of Violence Against Women (EVAW), codify-
ing legal protections from domestic and even societal abuse
of women, much of which is still widely accepted as a cultural norm. But according to a United Nations report issued

---

* Despite these gains, women in authority in Afghanistan are high on the Taliban's hit
list: "The killings of four female police officers since July and the abductions of and assassination attempts against female members of Parliament and their families in Ghazni
Province last year have aroused concerns that the Taliban are singling out women for
violence and intimidation, though all government officials, male or female, can expect to
become targets." Rod Nordland, "Taliban and Government Imperil Gains for Afghan
Women, Advocates Say," *New York Times*, February 7, 2014.

in the fall of 2013, reported cases of violence against women have gone up by nearly 30 percent, while prosecutions have increased by only 2 percent—a clear indication the law is not being enforced.*

There have even been efforts within the current government to roll it back. In May 2013, the Afghan parliament debated the EVAW decree, some questioning whether rape should even be considered a crime and whether there was need for a minimum marriage age for girls. According to Human Rights Watch, an ex-Taliban member picked by President Hamid Karzai to be part of the Human Rights Commission said EVAW violated Islamic law and should be repealed.

Human Rights Watch also estimates that about 95 percent of six hundred girls in juvenile detention have been jailed for "moral crimes," including having sex outside of marriage or fleeing their homes. Some of the evidence used against them is based on "virginity tests," examinations conducted in government clinics to determine whether a girl's hymen is intact.

"All of this would be horrific enough if it weren't bad science, but it is," wrote Heather Barr, senior Afghan researcher for Human Rights Watch in a December 2013 op-ed for the *New York Times.*† " 'Virginity' tests have no medical validity.

---

* United Nations Office of the High Commissioner of Human Rights, Afghanistan, "A Way to Go: An Update on Implementation of the Law on Elimination of Violence against Women in Afghanistan," Kabul, Afghanistan. December 2013. http://unama .unmissions.org/Portals/UNAMA/Documents/UNAMA%20REPORT%20on%20 EVAW%20LAW_8%20December%202013.pdf.

† Heather Barr, "In Afghanistan, Women Betrayed." *New York Times*, December 10, 2013.

A medical examination cannot determine, with any level of accuracy useful to a court, a woman's sexual history."

Along with these degrading practices is even more evidence of the Afghan government's efforts to curtain the rights of women. A proposed new law, Article 26, would make it virtually impossible to prosecute perpetrators of domestic violence by preventing family members who have witnessed it, as well as medical doctors and psychiatrists, from testifying or providing evidence at any criminal proceedings. Article 26 passed both houses of the Afghan parliament in February 2014, but after intense international lobbying, President Karzai said he wouldn't sign the bill without substantial amendments.

Unfortunately, the tide seems to be turning against Afghan women again, and as some analysts have pointed out, that fact will likely further erode what's left of the American public's support for the war effort, much of which was sustained by the desire to safeguard by preventing the Taliban's return. Sadly, Afghan women like Dr. Farzana Nawabi may have cause to be afraid even if the Taliban do not return.

17
LAWYERS, GUNS,
AND MONEY

||||||||||||

Money changers working the crowded streets of central Kabul.

When the Taliban first came to power in 1996, many Afghans like Haroon were cautiously optimistic. Since the Russian withdrawal and the fall of the communist government of Muhammad Najibullah in 1992, there had been incessant corruption and intensified fighting among warlords. Kabul had nearly been destroyed in the process. But in the regions that they controlled before taking the capital, the Taliban had proven to be effective administrators, curbing corruption and protecting roads and businesses so commerce could again flourish. Most critically, the Taliban applied the rule of law in a nation that had become lawless. Their courts heard grievances quickly and meted out justice just as swiftly.

The law the Taliban applied was sharia. Literally meaning "path to water" in Arabic (its necessity being as essentially to life as the path to water in the desert), it is based on a fundamentalist interpretation of Koranic verse and examples of the life of the Prophet Muhammad. Sharia's moral code is broad, addressing issues of crime, economics, and politics, as well as personal issues of diet, hygiene, prayer, and sex. Although its interpretation varies from country to country, the Taliban considered it the infallible law of God. Their interpretation was infamously harsh and prescribed medieval punishments: cutting off hands for theft, flogging and stoning death for adultery, hanging for rape and murder. Executions were often carried out in public; in Kabul, they were done before thousands at the former Olympic soccer stadium.

But while these methods were brutal, a good many Afghans could still see God's justice in them. Rather, it was the enforcement of myriad lesser dictates that began to diminish local support for the Taliban. Television was banned, as was music, dancing, pet ownership, and the depiction of humans or animals in photographs or drawings. Religious police from the Taliban's Committee for the Promotion of Virtue and Prevention of Vice would beat men whose beards weren't long enough (a fist length from the chin) and women who were not completely covered from head to toe in burkas. Women were eventually forced off the streets completely unless accompanied by a male relative, becoming prisoners in their own homes; this caused Physicians for Human Rights to issue a statement in 1998 declaring "no other regime in the world has methodically and violently forced half of its population into virtual house arrest, prohibiting them on pain of physical punishment."[*]

When the Taliban were driven from power in 2001, people, especially in the capital, were eager to embrace the freedoms that they had lost. Women began to participate in society again, although not without continued challenges to their rights. Music and art reemerged, and the Afghan media exploded with newspapers, news agencies, and dozens of tele-

---

[*] Vincent Iacopino and Zohra Rasekh, "The Taliban's War on Women: A Health and Human Rights Crisis in Afghanistan." A report for Physicians for Human Rights, August 1998.

vision stations—as many as seventy-six by some estimates—
many of them focusing on programming for specific ethnic
communities. But while the Taliban's legal and judicial ideology has been mostly abandoned in the past twelve years,
many Afghans still feel that the pursuit of real justice is impossible under the current government.

As former Northern Alliance commander Moammar
Hassan said to me during our talk in Taloqan earlier in my
journey, the bribery-infested Afghan justice system had frustrated citizens so much that many actually preferred settling
their disputes with the Taliban's traveling sharia law courts
instead of relying on the government.

Many Afghanistan watchers believe that the public's perception of a justice system, once again paralyzed by corruption, is one of the issues that will determine whether the
Afghan state survives in its current form following the withdrawal of U.S. forces in 2014.

The United States had become so concerned about the issue
of equal justice that the State Department created the Justice
Sector Support Program (JSSP) in 2005, which brought in
U.S. attorneys to help mentor their Afghan counterparts.
And in 2008, a Milwaukee criminal defense attorney named
Kimberly Motley, who had never before traveled outside the
U.S., decided that she would give the program a try for a
year, despite having to leave her husband and three children
behind.

Her lack of overseas experience hardly meant that Motley would be an innocent abroad. She had grown up in a rough part of Milwaukee, one of four children of an African American father and a Korean mother. Her father was stationed in Korea with the air force when he met and married her mother in Seoul, after which they returned to the States to start a family.

After he left the military, Motley's father was seriously injured in a car accident, and because the insurance company denied his claim, the family fell on difficult times. Still, Motley recalls, her parents instilled in their children a sense of independence and an entrepreneurial spirit. She helped support the family with a paper route and the money she earned from dozens of essay contests she regularly entered.

Motley says the insurance company's unfair treatment of her father inspired her to study law, and after graduating from Marquette Law School, she became a public defender, representing indigent clients accused of drug-related crimes, gun violations, and murder. Between cases, she found time to get married and have children. But family life didn't diminish her ambition, and on a dare by a friend, she entered and won the Mrs. Wisconsin beauty pageant and went on to win the national contest, taking the title of Mrs. America in 2004.

This may seem to make Motley an unlikely candidate for a full-year deployment to a war zone, but as she's since proved, she enjoys defying people's expectations.

She found chaos awaiting her in Afghanistan. While with JSSP, Motley spent a lot time speaking with Afghan judges attorneys and visiting prisons and detention centers. She says she routinely saw the rights of defendants violated; many were denied access to lawyers or even the right to speak in court to offer their own defense. She'd even seen people convicted with little or even no evidence against them.

"There was a lot of unfortunate corruption in the system," Motley said in 2012 BBC interview. "People would pay to get lesser sentences, and it was pretty obvious."*

Motely says her work with JSSP seemed to make little difference, and she became disillusioned with what she considered a hands-off approach. "We spent a lot of time writing reports on capacity-building," she recalls.

The Special Investigator General for Afghanistan Reconstruction (SIGAR) has criticized the State Department's Justice Sector Support Program as well, stating that their interviews with contractors like Motley found that "some JSSP contract requirements were poorly defined, resulting in useless deliverables."

In other words, the program's impact was questionable. But JSSP's website paints a different picture.

"The program's main goal," it states, "is to help create sustainable improvements in the Afghan government's supply of justice to the Afghan people. Together, we have trained over 2,000 Afghan investigators, prosecutors, judges, and defense attorneys within the Ministry of Justice (MOJ), Attorney

---

* Stephanie Hegarty, "Kimberly Motley: Making Waves in Afghanistan's Legal System," *BBC News Magazine*, March 13, 2012, http://www.bbc.com/news/magazine-17233778.

General's Office (AGO), Ministry of Interior (MOI), and the Supreme Court."*

There were a lot of foreigners languishing in Afghan prisons, clogged in a process too byzantine for them to navigate. And in that misfortune that Motley found a business opportunity. She remained in Afghanistan after finishing her obligations to JSSP, taking on some of those imprisoned foreigners as clients. One of them was a former British military officer turned security contractor named Bill Shaw, who had been accused of attempting to bribe Afghan authorities to release vehicles they impounded from his company, G4S. While the British Embassy seemed unable to do much for him, he credits Motley with negotiating his release back in July 2010, after he spent five months in Afghanistan's notorious Pul-e-Chakri Prison.

The case won her the respect of the expat community, and in the five years since she first hung out her shingle in Afghanistan, many more victories have followed. She claims a 90 percent release rate for incarcerated clients and is on the mobile phone speed dials of so many embassies and foreign workers there that she's been nicknamed "9-1-1."

Securing the release of high-profile criminal defendants like Shaw helped bring in paying clients, and Motley knew the public relations value of pro bono work. While working behind the scenes for jailed expats, she's garnered global

---

* "Afghanistan Program Overview," website of the U.S. Department of State, http://www.state.gov/j/inl/narc/c27187.htm.

headlines with cases on behalf of Afghan child brides and rape survivors.

One of the most celebrated is the 2012 case of a woman named Gulnaz, jailed for adultery after she'd been raped by a member of her extended family. Motley submitted a pardon request to Afghan president Hamid Karzai, and after turning up the heat by doing dozens of interviews with the international media, succeeded in winning a pardon. It was Karzai's first pardon in a case considered a "moral crime."

Motley says that two-thirds of her cases are pro bono, while her work representing the business interests of international corporations and embassies brings in the money. While she collected fawning profiles in high-end publications like *Vanity Fair* that played up her altruistic beauty queen credentials, it was Motley's business model that fascinated me: not only was she was making bank in Afghan's war zone economy, but the very existence of her practice highlighted the legendary corruption of the Afghan legal system and the failure of the American mentoring programs to turn it around. I wanted to meet her.

I made arrangements for Haroon and I to go to her office in the Saripul neighborhood of Kabul, not far from the American Embassy. When we arrived, she was talking with one of her assistants, trying to arrange to get her air-conditioning repaired. Her office was impressive, covered in Persian rugs with a large, ornately carved wooden desk in the center of the room. She wore a loose tunic over jeans, and her hair was pulled back to reveal cylindrical metal earrings the circumference of oatmeal cookies. She had a broad smile and a casual manner. We sat and talked for a bit before went on some legal errands around Kabul. Haroon and I tagged along.

She negotiated Kabul's streets and courts gracefully—and without a headscarf. While she'd worn one initially, she found that in the legal system, men respected her more without it. And with Motley, that respect went both ways.

"Before I took a single case," she told me, "I went to the Afghan Supreme Court, the attorney general's office, the Afghan Bar Association, and the Ministry of Justice to pay them the proper respect by letting them know what I was doing."

She said none of them had a problem with her working in the Afghan courts despite not being a member of the bar or an expert in Sharia law.

"I don't know everything about Sharia law and frankly I don't have to," she said. "That's not my job."

She speaks neither Dari nor Pashto, Afghanistan's two main languages, and relies on computers and her legal assistant to translate legal text and passages from the Koran. She is currently the only Western trial lawyer in Afghanistan, and she makes no apologies or excuses that her practice is a for-profit business.

Her activities have earned her plenty of enmity—weekly threats of kidnapping, rape, and death. (A grenade was thrown into her compound in February 2014 but did not explode, and no one was injured in the attack.) Motley nonetheless moves around Afghanistan's capital and outlying areas as if she's untouchable. She's received eight arrest warrants issued by various government entities, all of which she's gotten dismissed as harassment by a boys-only club not sure what to make of a female American lawyer running circles around them in their own courts.

Our first stop was the custom's office, where the Afghan government had impounded the de-mining vehicle of one of her clients. She's come to find out what it's going to take to get it released. As we passed through the gates, one of the guards told her he'd seen her on television—not in a courtroom but on a cooking show. Motley has become a bona fide celebrity, from the Afghan airwaves to the headquarters of the International Security Assistance Force, where she teaches a spinning class.

Inside she charms one of the clerks, giving him more attention then he's probably had in his whole career. When they're finished, she has information she can use and makes a note of the legal paperwork that will need to be filed to get the process started.

Our final stop for the day was Pul-e-Chakri Prison, where Motley took us to meet with one of her clients. Also known as the Afghan National Detention Facility, the prison was constructed in the 1970s. From the air, the compound looks almost like an "alien" crop circle—a giant, rectangular stone wall encasing an eight-spoked wagon wheel. Each of those spokes is a lettered cell block, A through H. The prison was notorious for institutional torture and executions. A mass grave was discovered near the prison in 2006; it held the remains of some two thousand people, believed by the Afghan government to have been killed between 1978 and 1986 during the Soviet-backed communist regime.

Haroon and I had first come to Pul-e-Chakri for a story back in 2001. At that time the entire facility was empty. Retreating Taliban had abandoned it, and all the inmates escaped soon after.

It was an eerie place. We walked through the dank, moldy, vacant cells, sifting through the clothing, shoes, and personal belonging that prisoners had left behind. What looked like the solitary confinement area was a series of tiny cells, no larger than shower stalls, with barely enough room to lie down. I walked into one, and Haroon closed the gate behind me. It was claustrophobic, even for the few minutes I was confined.

Since that time it has been renovated by the U.S. Army Corps of Engineers, and it is once again filled with prisoners. The one we came to see was Bevan Campbell, a former major in the South African Air Force turned Afghan security contractor, who had been sentenced to sixteen years after being apprehended at the Kabul Airport, allegedly for smuggling six kilos of heroin. Campbell said he thought the substance was protein powder, which he'd been given by a friend.

Motley said that through a reduction in sentencing, Campbell, who had already served nearly six years, was scheduled to be released that week, but it hadn't happened. She came to find out why.

Campbell was being held in a special unit outside for expats, political prisoners, and terrorists, including Taliban,

Al Qaeda, and suicide bombers. Campbell was a big burly guy with shaggy hair wearing a rugby shirt, track pants, and flip-flops. He looked as though he had just woken up even though it was late in the afternoon.

"So tell me what happened," Motley said to him.

He sighed loudly, then explained he had been taken to another facility and was about to be released when an officer demanded US$10,000 before the senior prosecutor would sign the release papers. Campbell said that it had happened so many times that it had become a running joke.

"I'm not paying a cent," Campbell said angrily, "I've been here too long already. When the Taliban come back to power, that's when I'll get out. I get along with them better than the rest," he told me. "They're disciplined and clean at least, better than the rest of the garbage in here."

But Campbell reserved his greatest contempt for the Afghan justice system and what he considered the weak international effort to reform it.

"When I think of whoever is in charge of mentoring these guys or trying reform the system, it's a fucking failure," he said. "It's just wallpapering. Nothing's changed, and that is why the Taliban will be able to come back."

Motley asked him a few more questions, scribbled some notes, and told me she needed to head out to another meeting. I asked if we could see his cell before we left. He took us down the concrete hallway and stopped in front of a room crisscrossed with iron bars, the kind covering the cells in old prisons like Alcatraz. He shared the cell with an Australian, another of Motley's clients, a security contractor accused of murder that didn't want to be identified.

Inside the room were two small beds, some pots, and a gas cooking stove. There was a small compartment on one side with a toilet and an area to bathe with a bucket and water from the tap. Campbell had covered two walls with hundreds of dates in neatly penned columns, days, he said, when the system "had really fucked him." He didn't elaborate, but Amnesty International, which also took on his case, argued that he'd been subjected to the equivalent of "mental torture": officials had gone through the motions of releasing him on one hundred different occasions only to return him to his cell. Campbell had been in Pul-e-Chakri long enough that he had become fluent in both Dari and Pashto.

Once outside, I asked Motley about the bribes Campbell had mentioned. She said she was going to look into the allegations, but it wouldn't do any good to start off accusing people; in this system, subtlety was important. But she was unequivocal: bribes are not part of her business plan.

"I don't take bribes, I don't pay bribes. That's not how I roll," she told me, nonchalantly pointing out a guard shack where she said she once had to stay during a prison riot at lock down. "They had *Sesame Street* on the television, so we watched Elmo while guards in riot gear ran by."

No place for a beauty queen, I thought. But I knew that being so reductive was an insult to all she had accomplished. She was using an outsider's perspective to get things done, and while she has been criticized by some in the Afghan Ministry of Justice for grandstanding and profiting from a developing system still in disarray, she is doing exactly what she'd set out to do: create a profitable business with some do-gooder stuff on the side. What her critics seemed most angry about was that she had also exposed their failures in the process.

"It is my responsibility to point out the weakness in the system," Motley told me, "but I don't stand up on a soap box and criticize capacity-building programs. I do what I can."

It is her insistence on transparency, she said, that has made her so successful; it's the very thing Afghanistan is most lacking: In Transparency International's 2013 Corruption Perception Index, Afghanistan tied with North Korea and Somalia as the most corrupt nation on earth.

Motley believes that foreign investment in Afghanistan's natural resources, like precious metals, is the way out of its turmoil, and she's been approached by India, China, and other nations to represent their commercial interests.

"I'm not an activist. I'm an international litigator. I don't march, I go to court," she said, "What's going to help the country is economic development. And yes, I'm very blessed with the clients I represent—but I encourage them to become involved in Afghanistan by developing human capital as well. I tell them to invest in people because it's also good from a commercial aspect."

While she's made both money and headlines in Afghanistan, it's hardly been a cakewalk. She's had to leave her husband and children back in the U.S. for many months at a time. She says she will be in Afghanistan for a while after the 2014 withdrawal. "I still have clients that need my help," she said, "and it would appear a little opportunistic to head out right away."

But she also said she feels like she's perhaps reached the limit of what she can safely achieve. She's already looking for new opportunities around the world, maybe in other failing states where she can both make some money and do some good; the need for a business like hers signals serious problems with a nation's legal system that others needed to know about. She could make it a trifecta, I thought, by heading to North Korea and Somalia next.

Bevan Campbell was finally released from Pul-e-Chakri prison on November 12, 2013, after Kimberly Motley secured a pardon for him from President Hamid Karzai. He returned to his home in South Africa after spending six and a half years in Afghan jails.

WOODEN CAGES

I may be clapping my hands, but I don't
belong to a crowd of clappers. Neither
this nor that, I'm not a part of a group
that loves flute music or one that loves
gambling or drinking wine. Those who
live in time, descended from Adam, made
of earth and water, I'm not part of that.
Don't listen to what I say, as though
these words came from an inside and went
to an outside. Your faces are very
beautiful, but they are wooden cages.
You had better run from me. My words
are fire.[*]

---

[*] Excerpted from the poem "Wooden Cages," from *The Soul of Rumi: A New Collection of Ecstatic Poems*, translation by Coleman Barks (Harper One, 2001).

PART III
JALALABAD AND
TORA BORA

A man on his way to Jalalabad waits atop his
truck for a massive traffic jam to clear.

18
THE ROAD

||||||||||||||

American MRAPs ("mine-resistant ambush-protected" vehicles) try to pass on the clogged Kabul-Jalalabad Highway.

The Taliban government collapsed November 12, 2001, and its leaders and followers went out much the same way they had come in: via Highway 1. They fled toward Jalalabad and to the mountains and caves to the south in Tora Bora. Al Qaeda leader Osama bin Laden and his followers were believed to be among them.

But the southern city of Kandahar, the last Taliban stronghold, had not yet fallen. Taliban leader Mullah Muhammad Omar, known as the One-Eyed Mullah because he'd lost an eye fighting the Russians during their occupation, was still hiding out there. To hasten its fall—and perhaps capture Mullah Omar—the U.S. landed one thousand marines in a desert south of Kandahar during an air assault mission that employed Super Stallion helicopters and C-130 Hercules aircraft. There they set up Camp Rhino, a forward operating base on the Taliban's home turf and the first significant presence of U.S. troops in Afghanistan since the beginning of America's involvement in the war on October 7.

I desperately wanted to get out of Kabul and go to Kandahar or Tora Bora to see up close what I thought would be the end of the war. My first attempt was inspired but dangerous—I tried to operate in an independent, self-sustaining "mobile news bureau" created from the shell of an old 20-foot passenger bus. It was innovative, but ultimately unsuccessful, as I detailed in my journal:

DECEMBER 2001: THE BUS

With reports that Kandahar will fall any day now, the conflict story is moving south. There's little left to report on in Kabul but politics, rebuilding, and features on Marjan, the zoo's indomitable lion. [NBC Correspondent Jim] *Avila and I are eager to make a run on Kandahar. And I just got the green light from NBC's foreign desk to buy a 25-person bus for exactly that purpose. It will be, I envision, a kind of Afghan caravan from which an advance crew can pursue this story whenever and wherever it moves. We will invoke the spirit of* CBS *Sunday Morning's Charles Kuralt in possibly the world's most lawless nation. My plan is to hollow the bus out, have wooden bunks installed, and desks and storage boxes for production equipment and personal gear. Local welders will attach a platform to the roof rack where a cameraman can shoot "beauty shots" and correspondent stand-ups from anywhere. A place where we can eat, sleep, and work—without having to worry about where we're going to stay each night. Armed guards will travel with us to ward off bandits or Taliban or both. Depending on our destination, maybe we will call it the Kandahar Express or the Tora Bora Bus. It cost $5,000.*

But there are problems before we even get started. The NBC engineers are not convinced, don't like the idea of driving the road to Kandahar, a road that is legendary for being one of the most dangerous in Afghanistan. Then our crew tells us they've heard from too many sources that this

*isn't even a fool's errand, it's a suicide mission. But even
so, Avila and I are committed and quietly decide to make
the trip alone. We've been given permission by the local
Northern Alliance commander in Maidan Shari to drive
south to the city of Ghazni, a third of the way to Kandahar. With a letter of permission from him and one of his
soldiers as an armed escort, we should be safe, he says, at
least that far.*

*It is morning and we are packing the bus for our
journey. It's a little rough, but close to what I envisioned.
Though the plan is Ghazni, we both are thinking that if
the path is clear, we'll make a run for Kandahar. Despite
the problems and warnings from colleagues, I'm excited
for the momentum, to be moving from Kabul, which
because of so much prior overstimulation, has become stale
for me. I'm looking for another rush of adrenaline. Fear,
I have learned, is the quickest fix. But I also feel some
anxiety beyond the dangers we may encounters. Without a cameraman, soundman, or engineer, I must now
become all three. I will shoot with a mini DV camcorder
and transmit using a 7E videophone. I have used them all
before, but not under this kind of pressure, not without a
supply line or tech support nearby.*

*We're going off into the wilds of Afghanistan again
and we have nothing and no one to rely on but ourselves.
While we are loading, Avila pulls me to the side. "We
need to make a pact," he says, "we need to be brutally
honest with each other once we get out there." Because*

neither Avila nor I have a reputation for mincing words or holding back, I am a bit surprised.

"I think you know that's not going to be a problem, Jim," I nod, continuing to pack. Before heading out, we stop at our driver's house, Yar Muhammad. Yar is a tough guy, quick-tempered, prone to occasional fits of road rage. Once when we were driving to a story and a bicyclist didn't move out of his way quickly enough, Yar stopped the van and confronted him. Within seconds fists were flying. I had to crawl over the front seat and out the door to break them up. But on a trip like this, into the danger zone, we are a bit more comfortable with his edgy nature. At his house, his ten-year-old son brings out a Kalashnikov and a harness filled with ammunition clips. He hands it to Yar, who hands it to me. We have done this before. As I lay it down on the backseat and cover it with my jacket, I see something I haven't seen before. Peeking out from one of the ammo pouches is a handle and metal ring about the circumference of a dime. My translator Ahmed sees it too. He puts two fingers to his lips and then touches them gently to the grenade. It is the Afghan version of "good boy, stay right where you are, please don't go anywhere."

But despite the preparation and dramatics, we don't get 50 miles outside of Kabul before we are stopped at a checkpoint and told to turn around and go home. A second commander in the region, a former Taliban who switched sides after the fall of Maidan Shar, doesn't care about our letter of passage and tells us we'd have only a 20 percent *chance of making it to Ghazni alive, let alone Kandahar.*

"Maybe you can try next week," he tells us in Pashto.
We are disappointed, but mildly so.

Less than three hours after we started, we are back
at the Intercontinental Hotel, unloading the "Kandahar
Express." Our colleagues look relieved to see us. Not one
says to us, "I told you so." Six porters varying in age from
20 to 60 appear to help us unload. They're wearing tat-
tered bellhop uniforms that probably looked great in 1973.
When they put down the last bag, I count out 100,000
Afghanis apiece and place them in each of their lined,
calloused, and dirty hands. A fine tip of about $1.50.
Kandahar was out. It was time to look at Tora Bora.

Twelve years later, I was ready to get out of Kabul again. I
hadn't run out of stories, I was just eager to see what was going
on beyond the borders of the capital. I had been to Kandahar and other areas in the south in 2010 and found the region
buzzing with violence and suicide attacks. With the staggered
withdrawal of America's NATO allies from the area, insurgent activity had only grown bolder. Dutch troops deployed
to Uruzgan Province withdrew from Afghanistan in January
2010; the Canadians, who had been operating mostly in Kandahar, began leaving a year later, leaving only a training contingent on the ground. The Australians would pull out at the
end of 2013. That left the British and Americans to carry on
the battle in the south, both with troop withdrawals scheduled
for 2014.

I was interested in seeing how the south had fared since I had been there last. Even now it was not a drive you could make safely from Kabul, so I put in a request to the headquarters of the International Security Assistance Force (ISAF) in Kabul to embed with U.S. forces in Regional Command South (RC-South), which seemed the only practical way to report from the region.

Unless you've been an avid Afghan watcher since the beginning of 2001, sorting out the current state of foreign military involvement in the country—even just trying to understand the difference between ISAF and NATO—can make you feel like you're playing Scrabble with a cheater.

Here's how it breaks down: ISAF is the UN security mission, mandated by resolution in December 2001 after the fall of the Taliban and part of the Bonn Agreement that created the power-sharing coalition government that replaced the Taliban. Its main purpose was to help rebuild government institutions and train the Afghan National Security Forces (ANSF), but it's also been actively engaged in fighting the Taliban and other threats to the nation's stability.

NATO (North Atlantic Treaty Organization) is a collective international military alliance formed in 1949 to thwart Soviet expansionism following World War II and has since been involved in conflicts and peacekeeping operations around the world, including Korea, Bosnia, and Kosovo. After the United States was attacked on September 11, 2001, Article 5 of the NATO Alliance was invoked; it requires member states to come to the aid of any other member state subject to an armed attack. It was the first and only time Article 5 has been used. That's what led NATO to take charge of the ISAF mission in Afghanistan.

As a part of the ISAF mission, Afghanistan was initially divided into five regional commands, which expanded to six after 2010; one of four NATO member nations took charge in each. The six regional commands were RC-North, led by Germany; RC-East, led by the U.S.; RC-West run by Italy; RC-South and RC-Southwest, both also headed by the U.S.; and RC-Capital, where Turkey is in charge.

ISAF says that it has more than 84,000 troops from 49 nations in Afghanistan—not all of them from NATO member states. While withdrawals change those numbers daily, the greatest number came from the U.S., with 60,000 troops, followed by the U.K., with more than 7,000, and Germany, with more than 3,000. By contrast, Iceland and Malaysia contributed 3 and 2, respectively.

Because of the withdrawal and restructuring, RC-South wouldn't accept any media embeds from the middle of July to the middle of August 2013. I didn't have time to wait them out, so just as I had in 2001, I looked to the east.

Even though it was the first day of the Muslim holy month of Ramadan, Haroon and Hakim agreed to drive me to Jalalabad in Nangarhar Province so I could see what was happening on the eastern border. I invited another American colleague to come with us, a young *Stars & Stripes* reporter named Alex Pena. He too had been hamstrung by the embed blackout in RC-South. Military embeds were the lifeline of *Stars & Stripes*, a U.S. government publication whose focus was news about the American military. Despite the affiliation, the paper reported independently and often hit harder with their stories than other media. This did not make them the most popular news agency among some military brass, who believed they should be a public relations entity rather than a watchdog.

Pena had emailed me a few years back, when he was still in college in Florida, and asked me to critique some freelance work he had done for CNN covering the Mexican drug wars. I was impressed, and we stayed in contact, but I had never met him until this trip. A Cuban-American from Miami, he left Florida immediately after he graduated and went to work in Africa as a freelancer for *Voice of America* and ABC News, earning a lot of street cred before most young journalist got their first byline. Now he was working for *Stars and Stripes* in Afghanistan, gaining more experience while receiving a regular paycheck. He was just beginning his career as a foreign correspondent; I knew mine was closer to its end. Collaborating seemed to me a good way to pass the torch.

Since the east is much more conservative than Kabul, we decided to dress in traditional clothes. At the Safi Landmark Hotel, I put on the *shalwar kameez*, sandals, scarfs, and a *pakool* cap Matin got for me in the north. I was taller and had lighter hair and skin than the Afghans in the east, but I would at least be somewhat less conspicuous in the attire and wouldn't draw as much attention in the nondescript blue station wagon we'd be driving—a loan from Haroon's brother.

When Haroon and Hakim arrived, Haroon texted me, and Alex and I met them on the street below. Just as I had been years ago before setting out in the Kandahar Express, I was eager but aware of the risks. Haroon said the drive to Jalalabad was safe during the day, but our plan was to go beyond Jalalabad and into much more dangerous territory. I wanted to go to Tora Bora.

To get there we would have to take the Kabul-Jalalabad Highway, a 93-mile (150-kilometer) west-east section of Highway 1. This was Afghanistan's ring road, the nation's only major thoroughfare linking 16 of the country's 34 provinces and most of its major cities. It's also the nation's connection to its Cold War history.

Highway 1 is 2,000 miles (3,360 kilometers) long, and three-quarters of Afghanistan's population lives within about 30 miles of the road. Most of the two-lane highway was built with the help of the United States and former Soviet Union in the 1960's, both countries vying for influence in Afghanistan. The Soviets built the Herat-to-Kandahar section while the Americans constructed the stretch from Kandahar to Kabul. Canadian defense analyst Anton Minkov told *Walrus* magazine that he believes the Soviets were contemplating invasion even then, almost a decade before their Christmas 1979 attack. Minkov notes that they had paved the connections across their own border and that the road was designed for heavy military transport.[*]

---

[*] Hugh Graham, "Road of Fire: The War in Afghanistan Will Be Won or Lost on Highway 1," *The Walrus*, December 2007.

The Soviet invasion strategy had been to take the main cities and hold the ring road that connected them. But Minkov said the Soviets ran into the same problem the ISAF had today: the Taliban had made convoy attacks a major tactic in their insurgency. Minkov claims that every single Soviet convoy that drove along Highway 1 was attacked, with a loss of 11,000 military trucks. The cost was so great that 25 percent of the Russian forces had to be used exclusively for ring road defense.

The Kabul-Jalalabad section that we would take was not part of the actual ring, but a trailing west-east span that followed the Kabul River Gorge for about half its distance, climbing 2,000-foot cliffs and descending into the valleys below. It is considered one of the most beautiful—and most dangerous—roads in the world. Afghan officials said that nearly 200 people were killed and 5,000 injured in traffic accidents just between March 2012 and March 2013. Many of the casualties were blamed on overloaded cargo trucks using the road to haul goods to and from Pakistan. The trucks were so slow climbing the grade that cars and passenger buses attempted to zip around them often plunged off the road, and people met their deaths thousands of feet below.

Haroon's good planning got us on the road early and we bypassed much of the traffic, enjoying the magnificent landscape of the roaring river and soaring cliffs. We used the time to reminisce, talking about friends and acquaintances and where they were today. While we laughed much of the time, there was one story that filled the car with silence after.

In early 2002, after NBC moved its bureau out of the Intercontinental Hotel to the house in Kabul's Wazir Akbar Khan neighborhood, a young houseboy named Rafi worked for us. He was about sixteen, a sweet, innocent kid eager to learn English and curious about how to use our gym gear.

Rafi would have dramatic mood swings, happy and talkative one day, quiet and sullen the next. I didn't learn the reason until told later by a colleague after I had already left Afghanistan following my second trip there: the man we'd hired to take charge of our house security, a dead-eyed Tajik from the Panjshir named Hamid, had been raping Rafi in one of the backrooms of the house. It was discovered only when one of the staff walked in on him in the act.

Hamid was a nasty piece of work. He had been foisted on us by the Panjshir "mafia," which was taking control of Kabul real estate and other profitable business enterprises in the wake of the Taliban. The NBC Kabul bureau chief, Babak Behnam, an Iranian whose family had sought asylum in America after the fall of the shah, fired Hamid. But the damage had already been done. Haroon gave me the details during our drive to Jalalabad.

"Rafi's father was dead and his mom remarried," said Haroon while driving, "but the stepfather took all of the money that Rafi earned from working at the NBC house and ran away, leaving both of them behind. It was all too much for Rafi, and he got a gun and shot himself." Hakim nodded silently, confirming the story.

Though I had heard the tragic tale of Rafi's suicide in bits and pieces prior to our drive, its details weighed heavily on me. The injustice seemed analogous to some of Afghanistan's own historical tragedies: a nice kid who gets an opportunity to get out of poverty by working with generous but oblivious Westerners instead ends up being raped and robbed and takes his own life in despair.

I wish I'd known what was going on while living in the house and wonder what I would've done if I had been the one who walked in on Hamid. Would I have beaten him? killed him? helped Rafi to take revenge himself? I will never know. It is in recounting stories like his that Afghanistan seems relentlessly savage and cruel. Although I know it's really not so different from any other place in the world, the thought of Rafi's abuse and despair made it seem so.

There is, in fact, a long-established, controversial culture of the sexual exploitation of boys in Afghanistan. Warlords, the wealthy, and other powerful individuals are able to take what they want without consequences. There's even a name for it—*bacha baʐi*, which literally means "boy play." *Bacha baʐi* boys are kept almost like pets, a status symbol for their "owners," who sometimes dress them in women's clothes and makeup with bells on their hands and feet and have them dance and perform for guests. Afterward, they may be required to have sex with the guests or their "owner."

Some claim that Afghanistan's institutionalized sexism, which makes women almost completely unapproachable, has created this culture, which preys on "female substitutes" who are both vulnerable and available. Afghanistan's poverty and large number of displaced children provides a steady supply of boys, who are usually kept while they remain "beardless" or until they turn eighteen.

While homosexuality is illegal in Afghanistan, sex with *bacha bazi* boys is not seen as homosexual by the men who engage in it, partly because their partners are boys, not other men, and partly because they assume the active—traditionally "male"—role in sex.

Human rights campaigners don't see it as homosexual behavior either: they consider it rape. But victims rarely report it because of the stigma and fear of honor killings or imprisonment. (Even female rape survivors are often jailed.) Some of the boys find the life preferable to poverty, as they are usually provided with food, clothing, and gifts.

Bachi bazi used to be confined to the rural areas of the south, but it has spread throughout the country, according to Suraya Subbrang of the Afghanistan Independent Human Rights Commission.

"When you don't have a strong central government or rule of law, and the culture of impunity exists and laws are not implemented, many things happen," she told the UN's IRIN news agency in September 2013.*

American soldiers have long been aware of *bachi bazi* as well, according to Ben Brody, a journalist and former U.S.

---

* "Afghanistan's Dancing Boys," *IRIN*, September, 18, 2013, http://www.irinnews.org/printreport.aspx?reportid=98776.

Army sergeant, who included this entry in a glossary of current U.S. military slang for the *Global Post*:

> "Man-love Thursday": Soldiers use this phrase to half-joke
> that on Thursdays in southern Afghanistan men custom-
> arily have sex with each other so that they will not be dis-
> tracted by lustful thoughts on Friday, the Muslim day of
> prayer. Sexual relationships between boys and men are no-
> torious in Kandahar, but the stories of Man-Love Thursday
> are likely apocryphal. A regional proverb goes, "A bird flies
> over Kandahar with one wing covering its butt."*

When the Taliban rose to power, Mullah Omar and his followers allegedly rescued a *bachi bazi* boy from a warlord who had
taken him from a local village to be his sexual plaything, making
the Taliban principled and trustworthy in the eyes of an Afghan
public weary of the excesses of the warlords.

With most interaction between men and women pro-
scribed by Afghan society, how do regular Afghan men, the
kind who don't bugger little boys, learn about sex, I asked
Haroon.

"Sometimes they go to prostitutes," Haroon told me matter-
of-factly.

"But how do prostitutes do businesses in a place where
adultery is still punishable by stoning?" I asked. "How can

---

* Ben Brody, "The Definitive Glossary of Modern U.S. Military Slang," *Global Post*, December 3, 2013, http://www.globalpost.com/dispatches/globalpost-blogs/groundtruth-
afghanistan/us-military-slang-glossary.

an Afghan man connect with a prostitute? You can't go to a bar or a nightclub and pick one up."

"Of course not," he said, "Everything is done through contacts here. One of your friends knows someone who knows someone who is a prostitute."

"But how does someone get into that life here," I asked, feeling like a thirteen-year-old boy talking to his father about sex. "I mean, sex isn't talked about here, and prostitution would be dangerous work, I imagine, what with the tradition of honor killings."

Honor killings are a noxious practice in some parts of the Islamic world. A woman's perceived adultery—anything from an unmarried couple meeting without a chaperone to premarital sex, unfaithfulness, even rape—brings shame on the entire family. Husbands, fathers, brothers, and uncles therefore have a responsibility to kill their wives, daughters, sisters, or nieces to reestablish the family's honor.

The Afghan Independent Commission on Human Rights documented 240 honor killings and 160 rapes reported between 2012 and 2013. Even more disturbing were its conclusions about who committed the crimes. The Commission claims that more than 17 percent of the honor killings were carried out by the victim's relatives, 10 percent by one of the parents, 2 percent by the victim's brothers, 1 percent by uncles, and another 4 percent was by neighbors, 1 percent by marriage advocates—and that 14 percent of the honor killings were actually carried out by the Afghan National

Police.* The Ministry of the Interior, in charge of the Afghan National Police, denied the allegations and called the report "far from reality."

Haroon told me there were a lot of reasons women become sex workers in Afghanistan. But poverty is the major driver: widows with no other means of support, orphan girls, and women who are trafficked from poor rural areas or from Iran and Pakistan.

"Where we are going now," Haroon said, "actually has a 'wives market' where men can buy a wife or sell ones they are tired of. Sometimes they even swap them with another man. It's been going on for a very long time."

I shook my head in disbelief.

"No, it's true," he said.

"Can we go to one of the sales," I asked?

"We can try," Haroon said, "but I don't think they'll be happy with outsiders there.

Subsequent research confirmed that he hadn't exaggerated. In certain districts of Nangarhar Province, where people from the Shinwari tribe live, buying and selling of women is a long tradition, less widespread today than in the past, but still common, according to the Afghan Independent Human Rights Commission.

The respected journalism blog *Afghanistan Today* quoted a local resident, Qari Gul Muhammad of the Ghani Khel district, who said the sales were still common in his region.

---

* Aazem Arash, "406 Cases of Honor Killing, Rape Registered in Afghanistan: AIHRC," Tolo News, June 10, 2013. http://www.tolonews.com/en/afghanistan/10805-406-cases-of-honor-killing-rape-registered-in-afghanistan-aihrc

"When someone visits, everyone knows and can provide them with the name and address of a girl for sale."* Gul Muhammad said the price of a girl can range from 80,000 to one million afghanis (US$1,600 to US$20,000), depending on their beauty.

The blog also quoted another resident, Gholam Habib, saying that poverty drives some of the sales, but others occur because men become tired of their wives or families want to be rid of daughters or widows.

Sometimes the women are taken across the border into Pakistan and sold multiple times.

"We have five or six cases where a single woman was sold three or four times," Zubair, the head of the district court in Ghani Khel, said.

Efforts to stamp out the practice are beginning to have some effect. The official said a man was recently sentenced to three years in jail for selling his wife.

Given that the practice has been ingrained in society for generations, it may take a few more generations to end. From *bachi bazi* to prostitution to wives markets, there are as many societal inconsistencies about sexual mores in conservative Afghanistan as there are in the next country—they just manifest a little farther underground.

---

* Abdul Rahim Mohmand [pseud.], "What Price for a Woman?" *Afghanistan Today*, http://www.afghanistan-today.org/helper/articleprint.php?id=207.

19
ADDICTION AFFLICTION

||||||||||||

There are fewer than two dozen drug treatment centers in all of Afghanistan. These children live at a residential center for women and children run by the Welfare Association for the Development of Afghanistan (WADAN) while their mothers are treated for opium addiction. Some of the children are addicted as well.

When we arrived in Jalalabad we were hungry and thirsty, having observed the Ramadan fast, which calls for abstinence from not only food but from water, cigarettes, sex—almost everything—from sunup til sundown each day of the month-long period. As non-Muslims, Alex and I didn't plan on fasting for the entire month, but out of respect for Haroon and Hakim, we decided we were game, at least that first day.

Despite spending so many years reporting in the Middle East and Afghanistan, I continued to be fascinated by Ramadan. It falls on the ninth month of the Islamic lunar calendar, and so it moves forward approximately ten days every year, as the lunar and solar calendars do not align. In fact, the beginning of Ramadan can vary from place to place, as it is measured from new moon to new moon.

Fasting, or *sawm*, during Ramadan is one of the Five Pillars of Islam (the others are *shahadah*, the profession of faith; *salat*, ritual prayer five times a day; *zakat*, or charity; and *hajj*, the pilgrimage to Mecca).

It takes extraordinary discipline to fast all day, every day for a month, and among Muslims it creates a special bond and is intended to instill a sense of humility, patience, and spiritual awareness; Ramadan is a time to focus on God and cleanse one's soul through acts of self-control and selflessness.

The most remarkable Ramadan I have experienced took place while I was embedded with an American army airborne unit at a forward operating base (FOB) on the western border of Iraq in November 2003. When I first arrived, everyone was in a sour mood: a patrol had been ambushed the night before, and a popular staff sergeant had lost his leg to an RPG and was now struggling for his life.

The battalion commander, a colonel, was a tall, power-fully built man who at one time had been a state champion wrestler and Olympic hopeful, but a bad knee ended his wrestling career. The following night he allowed me to tag along as he led his men on a raid against a suspected insurgent leader. His soldiers swarmed a multi-house compound in the 4 a.m. chill. They kicked in the doors and roused the family. In one of the back bedrooms, a specialist peeled back a blanket to reveal two young boys curled around each other, so small they looked like puppies.

The head of the household was taken to the main room and forced to lie on his stomach on the cold concrete. One soldier put a boot between his shoulder blades while another threaded his hands through plastic flex-cuffs, joining his wrists behind his back. He was made to stand and held in a corner. A light machine gun was pointed at his chest while his wife and children huddled under thick blankets as the house was searched.

The colonel decided he had gotten bad intel: nothing in-criminating was found. A soldier sliced off the cuffs binding the man's hands, releasing him just as the sun begins to rise.

Because it was Ramadan, now neither he, his wife, nor any other adult members of his extended family would be able to eat or drink anything until sundown.

The colonel apologized to the man and the soldiers loaded up their Humvees and headed back to their forward operating base. As we began to pull away, I saw the man, who only moments before had been held at gunpoint, approach the colonel. He placed his hand on his heart and asked the officer to bring his men back to his home so that his family could prepare breakfast for them before they left.

It was that moment of forgiveness and grace that underscored just how sacred this time was for Muslims.

We had come to Jalalabad mostly to take the temperature of Afghans in the east and gauge the security situation, but we also planned to visit one of the few drug treatment clinics in the country, the WADAN Residential Center for women and children. WADAN, which stands for the Welfare Association for the Development of Afghanistan, is one of the largest and most successful and sophisticated local NGOs.

After our visit to Heroin Hell under the Pul-e-Sokhta Bridge in Kabul, I had met and interviewed WADAN's founder and chairman, Muhammad Nasib, and its executive director, Jean Kissell. Through a patient, persevering approach, WADAN had found a way to work in some of the more hostile regions of the country, including Taliban strongholds in the east and the south. They claimed to have one thousand staff members across the country involved in everything from connecting local leadership to the national government through a program they call the National Association of Maliks (community leaders), as well as conflict resolution, education, women's rights, and drug treatment programs like the one we were going to visit. WADAN received funding from the U.S. Agency for International Development (USAID) and the United Nations Office on Drugs and Crime (UNODC), among others.

Nasib arranged for us to visit the women and children's center as well as overnight at their local staff house. When we arrived, we found a clean, gated compound where women and their children could take refuge while they struggled to overcome their addiction. In many cases, the children were addicted, too. About twenty kids, boys and girls together, were seated on the ground in a patio area, eating lunch as if it were just a regular school.

Staff at the center set up interviews with a few of the residents. One of them, Saira, was brought in to an office where I could speak to her with some privacy, but still in the presence of Dr. Jahan Noor, the Jalalabad program coordinator, and Fazel Wahid, the Center's administrator.

Saira kept her face covered with a veil while she told me that she and all three of her children—Fazel, 8; Eshanulla, 7; and Mariam, 3—were addicted to opium. She became addicted two years ago after being exposed to it by her husband, who had begun using it after losing his job several years ago. She then explained how the children got hooked.

"Sometimes they would complain of stomach pains and other sickness, and I would boil the skin of the poppy to make a tea and give it to them. Now when they don't get it, they cry and can't go to sleep," she said. "It is the same for me. When I don't use it my body hurts, but I want to stop using it."

Cheap and plentiful, opium has long been used for medicinal purposes in the region; many rural Afghans consider it a necessity, especially in the absence of any real medical facilities. But often its routine use as a pain medication or sedative turns into a full-blown addiction that incapacitates entire families—which is why Saira and her children were here.

WADAN runs treatment programs for both men and women, but this facility was only for women and children. Saira's husband would begin treatment once hers was completed. That was by design—part of WADAN's relapse prevention strategy was to get all family members clean before they resume living together.

According to Dr. Noor, the in-patient treatment for men lasts ninety days but only forty-five days for women because they have too many family obligations to keep them away from home for any longer.

We talked to another patient, Lailuma, who starting taking opium to help her sleep after her husband died ten years ago. She said one of her sons had already died from opium addiction and another is still hooked. He's already thirty and she worries he'll never get married because "girls don't like men who use opium."

"Patients come in with all kinds of symptoms from their drug use," Dr. Noor said, "Their hygiene is very poor, they have diarrhea, sometimes they are shaking. We have room for twenty new patients every forty-five days, but the waiting list is double that amount," she said.

I asked how the program worked, but the answers from Noor and Wahid were contradictory. While Noor said the patients were sometimes given some opium during the initial fifteen-day detox process, Wahid clamed it was done cold turkey.

"Eighty percent of the treatment is mental," said Noor, in an effort to smooth out the disparity, "while 20 percent is physical. It all starts with a good shower and scrubbing, followed by counseling and meetings with health care and social workers."

While addicts in Afghanistan often become pariahs in their own communities, Noor said the Center is accepted by this conservative community because the mullahs and Islamic education are part of the program. While the Koran says drug use is *haram*, or bad, the Center is trying to get the community to see these individuals not as bad Muslims but as being ill, having a disease like diabetes or high blood pressure.

And while opium helped fuel the war in Afghanistan, drug addiction didn't take sides in the conflict.

"Fifty percent of the Taliban are addicted to opium," said Fazel Wahid, the Center's administrator, who once worked in one of WADAN's men's treatment centers where many of the residents were members of the Taliban.

"I once treated a Taliban soldier at the Wardak men's treatment center," he continued. "He left clean and eventually made a pilgrimage to Mecca for hajj. He called us and thanked us for what we had done for him, saying he was able to make the hajj only because of us."

While it was encouraging to see drug treatment programs in Afghanistan that seem to be helping people, the programs were impossibly outnumbered by the problem. The Jalalabad Residential Center was just one of less than two dozen treatment centers in a country with an estimated one million addicts. WADAN had at least created a treatment center blueprint that could be scaled up across the country. Given the proper resources that might be possible—if the war ever ended.

That night, Haroon, Hakim, Alex, and I broke the Ramadan fast with a ritual meal called *iftar*, joining some of the WADAN workers at the staff house. By that time we were all hungry, but in the very hot and humid environment of Jalalabad, thousands of feet lower in elevation than the mountainous capital, we were more dehydrated than anything else.

The staff turned on the television in the guest room where we were staying, and the food and drinks were spread out on the *dastarkhwan*. But it wasn't yet time to eat: an imam would announce the precise moment on TV.

The food was tantalizing and plentiful. There were dates, kebabs, *kabuli* (chick peas), *pilaw*, meat- and vegetable-filled pastries, and desserts. And there were pitchers of a tamarind and honey drink that Haroon said would help to rehydrate us and prepare our digestive tracts for the meal.

When the TV imam said it was time, Haroon, Hakim, and the WADAN staff recited the break-fast prayer, which is spoken in Arabic in a similar version to this all over the world:

Allah! I have fasted for your acceptance and I am breaking my fast with your provision.

Then we all picked up a single date and ate it first, as is believed the way the Prophet Muhammad broke his own Ramadan fast. It was a remarkable moment, even for a non-Muslim, doing this together with everyone in the room and with millions of others in our time zone. There had been a sense of unity in fasting together, and now also in breaking the fast together, that made the hardships of the day worthwhile.

When we began eating, each of the dishes seemed, of course, the most delicious thing we'd ever tasted. Abstaining from food and drink, even for just a day, heightened the pleasure of eating and drinking and reminded us to be grateful for our daily sustenance.

Aside from the sounds of chewing, we were quiet during the meal, concentrating on the task before us. When we'd eaten everything, we pushed away from the *dastarkhwan*, pulled up cushions behind our backs, and sipped steaming chai, our bellies uncomfortably full.

It was then that we began talking to one another. Haroon told us about a series of trips he had taken for a USAID project. He was hired to take Afghan Sharia law scholars and judges overseas to observe the legal process in Western nations. Many of the men he said, had never traveled out of Afghanistan and were awed (or sometimes dismayed) by their experience at Western hotels.

On one occasion, at the Mariott Hotel in Cairo, one of the scholars wanted to see the hotel gym and pool, so Haroon took him. Once inside, the man wanted to test out the treadmill, and Haroon helped him on and set the machine to a gentle walking pace.

"But within a minute," Haroon said, "We were surrounded by the gym staff, who said the scholar could not use the machine wearing what he was wearing."

"What did he have on," I asked?

"A *shalwar kameez* and sandals," said Haroon. "What else? He doesn't have gym shorts and sneakers." We all laughed.

"And then after this guy had gone to the gym, he told all the other guys, so the next day the gym is full of all these guys with long white beards and *shalwar kameezes* using the treadmills and weight machines or just watching the other guests working out in their tight gym clothes." The image was hilarious.

But Haroon said some of the funniest moments came at the end of the trips, when the hotel bills arrived.

"A friend of mine was chaperone for them on a trip to Paris," Haroon said, "and he got a bill for one of the guys that included $1,000 in wine. So my friend asked him why this big bill for wine. And then he explained: 'On the first day they put a bottle in my room and I don't want it, so I pour it out into the sink. But then the next there's another bottle, so I believe they're insulting me, so I pour that out, too. And the next day as well, and so on.'"

We were rolling on the carpet laughing now, thinking of this bearded sharia law scholar thinking the hotel was purposely sending something *haram* or bad to his room each day to insult him. Well, he showed them.

It was a great insight into how culturally isolated from the world so many Afghans still were—even those in leadership positions responsible for carrying out justice in their communities.

We pulled up some chairs on the balcony next to the guest room and, careful to keep our heads beneath the balcony walls so we wouldn't be seen by the neighbors, knowing foreigners in a residential neighborhood would certainly arouse suspicions, smoked cigarettes and talked late into the night, wondering if we'd be able to get to Tora Bora the next day.

20
TORA BORA RUNAROUND

||||||||||||

American soldiers wait to board a Chinook helicopter at Forward Operating Base Airborne in Wardak Province.

The nights were hot in Jalalabad, and although we had a ceiling fan in the guest room to help cool us, we all woke up very dehydrated.

Making it to Tora Bora meant we were facing a marathon, and I told Haroon that at the very least we needed to drink if we were going to keep our wits about us. The last thing we wanted was to be lethargic and disoriented if we got into trouble in Taliban territory.

By the time we left the WADAN staff house it was already over 100 degrees. The road to Tora Bora was as dangerous as the one from Kabul to Jalalabad, but not because of traffic accidents: the hilly terrain created a perfect environment for bandits and the Taliban to wait in ambush.

We knew that to get to Tora Bora safely we'd need the help of the Nangarhar provincial governor, an outsize and controversial figure named Gul Agha Sherzai. Originally from Kandahar Province, Sherzai was the son of a teashop owner and dog fighter who became famous as a mujahedin commander against the Soviets.

When Mullah Omar holed himself up in Kandahar after his government in Kabul collapsed in 2001, he was pursued by two different Pashtun tribes: the Popolzai, led by Hamid Karzai, and the Barakzai, led by Sherzai. Both were assisted by U.S. Special Forces, who directed air strikes against Taliban positions.

When Kandahar fell, Karzai went on to become the new Afghan president; Sherzai was named governor of Kandahar Province in 2004. But his tenure was short-lived: he was removed after allegations surfaced that he ruled the province like a warlord, committing widespread human rights abuses, using checkpoints on Highway 1 to extort money from travelers, setting up protection rackets, and trafficking in opium. Despite this, he remained a close Karzai ally and was eventually named governor of Nangarhar Province (a post he resigned in October 2013 when he announced his candidacy for the Afghan presidency in 2014).

Haroon had contacted Sherzai's press secretary, and we'd arranged to meet him outside the gates of the governor's compound that morning. But when we arrived, the press secretary told us that Sherzai had been summoned to Kabul by Karzai for a special meeting; he didn't know when he'd return to Jalalabad.

We explained that we wanted to go to Tora Bora and that Governor Sherzai had in the past provided a security escort to journalists trying to get there. Would he do the same for us? The press secretary called his counterpart at the Afghan National Police provincial headquarters a few blocks away and arranged a meeting with the deputy chief of police, Muhammad Massum Hashimi.

My journey to Tora Bora in 2001 had been the culmination of the trip that began when I crossed the Amu Darya from Tajikistan into Afghanistan. After my failed attempt to drive that converted bus to Kandahar with Tony Avila, we regrouped and made a plan to go to Tora Bora instead. It was there that Taliban and Al Qaeda fighters had retreated, possibly on their way to refuge in the tribal areas of Pakistan. The Americans had already begun daily air strikes on their positions in the mountains.

Like our shelved attempt for Kandahar, this would be a dangerous trip. On November 19, 2001, just a few weeks earlier, four foreign journalists had been killed in an ambush while traveling in a convoy from Jalalabad to Kabul: Italian reporter Maria Grazia Cutuli, Spanish reporter Julio Fuentes, Afghan photojournalist Azizullah Haidari, and Australian photojournalist Harry Burton.

But Avila, videographer Tony Zumbado, and soundman Manny Garcia and I made it there safely after a harrowing drive that took the entire day aboard our newly christened "Tora Bora Bus."

In my journal, I wrote about what we witnessed after we arrived.

DECEMBER 2001: GUNFIRE LULLABIES

The White Mountains soar 12,000 feet into an azure-blue sky. They are snowcapped, jagged, princely. And because America's blood enemy, Al Qaeda, is burrowed into their crevices, they are being blasted away, slowly but relentlessly, with every passing American B-52 and B1-B bomber.

You hear the planes before you see them—and then it is just their contrails: dual streams of smoke sketching arcs overhead. They drop their payloads and bank south, back across eastern Afghanistan, back across the Indian Ocean to their bases at Diego Garcia. They fly so high their crews cannot possibly know what their bombs look, sound, smell like, when they finally hit the ground. The kill zone. This is what they look like: they look like birds, their black smoke plumes look like birds to me. In one I see a rooster, in another a swan. Distinct silhouettes, battlefield Rorschach tests, ink blots of ordinance against the Afghan horizon.

The shock waves of the explosions are dulled as they cross the valley toward us. But they are still persuasive, their concussions a silencing voice, ripe with anger, full of vengeance. We watch from a forward front-line position. There are dozens of other journalists here. It is a theater of war and war as theater. Tripods, microphones, lenses are all pointed toward the action. Only the faces of the television correspondents look away—looking back into their cameras with the detonation of thousand-pounders providing the backdrop. The very ground we stand on was, only a week ago, an Al Qaeda camp. But that was before the BLU 82. Before the Daisy Cutter. The largest non-nuclear bomb in the American arsenal. It detonates just prior to hitting the ground, sucking up all the surrounding oxygen and leaving a path of destruction five football fields wide in the pattern of a daisy. The U.S. bomber dropped one here, and now there is nothing but scorched earth. Trees burned down to their roots—trucks, tanks, weapons incinerated.

The mujahedin fighters, or muj, allies in the American effort to rid Afghanistan of the Taliban and Al Qaeda, look at the journalists with a mix of amusement and contempt. They laugh as reporters who can't tell the difference between outgoing and incoming duck or fall to the ground when muj tanks fire into the hills. They laugh louder when reporters scramble for their cars when the occasional Al Qaeda mortar and machine gun round does whiz overhead. While I shoot the latest explosion with my mini DV camera, a print reporter on my right is hugging the ground in a fetal position. The muj tease him, imitating rocket fire by making whistling noises. They are, after all, children of war.

I talk to a soldier named Zacara. He says he is fourteen but can't be more than twelve. He says in his entire life he has not known a day without war. A generation raised on gunfire lullabies, most trained to do nothing more but clean and fire their Russian PKM machine gun or rocket-propelled grenades. These men—and boys—are as rough as the landscape, calloused to the fears of battlefield dilettantes. But the contempt is mutual. Most reporters must hire the same muj from local commanders for their own protection against bandits, landscapes littered with landmines, cluster bombs, and other dangers. Some are honorable, duty bound, willing to risk their own lives for those

*in their care. Others are mercenaries, ready to fight
for paychecks rather than principles. Willing to side
with the Taliban, Al Qaeda, or America if the price is
right.*

The office of Deputy Chief Muhammad Massum Hashimi
was long and narrow, with sixteen chairs, eight on each side,
leading up to his desk at the end. On the wall behind him
were the requisite pictures of President Karzai and Ahmad
Shah Massoud. Men were already seated in most of the chairs
closest to Hashimi when we were brought inside the office.
We shook hands with him and a few of the men on the right
side nearest the deputy chief's desk, uniformed officers who
got up and relinquished their seats for us in a display of typical Afghan hospitality. We sat down and were offered chai
and waited while Hashimi finished the three or four different
conversations he was having with his men—all while taking
phone calls.

When he was through, I introduced myself and explained
what we wanted to do. Haroon interpreted. When Tora Bora
was mentioned, Hashimi's calm, relaxed expression turned
into pretend exasperation. The road to Tora Bora, he said,
was watched closely by criminals and the Taliban and often
mined with improvised explosive devices. There had just
been an attack on the road last week, he told us.

"That's why we need your help," I explained. "Is it possible to get a police escort from here to Tora Bora?"

The deputy chief considered the question. Then his phone rang and he answered it. He excused himself and left the room. That's when the remaining men, some of his senior staff, began asking us questions: Why did we want to go to Tora Bora? What would we do there? And some personal questions as well: Were we married? Any children? How old was I? Really? That old? But you have the body of a twenty-five-year-old. Then Hashimi came back into the room and sat behind his desk.

"How important is it for you to go to Tora Bora?" he asked me.

I exaggerated, implying that what I reported from Tora Bora could impact the U.S.-Afghan Bilateral Security Agreement. Almost universally, Afghan National Security Forces wanted some kind of continued help from the U.S. military and its allies after the withdrawal. The bilateral agreement would spell out exactly what kind of help that would mean: air power, ground forces, more weapons, supplies, spare parts? Hashimi raised his eyebrows at my answer.

"In that case," he said, "I must do my very best to help you. But the road is very dangerous."

"What about a helicopter?" I asked "That way we could avoid the road completely." Hashimi nodded slightly and told us to come back the next day after he discussed the issue with the Nangarhar police chief. While I didn't want to lose a day, I was committed to making the trip safely, especially since it wouldn't be just my life at risk. A helicopter was the smartest move, and based on Hashimi's response I was cautiously optimistic.

We left his office. We still hadn't had anything to drink, and we were all parched. I told Haroon that he and Hakim had exceptions to the fast since the Koran allows travelers to forgo fasting during their journey. He agreed. But we still didn't want to be conspicuous. Hakim drove around to several different shops until we found one with a refrigerated beverage cooler. Because we were so sapped of energy and dehydrated, we bought a half-dozen large cans of Hakim's favorite, Monster Energy Drink (energy drinks have become very popular in Afghanistan since the Americans arrived) and equal amounts of water. Then we drove around town looking for a place to drink them without being seen.

Hakim pulled under the shade of some trees next to a riverbank where local boys were cooling off and swimming. With our backs to them, we tilted the cans and took huge gulps of the sugary, heavily caffeinated sodas.

"I feel like were all teenagers in high school sneaking away to drink a six-pack of beer," I said, and we all laughed and continued to drain the cans, getting some of our energy back.

After finishing his drinks, Alex got out of the car and walked up to the riverbank. Almost immediately, some young boys began talking to him. Because of his Cuban heritage, black hair, and olive skin, a lot of people had already mistaken him for a local: people here had darker complexions than those in Kabul.

We could see what was happening through the rearview mirror.

"Better go up and save him, Hakim," I said, "before he gets into trouble." Hakim got out of the car and walked over.

"Those people in the restaurant over there are watching us, too," Haroon said, pointing to a small complex of mud-brick building behind us. "They probably think we're bad Muslims, drinking and smoking."

"Probably," I nodded. "But if they really knew who we were it could be a lot worse."

We laughed, but I was starting to feel anxious about our chances of getting to Tora Bora. I had learned that the longer things took, the less likely they were to happen. Tora Bora seemed an essential piece of this story, the place in which a dozen years ago we thought we would see the destruction of the Taliban and maybe even the capture of Osama bin Laden. Back then I believed I might be witnessing the end of the war. But how wrong I was.

What was it like today, I wondered. Who was in control? When I'd worked for the major American television network NBC News, my bosses were obsessed with the caves of Tora Bora. It was there, after all, inside the White Mountains, that Osama bin Laden had reportedly built a multilayered underground fortress with room for thousands of fighters, an elaborate ventilation system, an munitions depot, a hospital, roads, even a hydroelectric plant to power it all. Was it real or just myth? We felt pressure from New York to find out.

I detailed one of our attempts that ended in utter folly:

DECEMBER 2001: THE CAVES

Our fixer has introduced us to a wily muj named Attica. Attica has a penchant for showiness that's evident almost immediately from the double-barreled sawed-off shotgun he carries, hanging from a shoulder sling. Attica says he got the shotgun from a captured Al Qaeda cave— and if we're ready, he can take us to one.

"But it is so dangerous," he tells us. Jim Avila, the NBC correspondent I am working with, looks at me and raises his eyebrows. We both know this mean the price is going up. To get anywhere, to do anything in Afghanistan, you must pay for a guide. By the time we get done negotiating, Attica has spelled out the multiple perils that may befall us from U.S. bombs, stray Al Qaeda fighters, or even other muj. We've topped four figures.

"Afghani-scam," I say to Avila. He nods. But the caves are not just a story in Tora Bora, they are an obsession. After nine weeks of American bombing, they have developed an almost mythical quality. The last hideout of Osama bin Laden. What did they look like? How do the Al Qaeda live in them? Do they have cable? Everyone wants to peer inside the caves, including our bosses at NBC. We have to find someone who can take us in. Attica says he can—cash on delivery. Two people only: Avila, a handheld camcorder, and me. But there's more. We have to dress like Afghans. "Otherwise it is too, too dangerous." Attica repeats his mantra. We believe he is simply

*toying with us. Shelling out the cash is not enough; he
needs to make us look silly as well.*

*An hour later we are driving toward the front lines and
the supposed captured Al Qaeda caves. Jim is dressed like
a Pashtun, with a long flowing shirt and baggy pants. I'm
given some fatigues and a heavy shawl, called* a patu, *to
cover up my camera. We're both wearing* pakools, *traditional
wool caps, to cover our heads. According to the guards at our
compound, neither of us looks very convincing. But soon,
we'll discover, it won't matter at all. When we drive by the
hordes of media covering that day's bombing runs, despite
our disguises, a few of them recognize us. Soon they are all
in their vehicles, following us down the road. Our secret tour
of the captured Al Qaeda caves has now become a fifty-car
convoy. In the confusion, Attica slips out of our truck and
disappears. The whole thing is off. Thankfully, no money has
changed hands, but Avila and I, all dressed up with nowhere
to go, are left leading a parade of story-hungry journalists
down a road that will end in ridicule.*

The next day, when we return to the deputy chief's office, he tells us the only safe way to Tora Bora is indeed by
helicopter—but the national police in this province don't
have one.

"What if we drove by ourselves," I asked, "could we get
there safely?"

"You might get there," Hashimi said, "but I don't know what might happen after that."

"Why?" I asked.

"Because the Taliban control Tora Bora," he said, shrugging his shoulders slightly.

And so there was the answer. The Taliban's revolving door in and out of Afghanistan, shut down at the beginning of the war, now seemed to be back in operation. Not only had they not been defeated there twelve years ago, but many of them, along with Osama bin Laden and his Al Qaeda fighters, had escaped. That might not have mattered, I thought, had the Afghan government been less corrupt and a little more effective in all the years since.

While the government hadn't lost the military war, primarily because of the tens of thousands of international troops that had been keeping them in power, they had lost the public trust and their faith that what the government could offer was substantively different or better than what the Taliban could provide. That doubt had created a hole large enough for the Taliban to slink through, and they had once again become a viable threat. Back then, I had believed things would turn out so much differently. Even the myth of bin Laden's caves had been destroyed. So how could the war not be over?

From my journal:

DECEMBER 2001: SMOKE PLUME BIRD

These are the faces of the enemy: Al Qaeda prisoners captured by the muj. At Commander Haji Zahir's mud-

hut compound, they are paraded in front of the media like the latest fashions from Paris. Shutters click, cameras whir. But these are not the wild-eyed fanatics we had created in our imagination. These are not the single-minded, suicidal killers we half expected to see. Instead, the muj lead out groups of bandaged and broken men and make them sit on wooden bed frames. They looked disoriented, shell-shocked, ready to call it quits and go home. One man has a bandaged head, another a bandaged foot. One covers his face with his hands, another with a scarf. It is a Taliban/Al Qaeda perp walk. No questions allowed. The men are simply introduced as Arabs. There are nine in the first group, all wounded in some way. Then a second group of nine is led out all at once. Their hands are bound behind their backs with red rope. They look somewhat healthier, but no more fearsome. They are subdued, defeated for the moment. A Western correspondent next to me looks on them with disdain, says with satisfaction, "Death to America, huh?"

The local commanders here say the war is over. The back of Al Qaeda is broken. The caves overrun. Although usually prone to gross exaggeration, they do have some evidence. U.S. bombing backed up by muj fighters and U.S Special Forces on the ground have left hundreds of dead Al Qaeda fighters in the White Mountains and hundreds more running for the exits, Osama bin Laden among them. Two captured Al Qaeda fighters say they saw bin Laden ten days ago, that he shaved his beard before bidding them farewell.

*Today we have driven an hour into the White Mountains
to another captured Al Qaeda base. There are deep craters
everywhere. Acres of twisted metal, burned-out tanks and
trucks, shreds of clothing, shoes, an ammo belt, a Taliban
black turban, bits and pieces of the Koran. And there is a
cave. It is very close now, just a short climb up a steep hill.
When I reach it, I see a teardrop opening dug into solid rock.
I turn on the light on my camcorder and step inside. It is nothing more than a rabbit's burrow, 6 x 8 at the most. Not even
high enough to stand up. A hole in the side of the mountain.
Simply a place to run for cover. It is filled with nothing more
than a pile of spent machine gun rounds. It is interesting,
eerie even, but far from mythical. And no signs of Osama bin
Laden. He was gone, long gone, disappeared, like the smoke
plume birds made by the American bombs.*

But bin Laden wouldn't escape forever, although for years after, it did seem that he had. In the early morning hours of May
2, 2011, twenty-five U.S. Navy Seals lifted off from forward
operating base Jalalabad in two modified Blackhawk helicopters. The operation's reputed code name: Geronimo;* their

---

* U.S. officials have refused to confirm this was the code name of the operation and if
so, why. (In various news reports it was also referred to as Operation Neptune Spear).
Geronimo was the nickname of the Native American Apache warrior Goyahkla, who
led raids against Mexican and U.S. outposts on the western frontier throughout the
1870s and 1880s. Geronimo was legendary for eluding capture. His exploits include escaping pursuing troops by entering a mountain cave and simply "disappearing." It's a
tale similar to Osama bin Laden's 2001 escape from Tora Bora and posited by some as
the genesis for the code name.

destination: a mysterious compound in Abbottabad, Pakistan.

In a forty-minute assault during which one of their helicopters crashed, they killed America's most wanted man, Al Qaeda leader Osama bin Laden, ending a manhunt that had lasted nearly a decade. One of bin Laden's sons, two other men, and one woman were also killed. Inside the compound, the Seals collected five computers, ten hard drives, and dozens of other storage devices—a jackpot of intelligence on the inner workings of Al Qaeda.

Bin Laden was given a burial at sea, dropped from the deck of the American aircraft carrier USS *Carl Vinson* into the Arabian Sea. His body was prepared in accordance with Islamic law, according to U.S. officials.

In August 2013, a few weeks after I left Jalalabad during my most recent trip, I heard from contacts in the area that the Afghan National Police in Nangarhar had fought a two-day battle with the Taliban just outside Jalalabad. Twenty-two officers were reportedly killed in the firefight, along with seventy-six Taliban. Contrary to what I had witnessed a few weeks earlier during the protests in Taloqan City, some of the ANP were still willing to fight. But which battles they would choose to engage was still anyone's guess.

21

DEAD MAN'S BED AND OTHER MYSTERIES

||||||||||||||

In conservative Jalalabad, we decided it was best to dress local. From left,
Stars & Stripes reporter Alex Pena, the author, Haroon, and Hakim.

On my last night in Afghanistan in 2001, after camping in our bus for a week and watching the battle of Tora Bora unfold, my crew and I handed off our responsibilities to another team and headed for what we hoped were hot showers and clean beds at the Spinghar Hotel in Jalalabad. The Spinghar was the only accommodation available to us and was full of other journalists commuting daily to the front lines.

After I got my team—Jim Avila, Tony Zumbado, and Manny Garcia—checked into the hotel, the front-desk clerk said that there was one room left for me. He told me I was lucky, because the room had just become vacant that morning. He handed me a key to room 215. I took it from him, pulled on my backpack, grabbed the rest of my gear, climbed the stairs to the second floor, and opened the door to my room.

The place was a mess. It had a dank, musty smell and hadn't been cleaned; there were dirty sheets and a used towel in the bathroom. But I was too tired—and the hotel staff too overburdened—to do anything about tidying up the room. After a lukewarm shower, I put my sleeping bag on top of the mattress and fell asleep.

That night I had some of the most tortured nightmares of my life—abstract swirling colors, pain, and shouting. When I woke up the next morning I was sick as a dog: diarrhea, vomiting—the works. When I told the story to my crew they said they'd heard rumors that a CNN satellite technician had died from a heart attack in that room just a few days earlier.

I felt too sick to investigate. We packed up, got onboard the Tora Bora Bus one last time, and drove over the border to Pakistan. My one-hundred-day journey into the heart of the Afghan war was over.

In 2013, just as we were about to leave Jalalabad, I became too curious to pass by the Spinghar Hotel without learning what had happened twelve years earlier, and I asked Hakim to take us there.

At the front desk, Haroon told my story to an old clerk, a man named Malang who has worked at the hotel for more than twenty years. He nodded as Haroon recounted the tale and then took us to the second floor. The hotel was cleaner and brighter than I had remembered it. The concrete floors were polished, and the doorframes and doors crisply painted.

"Yes, it was right here," Malang said, pointing to room 215. "He died in this room. He was a big man, and it took six of us to carry him out. All the rooms have been renovated since then."

"That day when I check in, not even the sheets had been changed," I said.

Malang laughed. "No, I'm sure they had not. We were so busy trying to keep up with all the foreigners coming from Tora Bora that we just rented the room as it was."

"Can we go in," I asked, eager to see the inside of the room.

Malang shook his head. The room was currently occupied. I was disappointed, but I understood: the occupant would unlikely be soothed by hearing about the room's history. I told Malang about the nightmares I'd had that night and how sick I was the next day, after sleeping not just in the same room, but on the very bed where that poor technician had died. I somehow felt that his unhappy spirit was still in there with me. But Malang said that no one who had stayed in the room since had ever complained of anything similar to what I'd experienced. Maybe, I thought, the spirit had found its way out of the room, the hotel, out of Afghanistan—and arrived in a more peaceful place.

I found out that the technician's name was Stephen C. Allen, forty-seven, from Woodstock, Georgia. He was found dead in the hotel bed on Sunday morning, December 9, 2001, fully dressed. I could only find a few listings about his death, most from ham radio groups he'd been active with. And there was one from CNN, a transcript to the opening of its *News Night* program with Aaron Brown dated December 10, 2001. It was a brief but heartfelt tribute to one of those individuals in television news who work behind the scenes and receive little fanfare, even in death.

AARON BROWN, CNN ANCHOR: Good evening again, everyone. Here's what's hard about writing this page each day. Some days, what's supposed to be important isn't. What's important today is the hunt for bin Laden, or that tape the government found and may yet allow the rest of us to see. That's what's important today.

But for us, it doesn't seem as important as a guy named Steve Allen, who died over the weekend. Steve was a CNN technician. His job in Afghanistan was to get the satellite feeds up so our reporters could feed their stories. The best stories in the world mean nothing if they don't get out, and Steve got them out.

He and his team were staying at a hotel in Jalalabad. Steve didn't show up for breakfast the other day. And when they checked his room, they found him dead, apparently from natural causes. There was nothing glamorous about Steve's job, no big salary. He wasn't out there show boating, no Geraldo stunts. Just set up the feed. Make the thing work somehow, anyhow. Get the story to Atlanta, and get it on the air.

I didn't know him. It's a big company and I've been here just a short time. But one of our guys died on the job, and nothing much else seems to matter to me tonight. We send our condolences to his family. We want them to know that tonight they are very much on all of our minds.

Now to all those other things. Tanks again bombarded the cave complex of Tora Bora, and today an opposition commander claimed al Qaeda fighters and Osama bin Laden had been forced into a one and a half square mile area . . .*

I asked Malang if there had been any other kind of paranormal activity in the hotel. He told us to follow him and guided us another to room on the first floor.

---

* Transcript of "NewsNight with Aaron Brown," CNN, December 10, 2001, transcripts .cnn.com/TRANSCRIPTS/0112/10/asb.00.html.

"There was a female journalist staying here after crossing the border from Pakistan," Malang said. "The next day she was planning to go to Kabul with a group of other journalists. But that night I remember that she got very cold and kept asking us to bring her blankets. She was so cold she called us twice that night to bring even more." Malang paused. "And the next day on the road back to Kabul, she was killed by bandits."

Her name was Maria Grazia Cutuli, the journalist for the Italian newspaper *Corriere della Serra,* one of the three killed in the ambush on the Kabul-Jalalabad Highway a few weeks before we drove in on the Tora Bora Bus.

I shuddered at the story and thanked Malang. Then we made our own way back to Kabul, on the only road that goes there: the Kabul-Jalalabad Highway.

About halfway there, maybe two hours into our drive, we found that traffic had backed up for miles near the Daronta Tunnel. An overloaded truck had tipped over inside—not an unusual occurrence—and an American military convoy was working to clear it out.

After about an hour of waiting with cars lined up two abreast in the westbound lane of the two-lane highway and a single lane of slowly snaking traffic on the eastbound side, we saw a convoy of American military trucks knows as MRAPs, for mine-resistant, ambush-protected, driving through the tunnel toward us. The overturned truck had been cleared, but now they were having difficulty navigating the maze of Afghan cars that filled up both lanes.

Alex and I got out of the station wagon and began taking photographs of the MRAPs. A young soldier—he looked no older than eighteen or nineteen—behind a .50-caliber machine gun in one of the MRAP turrets began waving and shouting at us.

"Hey! No fucking pictures, no pictures!" he yelled.

I turned to him and shouted back, "This is a road in Afghanistan. You can't tell us what we can and can't shoot. We've got permission to be here," and I held up my press credentials from the Afghan Foreign Ministry.

The soldier looked at me, confused—and then I remembered that both Alex and I were still wearing local clothes. We look like Afghans to this kid, and he was probably scared shitless, as the convoy was set up perfectly for an ambush, stuck between the Afghan cars.

"We're Americans," I continued. He looked at me even more puzzled then pushed his radio to talk to his commander. "Okay, okay," he said, after getting word. "It's okay." He gave us a thumbs-up. "Sorry."

We finally cleared the tunnel an hour later, and I thought about the encounter on the drive back to Kabul, disturbed by how much mistrust still existed between Afghans and Americans. I had, for just a few moments, felt what it was like to be an Afghan, an object of a young soldier's fear and suspicion, fear that translated into orders about what I couldn't do in my "own" country. I wondered how Haroon and Hakim might've felt had they been shooting photographs instead of me.

The truth is, they had likely already experienced something similar many times since this war started.

NOT HERE

There's courage involved if you want
to become truth. There is a broken-
open place in a lover. Where are
those qualities of bravery and sharp
compassion in this group? What's the
use of old and frozen thought? I want
a howling hurt. This is not a treasury
where gold is stored; this is for copper.
We alchemists look for talent that
can heat up and change. Lukewarm
won't do. Halfhearted holding back,
well-enough getting by? Not here.*

* "Not Here," from *The Soul of Rumi: A New Collection of Ecstatic Poems*, translation by
Coleman Barks (Harper One, 2001).

PART IV
WARDAK AND
LOGAR

A U.S. Army and an Afghan National Army soldier on an early morning joint patrol in Wardak Province, one of Afghanistan's most dangerous regions.

22

HUMAN TERRAIN TEAMS

|||||||||||||

Afghans watch a group of American soldiers pass by on
the streets of Maidan Shar in Wardak Province.

When we got back to Kabul, I wasn't eager to be locked back into the isolation unit that was the Safi Landmark Hotel, so Alex found me a spot where he was staying, a place known by local taxi drivers as Mr. Tom's House because a freelance journalist named Tom Peter had rented it for years as a gathering place and haven for freelance foreign journalists. Tom was gone, working in Syria and other hot spots, but it was still occupied by a mix of Afghan locals, rotating staff journalists, a few administrators from the American University of Afghanistan, and the occasional freelancer like me, who was just passing through.

The house was a welcome replacement for the Safi. Although gated and surrounded by high walls, it was in the busy neighborhood of Qala Musa, and the rhythm of Afghan life, from butcher shops to ice cream vendors, surrounded us. There was also a grim reminder of past attempts to conquer the country. Nearby Tom's House was the Kabre Gora, or "graveyard of foreigners," also known as the British Cemetery. The nineteenth-century cemetery holds the bones of around 160 soldiers from that era, just a few of the casualties from Great Britain's frequent wars in Afghanistan.

The first had been in 1839, a blatant act of imperialist expansion with the strategic goal of keeping Afghanistan out of Russian hands, part of the so called "Great Game" rivalry between the two for dominance in Central Asia. The British

took Kabul then, but two years later, after an Afghan uprising, sixteen thousand British and Indian troops, their families, and retainers were slaughtered during a retreat through
the Khyber Pass after being told they would be given safe
passage.

The British marched back in with new forces and burned
much of Kabul to the ground in retaliation, but they allowed
for much more Afghan autonomy in the aftermath. However, they invaded again later in the century, and many of
the soldiers now buried in the cemetery are from that period.
They came back a third time in 1919, but after a few years had
had enough of Afghanistan and signed a treaty granting the
nation its independence.

On the cemetery's south wall there are ten recently placed
marble plaques inscribed with the names of dozens of British
service members killed in Afghanistan since 2001. The list is
far short of the more than 440 British killed; there's no space
left on the plaques.

Like me, Alex Pena from *Stars & Stripes* had been shut down
trying to embed in RC-South, so he put in a request with
RC-East as a backup. They hadn't had a lot of attention in
the previous few months and were open to hosting some media embeds. He planned to cover the Human Terrain System,
the controversial U.S. military program that put teams of anthropologists and other social scientists in the field alongside
soldiers to help battlefield commanders better understand the

communities in which they were fighting. He'd also asked to go on some joint patrols with U.S. and Afghan National Army soldiers to see how the transition was working.

I asked to piggyback on his embed since my trip was winding down and I hadn't been able to do any reporting on the military hand-off. An absurd amount of time and money had been invested in equipping and training the Afghan military; I wanted to see them in action since so much was riding on their ability to secure their own nation once the Americans and other international forces left. Afghans could fight; history proved that. But could they now fight as a national army rather than a assortment of ethnic militias pledged to regional warlords?

Alex was able to add me to his embed application as photographer/videographer under the *Stars & Stripes* billet. While I wouldn't actually be reporting for them, it made the bureaucratic paperwork easier for everyone, especially the ISAF/NATO public affairs office. Within a couple of days we were on a fifteen-minute flight from Kabul to Bagram Airfield, a flight so short it felt like a single arcing trajectory from take off to cruising altitude to landing, with no actual flight time.

The airfield was about 40 miles north of Kabul in Parwan Province and had been a Soviet air base during their occupation from 1979 to 1989. The nearby village of Bagram had been around since the time of Alexander the Great; known then as Alexandria on the Caucasus, it became a key trading point along the Silk Road.

Bagram was America's largest military base in Afghanistan and the logistical heart of the war, pumping out planes, people, and supplies to all parts of the country. I had been to Bagram a half dozen times before, and with each visit it seemed to have grown exponentially. In 2009, Bagram underwent a reported $200 million expansion that turned it into a small city, at one time ballooning to a population of as many as 30,000 people. It had paved streets, traffic cops, shopping bazaars, and so many fast food outlets (Burger King, Popeye's, Subway, Pizza Hut, DQ) that author Robert Young Pelton once described it for a *Men's Journal* article as follows:

> Bagram is America's duty-free space station in the war on terror and may be the most culturally isolated outpost on the planet. The world's most effective killing machine has ensconced itself in a hastily constructed replica of a Midwest strip mall.*

But Bagram also had a darker reputation. It was home to the Parwan Detention Facility (also known as the Bagram Theater Internment Facility), a prison run by the U.S. military until it was handed back to the Afghans in March 2013. It held between 600 and 1,800 prisoners at a time and became a flashpoint for controversy when the 2002 torture and killing of two Afghan men being held there was brought to light through a 2,000-page report leaked to the *New York Times*.

---

* Robert Young Pelton, "Afghanistan: The New War for Hearts and Minds," *Men's Journal*, February 2009.

The two prisoners, known as Habibullah and Dilawar, were reportedly chained to the ceiling and beaten to death. The trauma to the prisoners' legs was so severe that autopsy reports compared them to being "run over by a bus."*

Dilawar was described as a nonviolent twenty-two-year-old taxi driver who weighed 122 pounds. Leaked documents stated that his legs had been pulpified by the beatings and that had he lived, they would have had to be amputated. (The story of his death was made into an award-winning documentary, *Taxi to the Dark Side*, in 2008.)

The *New York Times* also reported about a secret prison near Bagram known ominously only as "the black jail," run by the CIA and Special Forces operatives:

> The site, known to detainees as the black jail, consists of individual windowless concrete cells, each illuminated by a single light bulb glowing twenty-four hours a day. In interviews, former detainees said that their only human contact was at twice-daily interrogation sessions.†

After the Parwan Detention Facility came under Afghan control in March 2013, a three-member Afghan detention commission released 560 prisoners. And in January 2014, a spokesman for President Karzai said that the Afghan govern-

---

* Tim Golden. "In U.S. Report, Brutal Details of 2 Afghan Inmates' Deaths," *New York Times*, May 20, 2005.

† Alissa J. Rubin, "Afghans Detail Detention in 'Black Jail' at U.S. Base," *New York Times*, November 28, 2009.

ment planned to release 72 of 88 prisoners at Bagram that the United States still considered dangerous and a threat.

"We cannot allow innocent Afghan citizens to be kept in detention for months and years without a trial for no reason at all," Karzai's spokesman Aimal Faizi told Reuters.* We know that unfortunately this has been happening at Bagram, but it is illegal and a violation of Afghan sovereignty, and we cannot allow this anymore."

The U.S. State Department criticized the move. Spokeswoman Jen Psaki said that the detainees being released were "dangerous criminals against whom there is strong evidence linking them to terror-related crimes, including the use of improvised explosive devices, the largest killer of Afghan civilians."

The decision was another indication of the growing rift between the U.S. and Afghan governments already exacerbated by Karzai's reluctance to sign the Bilateral Security Agreement. (Karzai said he will leave that decision to Afghanistan's next president). The U.S. has threatened that without an agreement they may initiate the "zero option," a complete withdrawal of all troops from Afghanistan, as they did in Iraq. Karzai has called the zero option an empty threat. As for the black jail, I didn't know if it still existed, which is the way the CIA and armed services branch spooks from the Defense Intelligence Agency preferred it.

Unlike those who arrived at the base involuntarily, Alex and I were pampered at Bagram. As in-transit media

---

* Reuters, "Afghanistan to Free Most Inmates Seen by U.S. as Threat," January 10, 2014.

embeds, we were not supposed to do any reporting, only wait for the flights that would take us to a remote forward operating base (FOB) and eventually an even more remote combat outpost (COP). In the meantime, we were housed next to the Bagram public affairs office in a wooden barracks, or hooch, dubbed the Hotel California, with the option of filling our time by going to one of the multiple gyms on base, shopping at the bazaars and PX, eating fast food, and catching up on sleep.

The next day, while we waited for our flight out to join our embed units, an officer came into the terminal waiting area and told all the service members to come outside to pay their respects to an arriving hero. Curious, Alex and I filed out as well. Even though they were from different units, even different branches, the soldiers and marines lined up together in one formation just behind a chain-link fence. They snapped their right hands to their foreheads as the "hero" appeared—a coffin draped in a U.S. flag carried by six American soldiers in fatigues. The coffin was loaded into a large box truck with the words "Bagram Mortuary" on its side.

At the time there were few details about who was inside the coffin, but we learned later that the only American deaths reported around that time were two U.S. soldiers and a civilian advisor who were shot and killed by Afghan National Army soldiers in Paktika Province. This flag-draped coffin most likely contained one of the casualties, another victim of what the military called green-on-blue killings—when Afghan security forces killed their ISAF allies.

According to the *Long War Journal*, a blog of the Foundation for the Defense of Democracy, a conservative think tank, there have been 140 ISAF deaths from green-on-blue attacks since 2008. While in 2008 they accounted for only 2 percent of overall deaths of coalition forces, that number had soared to 15 percent by 2012, when 61 were killed and 81 wounded. Those numbers dropped to just under 10 percent of all coalition deaths in 2013, when 14 were killed and 29 wounded. The *Long War Journal* suggests the reduction may have to do with the "guardian angel" program, in which soldiers and marines act as armed bodyguards for U.S. troops working with the Afghan National Security Forces.[*]

NATO commanders blamed cultural difference and personal issues for the majority of the green-on-blue attacks; the Afghan government blamed them on infiltration by Taliban and foreign spy agencies, especially Pakistan's Inter-Services Intelligence (ISI), long suspected of supporting the Taliban in Afghanistan. Either way, when your allies are responsible for 10 percent of your overall combat deaths after a dozen years working together, there's a problem that needs fixing.

The Taliban were, in fact, quick to take credit for almost every green-on-blue incident, recognizing its propaganda

---

[*] Bill Roggio and Lisa Lundquist, "Green-on-Blue Attacks in Afghanistan: The Data," *The Long War Journal*, August 23, 2012, updated February 13, 2014, http://www.long warjournal.org/archives/2012/08/green-on-blue_attack.php

value. They even claim to have created a Call and Guidance, Luring, and Integration Department to encourage defections, which Mullah Omar said were a matter of religious duty for government and security personnel.

Our ride arrived shortly after the impromptu honor guard ceremony ended, and Alex and I boarded a U.S. Army CH-47D Chinook, the double-rotor, heavy-lift work-horse helicopter that can carry as many as 45 troops in full gear and as much as 26,000 pounds of cargo. Versions of this versatile bird have been in operation since the Vietnam War. Once onboard and strapped in, I tapped Alex on the shoulder and pointed to the ceiling; crew members had used lengths of olive drab paracord to secure a cardboard cutout of "the most interesting man in the world," the bearded, silver-haired actor from the Dos Equis beer commercials. Flying across the mountains to FOB Airborne in northeastern Wardak Province, his presence was a lighthearted counterpoint to the M240 machine guns mounted at forward openings on both sides.

When we touched down at Airborne we exited the Chinook with a burly, bearded American traveling with two large duffel bags and a big backpack. We thought he might be a manager for KBR (formerly Kellogg, Brown, and Root),*

---

* KBR is the American military contractor that built many of the bases in Iraq and Afghanistan; after their construction, they usually contracted to provide food, cafeteria workers, PX, and a myriad of other products and services on the base. The wars had

But it turned out that the American was a member of the human terrain teams we'd actually come to interview, a political scientist named Caleb Bartley. The son of a Vietnam veteran, Bartley had never been in the military himself: he studied it instead. He held a master's degree in defense and strategic studies from the University of Missouri; he joined the Human Terrain System program in 2009.

This was Bartley's third deployment to Afghanistan, and FOB Airborne would be his new home for the next year. We helped him carry his gear to the pickup point, where we were met by the other two members of the human terrain team at RC-East: Clarissa Bertha, an anthropologist and air force veteran who had served in Bosnia, and Polly Cegielski, another anthropologist; both had joined the program in 2010.

After a quick tour of the base, Bertha dropped us off at our hooch, two nearly bare but comfortable rooms adjacent to the FOB's Morale, Welfare, and Recreation Center, a building filled with computers and phones where soldiers could call or Skype their loved ones, or even just play computer games and surf the net.

My room had a fat single mattress and a chest of drawers ingeniously made of ammo crates; on an FOB, that's the equivalent of a room at the Ritz. There was also a broken vacuum cleaner, even thought there were no carpets.

---

made the company billions while miring it in controversies over everything from price gouging to the mistreatment of the contract workers it brought in from Third World countries like Bangladesh and the Philippines to serve food and clean toilets.

"It looks like Khalid Sheikh Muhammad was already here," I joked, pointing at the vacuum, while Bartley, Alex, and I inspected the rooms. They laughed, catching my reference to a recent AP story about the criminal mastermind behind the 9/11 attacks who also claimed to have beheaded *Wall Street Journal* reporter Daniel Pearl. Mohammed had been kept in a secret CIA jail and waterboarded 183 times. According to the AP, he had asked the CIA if he could design a vacuum cleaner while he was in detention. After he confessed to the attacks, the CIA, wanting to keep him occupied and sane, agreed to his request.* There were no follow-up reports on whether Sheikh Mohammed ever built his vacuum, but he had earned a bachelor's degree in mechanical engineering at North Carolina A&T University seventeen years earlier, so it's likely he was capable of the project.

After we settled in, we met Bertha, Cegielski, and Bartley in their office near the base's tactical operations center. While polite, they were clearly suspicious of us.

Bartley was direct: "Why are you interested in the human terrain teams?"

I could understand his caution. The Human Terrain System (HTS), the name for the U.S. military program of which the human terrain teams (HTTs) were the moving parts, had been neck-deep in controversy almost as soon as it was launched in 2005.

The two forces behind the HTS were American officers in Iraq who had complained to their bosses that they had no

---

* Adam Goldman, "The CIA and the Secret Vacuum Cleaner," Associated Press, July 11, 2013.

information about the local communities, and Montgomery McFate, a Yale-educated cultural anthropologist who saw social science as a tool for increasing the effectiveness of military operations. In 2005, McFate began building a database on the Iraqi population. Then the Pentagon teamed her up with a retired Special Operations colonel named Steve Fondacaro, who wanted to take the program farther by embedding social scientists within American combat units. The HTTs were created to map the social battlegrounds of Iraq and Afghanistan, much as the physical terrain had been mapped.

The HTTs were tasked with a range of sociological exploration: identifying community leaders, insurgents, and their rivalries for power; finding out which tribes and clans might be amenable to working with the troops and which were better left alone; and probing the dynamics of community conflicts, such as how land disputes might be exploited by insurgent groups.

The idea behind the HTS seemed well-grounded strategically. Not understanding cultures and communities was costing the U.S. both lives and local support. It was more than a hearts-and-minds argument, it was an efficiency standard that could help the military make better decisions about who to fight and who to negotiate with. Some combat field commanders were indeed impressed by early deployments of HTTs, claiming that in certain regions, the presence of social scientists reduced combat operations by as much as 60 percent; that freed troops to focus on civil affairs like building schools and health care clinics, projects that helped build confidence in and support for the government

But almost immediately, the HTS program had come under attack from the American Anthropological Association, which considered the work an unethical breach of trust: scientists were not just observing the people they were studying but providing information on them to the military that could result in their detention, danger to their physical safety, or even in their deaths.

Montgomery McFate defended the program. In 2007, she told the *New York Times*, "I'm frequently accused of militarizing anthropology, but we're really anthropologizing the military." She denied that the HTT anthropologists were like spies collecting intelligence and said the goal was to help the military "decrease conflict instead of provoking it."*

In truth, HTT information was collected in a giant database and could be used by battlefield commanders both to build a community a road and defeat it militarily. Anthropology is the observation and study of cultures, but that understanding isn't intended to be actionable, and doesn't typically result in bombing runs *or* construction projects. The American Anthropological Association called for anthropologists to refuse to serve with the HTS.

The environment for the HTS continued to get tougher, especially after an incident in 2008 that became the subject

---

* David Rohde, "Army Enlists Anthropology in War Zones," *New York Times*, October 5, 2007.

of *The Tender Soldier* by former *Chicago Tribune* reporter Vanessa Gezari.

Paula Loyd had come to the Human Terrain System with impressive bona fides. In addition to a degree in cultural anthropology from Wellesley College and a masters in foreign service from Georgetown University, she had done a four-year stint in the U.S. Army as a heavy-wheel vehicle mechanic. She had also been both a civil and military officer with UNAMA, the United Nations Assistance Mission in Afghanistan, and a field program officer for USAID. Loyd knew Afghanistan, and her work there earned her both praise and respect.

Gezari wrote that Loyd understood how important it was to read between the lines, that communication in a culture dominated by an outside power tended to become almost imperceptibly nuanced while still carrying important information.

In an opinion piece Gezari wrote for the *New York Times* she cited a passage Loyd had written in her Wellesley thesis years earlier: "people in these environments talk in 'jokes, metaphors, folktales, and codes,' artfully conveying meaning while preserving maximum deniability."*

On November 4, 2008, Loyd was in the village of Chehel Gazi in the Maiwand district of Kandahar Province with an American army foot patrol. She began a conversation with a man named Abdul Salam, who was carrying a jug of fuel he said was for his motorcycle. Loyd asked him, through her interpreter, what he had paid for it, but when the interpreter

---

* Vanessa M. Gezari, "How to Read Afghanistan," *New York Times*, August 10, 2013.

was called away, Salam, with whom she had been chatting amiably moments before, doused her with the liquid and set her on fire. She suffered second- and third-degree burns over more than half her body.

An eyewitness account recorded in court documents describes the incident:

> Engulfed in a ball of flame large enough to force those near her to involuntarily back away, Paula Loyd screamed in agony as the children that had surrounded her ran away. In the several seconds following the attack, no one could get near enough to Ms. Loyd to help her. Panicked, Ms. Loyd ran around briefly before those near her pulled her to the ground. One of the platoon medics tried to put the fire out with dirt, ultimately grabbing Ms. Loyd by her foot and dragging her into the nearby drainage ditch to douse the flames. By the time the fire was extinguished, all of Ms. Loyd's clothing had been burned off and only her helmet and body armor remained. Medical personnel would later determine that Ms. Loyd suffered second- and third- degree burns over more than 60 percent of her body.*

Salam took off. But when team member Don Ayala was informed of Loyd's injuries, he ran him down, forced him to

---

* United States of America v. Don Michael, Ayala, United States Court for the Eastern District of Virginia, Alexandria Division, Case 1:08-cr-00474-CMH Document 29 filed 5/01/2009, Criminal No. 1:08cr474, Sentencing Date: May 9, 2009, The Honorable Claude M. Hinton. http://fantlab.ru/files/messages/91/914/9142/914253/ayala_29_1_50109.pdf.

the ground, and secured his hands behind his back with flexi-cuffs. When Ayala learned how badly Loyd had been burned, he pushed his pistol against Salam's head and shot him, killing him instantly, according to a soldier's affidavit to the Army Criminal Investigative Division.

Ayala, a former army ranger and security contractor who had been Hamid Karzai's bodyguard on a previous deploy-ment, was charged with murder and shipped back to the U.S. for trial. He pled guilty to voluntary manslaughter, which could have meant more than sixty years in jail under federal sentencing guidelines. Instead, Ayala was sentenced to five years probation and a $12,500 fine. Loyd's family had pleaded for leniency on his behalf.

Loyd died from her injuries a month after her attack, on January 7, 2009. She was the third HTT member to be killed in the field.* To HTS supporters, she and the others were heroes on the same level as soldiers, contributing to national security. To HTS critics, the deaths indicated that when anthropologists shift from observers to participants, they endanger themselves, the communities they study, and the science itself.

More bad news followed. Internal army investigations of the program obtained by *USA Today* through Freedom of Informa-tion Act requests revealed a program beset by racism, sexism,

---

* The other two HTT members were Michael Bhatia, killed by an IED in May 2008 along with two soldiers while riding in a Humvee in Khost, Afghanistan, and Nicole Suveges, killed on June 24, 2008, along with eleven soldiers, Iraqi government officials, and U.S. embassy personnel by a bomb planted in a government office in Sadr City, Iraq.

and corruption. There were allegations of sexual harassment and degrading comments made to black employees; current and former employees admitting they filed timesheets for hours they hadn't worked, sometimes racking up salaries of $200,000 a year, equal to what Secretary of Defense Chuck Hagel earns.

Nonetheless, the Human Terrain Team at FOB Airborne—Clarissa Bertha, Polly Cegielski, and Caleb Bartley—believed in the value of the program and that their work had positive effects for both the military and the communities they observed.

"In my last unit, there were times we recommended *against* removing someone because doing so would have created a vacuum that'd make it harder to stabilize that area," said Bertha.

And in Bartley's view, HTS critics actually underscore the true nature of the program.

"If the critics say we help the Army be a more effective killing machine, I kind of hope so, because if you are ineffective, and you're killing indiscriminately—indiscriminate killings will create nothing but upheaval and more violence and further conflict," Bartley told me. "The difference is between academic anthropology and applied anthropology. The former has the idea that academic work that leads to killing someone is a heartless act of fascism. But we use our knowledge, skills, and abilities to make the organization we're committed to a more effective organization. That makes perfect sense."

Cegielski feels that some criticism of the HTS harkens back to an outdated, ultra-traditionalist view of anthropologists: Margaret Meade types who go to Samoa, New Guinea, and Bali, live among the natives, immerse themselves in their communities, and become their best friends. She said what the HTTs do actually leaves a smaller footprint. And when they do provide actionable information to battlefield commanders, it is, she believes, in the best interests of the community.

"While we do go out and meet with them, we're not living with them, we're not targeting them for information so we can kill them better—we're trying to help them so there is less kinetics [violence]," Cegielski said. "If we can target a specific person, it's going to make the environment safer for them as well as for us. There are definitely benefits on each side. We're not just being insidious and sneaky."

"Some people are really afraid of being labeled "intel," added Bartley, "and I always thought that was so ridiculous, because intelligence from the military point of view is taking in information, analyzing it, and then providing it to the commander so he or she can make better decisions. *Of course* we're intel: We gather information. We analyze it. And then we present it to the commander so that he or she can make better decisions."

Bertha jumped in. "We are trying to help them look critically at the big picture, if you will. So they can make the most complete and best-informed decision that they can." And she pointed out that what she's discovered while mapping the human terrain of Afghanistan is that people aren't getting what they need from their national government.

"There's not a whole lot of trust and faith in GIROA [Government of the Islamic Republic of Afghanistan]. There is a view and a sentiment that GIROA does not care about their people. It's not that they trust Taliban, but they see Taliban as someone who provides minimal civil services, whereas GIROA provides nothing. The Taliban has a presence, while GIROA does not."

Bertha continued, "They understand who can provide the basic benefits. And if they have to take if from someone whom they view as harsh, violent in some cases, and mean, they still need to get their basic needs met, because this is about survival: It's not about who we like best. It's not about who we trust, necessarily. But if one group is not meeting those needs, they'll look to someone who will."

And it may be that's how the Human Terrain System and human terrain teams will prove their worth—by gathering the very information that means not just winning the war but winning the peace as well.

Journalist Vanessa Gezari felt that fallen HTT member Paula Loyd had understood that and that she, like Bertha, Cegielski, and Bartley, had had the best intentions. But she also believed Loyd was part of a program destined to fail:

The Human Terrain System sought to bring a degree of anthropological and interpretive acumen to a military that badly needed it. But it came too late, alienated too many anthropologists, and was thrown together too quickly and sloppily to achieve many of its goals in Afghanistan. Taxpayers have spent more than $600 million on the deeply flawed program; it has occasionally benefited soldiers, but its slipshod construction and murky aims have also put Afghans and Americans at risk.

Nonetheless, Gezari believes the system should be overhauled, not abandoned.

"What happened to Paula Loyd reminds us that understanding what motivates our enemies and the people we're fighting among is a long and painful undertaking. But turning away from this effort, as many in the military did in the wake of Vietnam, ensures only that more Americans will die in other wars, in other far-flung corners of the world."[*]

---

[*] Vanessa Gezari, "How to Read Afghanistan," *New York Times*, August 10, 2013.

23

TARGETS

||||||||||||||

A member of a Human Terrain Team meets with female members of the Afghan National Police.

The next day, the battalion commander at FOB Airborne was scheduled to meet with the Afghan National Police chief of Wardak Province. Human Terrain Team member Polly Cegielski was going along to speak with three female police officers. Alex and I joined them to observe.

Though the police compound is just a few hundred yards walk from FOB Airborne, it's outside the wire, so we all put on our full "battle rattle"—Kevlar helmets, body armor, ballistic glasses, and ear protection—before we headed outside the gate. There was a traffic circle a short ways away, and a few soldiers stopped traffic so we could cross. They've seen this countless times before, and the locals stare at small troop movement without expression. We are in the district of Maidan Shar, the provincial capital, with a population of more than 35,000, the vast majority Pashtuns. Despite its proximity to Kabul, it's an extremely poor and conservative place. Most residents are farmers and herders. But it's rich in natural beauty, ringed by the Arghandeh and Paghman mountains. I was there in 2001, only a short time after first arriving in Kabul, to investigate reports of fighting.

From my journal:

NOVEMBER 2001: CROOKED LITTLE WAR

Maidan Shar is a crooked little fight in a crooked little war. The Taliban commander here has agreed to switch sides, wants to join with the Northern Alliance, but hasn't been offered enough money yet. So in between negotiations, they exchange fire.

Northern Alliance armor and artillery form in a crescent moon around this Taliban holdout on a mountain foothill. When my fixer Halim and I arrive at the front, we believe it is a more noble fight than that. We would not have risked our lives otherwise. We walk over to a Northern Alliance Katyusha rocket battery. The commander tells us they have fired at the Taliban position five times already this morning. I interview him, then begin shooting footage of the Katyushas. A crew member whistles to me, then points to the sky. There is a visceral sound of metal slicing through the air, a high-pitched Doppler effect scream. The Taliban have their own Katyushas, and they just fired one at us. It lands several hundred yards away, but close enough for all the Northern Alliance troops to scramble into a Jeep Cherokee and fly down the road, out of range.

After shooting footage of the rocket, Ibay, a colleague from Turkish TV, pulls up in a taxi. He tells me that he was all the way into the village of Maidan Shar earlier in the morning, no more than 100 meters from the Taliban. Did I want to see it? Did I want to go with him now? There are no answers to those kinds of question, those kind of moments.

We are in our van, moving past Northern Alliance troops and tanks into the town. They tell us not to go: it's

*too dangerous, they say. I'm looking for an out, anything,
but Ibay is resolute. Halim is not anxious to go but will
stay with me regardless. Same for our driver Yar Muhammad. The minute we drive into the town, I think we have
made a bad decision. We are heading to a Northern Alliance forward position in the Maidan Shar graveyard. In
between is a road and a mile of open space in easy range
of Taliban guns. We leave the van door open, in case we
need to roll out and look for cover. The town is deserted.
Then the open stretch. Yar Muhammad is driving very
slowly, I can only think of what a great target we are, a
large white van going 5 miles an hour.*

*We make it to the graveyard, and immediately the sound
of machine gun fire surrounds us. I've heard a lot of it in
Afghanistan, but none of it this close. It makes the ricochet
sound that bullets make when they hit dirt and rock flying
past their targets. I do a quick interview with a Northern Alliance soldier who is sprawled out on a grave, leaning against
a headstone. He tells me he has been here for five days. That
he is not afraid. He is so laid back, literally and figuratively,
I tend to believe him. Why, I wonder, as we talk, does so
much of the fighting here seem to take place in graveyards.
But that's an easy one: because there is so much, so many of
both. The soldier points to my head, tells me to keep low. The
Taliban have a bounty of $50,000 for any foreign journalist
killed. I have heard the story before, believe it is more rumor
than fact. Nonetheless, I am flattered. But only a little. I was
hoping for six figures.*

*Then, a rapid burst of machine gun fire. He points
behind us. I swing my camera around and see five Northern Alliance soldiers running across the same field we
had driven across. They are under heavy fire. They bob
and weave like boxers, sometimes diving into trenches
until they are covered by the incline of the hillside. Some
have machine guns strapped to their backs, others rocket-
propelled grenades, and they are all carrying something in
their hands, What are they carrying? Ammo? Grenades?
When they finally reach us they are huffing and puffing.
They put down their weapons and sit next to their comrades. Carefully, they unwrap their packages. I look closer,
curious about what's inside. It's bread. They were carrying
bread. They risked their lives under fire to carry bread
across the front lines.*

*We stay for another few hours. With no more sounds of
gunfire, we get back in the van and speed across the open
field. We make it out safe. We learn later from one of our
sources that a deal has been struck. When the Taliban
commander got his number* [the amount of money he
wanted] *peace broke out in Maidan Shar. A little too late
for the half dozen men from both sides who were killed
there in the last five days while the warlords negotiated.*

Maidan Shar seemed a much more peaceful place now, although the peace was uneasy. There were plenty of Taliban
and Taliban sympathizers in the area, and Airborne, like

most other FOBs, endured frequent mortar attacks, or as the soldiers called it, IDF—for indirect fire: anything lobbed at you rather than pointed at you . . . like the muzzle of a gun.

Once inside the police compound, we removed our gear and were taken into an office where we were introduced to the three policewomen: Razia Yaqoobi, a twenty-six-year-old from Gazni Province with four years on the force; Bibi Mobin, thirty-seven, a widow and mother of six who lost two of her daughters and a son-in-law in a suicide bombing in Kabul; and an irrepressible women named Roina Durani, who gave me a reproving look when I asked her age and who had been on the force for five years.

I had instant respect for all of them. The statistics showed that being a cop was the most dangerous job in Afghanistan. The Afghan Ministry of the Interior announced over the summer that more than 2,700 Afghan police officers had been killed or injured in the previous four months alone. And being a female cop was like painting a target on your back. In addition to the threat from the Taliban, many were sexually harassed and sometimes even sexually assaulted by their male colleagues. And they were often assigned to do nothing more than carry out body searches of other women at checkpoints, buildings, and airports. In southern provinces, women were often discouraged from or even threatened for taking jobs with the police, sometimes by their own family members. No wonder women made up only a dismal one percent of the total Afghan police force. According to an Oxfam study, in 2005 there were just 180 women out of more than 53,000 officers. By July 2013, the number had grown to 1,551 out of 157,000—still just a fraction of the overall force.*

To underscore the danger of such a career, the Taliban had chosen to assassinate some of the nation's top female cops as an example to others. In 2008, Afghanistan's highest-ranking and most prominent policewoman, Lt. Col. Malalai Kakar, was shot and killed in her car by two men on a motorbike while on her way to work in Kandahar. Her eighteen-year-old son, who had been driving, was seriously wounded in the attack.

The forty-one-year-old Kakar, a mother of six, was the head of Kandahar's Department of Crimes Against Women. She came from a long line of police officers who included her father and brothers, and joined the force herself in 1982, during the Russian occupation. She was forced out when the Taliban took over but was the first female police officer in the country to return to work after they were driven from power.

Her exploits were legendary, sometimes making it hard to sort myth from reality. She's credited with interrupting three men about to launch a suicide attack and killing them in the shootout that followed. Whether her exploits had been inflated or not, she was an iconic figure whose death frightened many and inspired some:

> In the no-man's-land of Kandahar Province in Afghanistan, Malalai Kakar was like a feminist action hero. Swathed in

---

* Louise Hancock, "Women and the Afghan Police." Oxfam Briefing Paper 173, September 10, 2013. http://www.oxfam.org/sites/www.oxfam.org/files/bp-173-afghanistan -women-police-100913-en.pdf

her burka and carrying a Kalashnikov in her hand and a 9-millimeter pistol on her hip, the region's top female police officer—and mother of six—apprehended thieves, killers, and wife-beaters. Once, in a shootout with a dozen Taliban fighters, she and three male officers held their own until the Taliban fled. Another time, she burst into a home, knocked down the husband, and rescued a woman and child the man had kept chained in a cage. Back at the station, Kakar mediated neighborhood disputes and even marital disagreements.*

On July 4, 2013, just two weeks prior to our arrival in Maidan Shar, the top female officer in Helmand Province, Islam Bibi, was killed, shot while she rode to work with her son-in-law on the back of his motorbike. The mother of three survived the immediate shooting but died at the hospital. She had been in charge of thirty-two female officers. Bibi had told a British newspaper that she loved being on the police force but that her family was so opposed to it that her own brother had tried to kill her to stop her from working. While the Taliban had claimed credit for Kakar's killing, no one ever took responsibility for Bibi's.

Following in Kakar's and Bibi's footsteps, the three policewomen in Maidan Shar were well aware of what they were getting into.

---

* "Murderous Message" [editorial], *Los Angeles Times*, October 19, 2008.

"When we accepted this job, we knew it was dangerous, but we accepted the risk," said Razia Yaqoobi. Bibi Mobin nodded her head in agreement; she understood the sacrifice personally, having lost family members in a suicide bombing in Kabul.

"In Chak district, the Taliban hanged a woman from a tree and shot her five times for working with a Swedish NGO," said Roina Durani. "The same thing could happen to us." But she remained undeterred.

"Since I was a schoolgirl, I wanted to be a policewoman," she continued. "I worked in the Ministry of the Interior when I was young and saw them and thought they were so special in their uniforms."

While she was mostly relegated to conducting body searches of other women, Durani said there were times when the work could be exciting.

"Two years ago, around the time of Ramadan, we went on a mission to Sheik Habad, and the insurgents attacked us. The male officers fought back with Kalashnikovs and RPGs. We were armed with Makarov (9-mm) pistols but were told to take cover inside the vehicles and not to shoot. I would've shot back if they had let me," said Durani. "After it was over, we went on with the mission and helped search the houses, but the Taliban took all their women and children to other locations before the attack, so they were mostly empty."

I asked her what I'd asked so many Afghans: "Is your life better now than it was under the Taliban?" She looked at me and raised both hands, indicating I'd asked a very silly question.

"When the Taliban were in power, we couldn't even leave the house without a male relative. We couldn't get jobs, girls couldn't go to school," Durani said. "The last twelve years, we've been like birds flying freely. If the Taliban come back to power, we will be in a cage again."

But while Durani fights against the prospect of that cage, she's ambivalent about her daughter, who has expressed in following in her footsteps, taking the same risk. And she has reason to be concerned. Just two months after the killing of Islam Bibi in early July, her replacement, Lt. Nigara, was shot while waiting for a government bus to take her to work by two pistol-wielding men on motorbikes. Like Bibi, Nigara survived the attack but later died from her wounds. No one has claimed responsibility for the murder, and police have no suspects.

The forty-one-year-old Nigara had been a police officer since the Russian occupation, and, like Kakar, had been forced out of work by the Taliban. And she had a similar fearless streak, telling the *New York Times* she once stopped a suicide bomber by putting him in a bear hug and wrestling him to the ground.* Her death, like the others, will almost certainly put a dent in female police recruiting, especially in the south, perhaps hastening the return of that Taliban cage Roina Durani spoke of instead inspiring others just as tough

---

* Rod Nordland and Taimor Shah, "Female Afghan Police Commander Dies After Shooting," *New York Times*, September 16, 2013.

and determined to take her place. In fact, one of Nigara's fellow officers told the *Daily Mail* that the Taliban have told them there will be more killings to come.

"They have given us warning that one of us will be killed every three months, and we will be killed one by one."*

---

* Helen Collis, "Helmand's top policewoman who bear-hugged a suicide bomber and ignored Taliban death threats is shot dead—two months after her female predecessor was also murdered." *Daily Mail*, September 16, 2013.

24

COMBAT OUTPOST
SOLTAN KHEYL

||||||||||||||

Two U.S. army soldiers, followed by a medic, run to the
combat aid station at combat outpost Soltan Kheyl
immediately after being wounded in a mortar attack on the base.

There's so much activity in Afghanistan during this drawdown of U.S. and NATO forces that the International Security Assistance Force has been using a fleet of civilian helicopters to move personnel, mail, and the like from one base to another. It's 10 p.m. when Alex and I board one for our departure from FOB Airborne just two days after our arrival. Having completed our reporting on the Human Terrain Systems, we headed to our next location, combat outpost (COP) Soltan Kheyl, a remote but critical base overlooking the Sayedabad district and Highway 1 in Wardak Province. There we'll embed with two American companies doing joint patrols with the Afghan National Army.

A ride on a bird in the Afghan night was usually calming for me; the gentle agitation of the helicopter's rotors worked like the pulsating lull of a shower massage, while a sky full of stars and the dark terrain below dully illuminated by kerosene lanterns hung from the mud-walled compounds made it seem like the whole universe was nothing more than tiny specs of light. But on this night something was wrong. This night I was playing that psych-out game that soldiers and other journalists have told me they sometimes play while riding in Humvees, MRAPs, or Blackhawks taking them deeper into the heart of conflict. The game of imagining their deaths.

While flying through the Afghan night, I obsessed that this would be the end of the line. That after all my time in war zones, the jig is finally up: the bird will crash or I'll be killed by a roadside bomb, or even worse, it will blow off my nuts and all my limbs, but I'll live. For fifteen minutes, I can't dislodge the feedback loop of my own misfortune, wondering if I should scratch out a letter to loved ones back home. Then we land at Soltan Kheyl, and the morbid rumination ends.

At the gravel landing zone we're met by Sgt. Jongin Choi, a twenty-four-year-old Korean American from New Jersey and part of 3rd Battalion, 7th Infantry, Alpha Company. Choi takes us to the tactical operations center on the combat outpost to meet his commanding officer, an easygoing captain from Connecticut named Jon Rembetsy, who carried himself with the confidence and competence of an officer with four Afghan deployments under his belt. After a quick introduction and briefing, Rembetsy scheduled us for joint foot patrols with his third and first platoons and squads from the Afghan National Army over the next three days. Sergeant Choi then took us to a warehouse subdivided into rooms by plywood walls and cutout doors. The rooms offered thin mattresses on steel and wire frames, some privacy, and little else. It was perfect.

The next day Choi shows us around Soltan Kheyl, an outpost built on a hill 8,000 feet above sea level. The base was shared by the Americans and the Afghan National Army, but wire fences and walls separated the two, an indication, I presumed, of ongoing distrust. And even though the U.S. is drawing down forces, Soltan Kheyl has been beefed up with soldiers from two different regiments of the 3rd Battalion because of the increased frequency of Taliban attacks at the beginning of the summer. The COP is tasked with keeping open a 50-mile stretch of Highway 1, a vital part of the military supply route that brings food, fuel, and ammo from Bagram to Kandahar, and a lifeline for local businesses and communities along its course.

The road's heavy truck traffic has made it a prime target for both the Taliban and bandits, who mine the roads, ambush convoys, and steal their cargo. Some are in collusion with crooked trucking contractors, running insurance scams: the trucks are unloaded and then set ablaze so the contractors can file claims.

A paramilitary group known as the Afghan Public Protection Force was created to help with convoy security in the wake of massive fraud and corruption endemic to the private security contractors that had been doing the job, but many American commanders felt the Afghan Public Protection Force was little better and likely colluding with the crooked truckers, Taliban, and bandits wreaking havoc on the roads.

American military leaders knew the Wardak section of Highway 1, the "southern gateway to Kabul," was critical strategically: the Taliban had used it on their march to take the capital in 1996. If the U.S. was unable to train Afghan National Security Forces to hold and protect Highway 1 after their withdrawal, it could lead again to the fall of Kabul.

We've asked to see the Afghan National Army 3rd Kandak (battalion) adjacent to COP Soltan Kheyl. Choi takes us first to meet Maj. Rob Howard, the American recently brought here to help the troubled unit regain its footing.

In army slang, Howard is a "maverick," an enlisted man who jumped across the divide to become an officer. Traditionally, mavericks are well-liked by the men and women they lead because they've been in their boots and represent the potential for career advancement. Howard would be no different—if he actually had his own men to lead. But his job at COP Soltan Kheyl is as an advisor, both to the Afghan officers and the sixty-two Czech troops assigned as trainers to the Afghan National Army.

When we arrived at his office, he had three laptops open on his desk. He shook our hands, greeting us sincerely as welcome arrivals rather than annoying burdens being foisted on him from further up the chain of command. Considering the difficulty of what he's been asked to do, Howard needs all the potential support he can muster, even if it means soliciting media types like us. He wasted no time cutting to the chase.

"The reason this *kandak* is not far enough along is because of leadership issues," he told us. "It's last commander was just relieved for not being aggressive enough, and the new one, Col. Mulinkadin, is really strong, but he's got issues we have to fix first."

Howard told us that Mulinkadin was really pushing his men and that he had gotten results, including lowering the number of attacks on Highway 1: in June, overall enemy activity had been cut in half. But some of his junior officers and

NCOs were chafing at the faster operational tempo and had made false accusations against him.

"In just a few weeks," Howard said, "he's been accused of releasing detainees for money, accused of selling fuel, and, get this, accused of selling hash for sexual favors. He's been cleared on all charges, but obviously this indicates the need for some housecleaning in the unit."

Howard said the colonel had also made sure that his Afghan National Army units were linking up with American platoons for joint operations each day, although Ramadan had reduced their activities.

"I really like this guy," Howard told us as we walked down a dirt road and through the gate to the 3rd Kandak's area of the base to meet Mulinkadin, "but I have to watch his back with his bosses."

Col. Atrafy Malinkadin's office was similar to those of the military and police commanders I'd seen all across Afghanistan: another dark room with heavy curtains, a big desk at one end, portraits of Karzai and Massoud, and chairs lined up against the walls on both sides. We took our seats and talked with Malinkadin through an interpreter about the challenges he faced.

"Corruption is preventing 80 percent of what we can do." Mulinkadin said, "One of the best examples is the convoy. The Afghan Public Protection Force is supposed to bring fuel trucks here, but they're selling the fuel in Kabul then staging attacks that destroy the fuel trucks. And they're insured, so they're making money off the insurance, too. And the Taliban are certainly involved."

Mulinkadin said he'd made improvements, both to the quality of life for his soldiers—they now had cots, mattresses, and even showers—but also to interagency communications. He'd created a communications coordination center on the base staffed by representatives of the Afghan National Army, the Afghan National Police, local police, and the National Directorate of Security, the Afghan domestic intelligence service. As a result information about improvised explosive devices (IEDs), convoy attacks, and other operational issues could be shared.

I asked Mulinkadin if he thought he could still take on the Taliban after the International Security Assistance Force (ISAF) and the Americans withdrew.

"Whether coalition forces are with us or not, we still have to do the job," he said, "but it's better if we build our house out of concrete rather than mud, and coalition forces are the concrete. I don't want to keep them forever," he laughed, "but every single person in the Afghan National Army still wants the coalition forces here after 2014."

As we left Malinkadin's office and headed back to the American side of the base, we heard helicopters overhead. We turned the corner just in time to see soldiers unloading a stretcher from the rear hatch of an MRAP. The small body on it was covered in metallic space blankets and immobilized by straps. Five men carried the stretcher while another held an IV bag and ventilated the patient, squeezing the bag valve mask covering his face. Alex and I followed them as they hustled the stretcher to the landing zone and shielded the patient with their bodies against the swirling dust from the landing Blackhawk medevac. Within two minutes, the patient was loaded and the helicopter lifted off again.

We learned later what had happened from Maj. Howard; it was not good news for him or anyone else on the base. The patient being airlifted out was a ten-year-old Afghan boy who had snuck onto the COP's rifle practice range to collect brass shell casings; a ricochet had struck him in the head. Howard said he was told the boy had died in-flight, but a medical source on the base told me he was likely dead before the helicopter even arrived. Later, looking through my photographs of the landing zone, I spotted something to support that theory: one of the Czech medics looking dejected, his chin on his chest, no longer attending to the patient.

A few days later, Howard told us there had been a JAG (judge advocate general) investigation, and a few dozen people had been interviewed. The conclusion was that either an Afghan National Army soldier or one of the trainers from the Czech Republic had fired the ricochet round, and it had lodged in the boy's skull.

But the bullet was never extracted in an autopsy to determine who had fired it, something that would've been evident from the type of ammunition used: the Afghans use AK-47 rifles that fire 7.62 x 39 mm rounds, while the Czech infantry rifle was the CZ 805 BREN that shoot NATO-standard 5.56 x 45 ammo. When I pressed him, Howard shook his head and said he didn't know why but seemed to agree with my presumption that it wasn't an oversight. No matter with whom the blame belonged, the killing of a child did not inspire confidence or support for either the Afghan National Army or their ISAF trainers. The boy's body was returned to his family with a solatium of $1,000 and some rice and cooking oil.

I attended a mission briefing a few hours later by 3rd Platoon, the unit we'd patrolled with that morning. The platoon leader, a young lieutenant, told his men to be prepared for retaliation.

At 4:30 the next morning I woke up, used the Porta-John, splashed some water on my face, went back to my hooch, and began putting on my gear. Choi would be there by five to walk us out to the east gate.

Like a soldier, I had a ritual before I went out on patrol. I laid my gear out the night before, charged the batteries for both my camcorder and my DSLR , adjusted my helmet straps, and checked the attachments on my body armor: the first aid pouch on the back left of the vest with a large compress, tourniquet, and paramedic shears. I had a quart-size canteen in a holster on the right, a pouch on the front right side for extra batteries and lens cleaning gear, a pouch with a rain poncho in the center, and two pouches on my left front for a head lamp, compass, Nomex gloves, and ballistic glasses with interchangeable lenses—clear for night, dark for daylight. I carried a monopod bow-style over my back and slung my two cameras—video on my left, still on my right—over my shoulders, with their straps looped through a climbing carabiner connected to my body armor in the back, which let me use one camera while keeping the other ready and in place. Finally, I wore kneepads so I could kneel on rocks or concrete for a better shot, or even just to take a breather. It had taken me a few years of experimenting, but I had assembled a kit that provided mobility and flexibility while still offering some protection. I laced my boots and met Choi and Alex outside. It was still very dark as we walked down the dirt path to the gate to join the rest of the platoon.

The Afghan unit had still not arrived when we got there, and 3rd Platoon was getting antsy; they wanted to get outside of the wire under cover of dark.

When the Afghan soldiers did arrive, it was just a squad, nine guys instead of the twenty-odd soldiers the Americans had assembled. As we waited in the darkness, I listened to the chatter from Choi's radio. The Afghans didn't have coms or night vision, so they wouldn't be able to talk to the Americans or each other if they got too far out of view, and negotiating the rocky descent down to the village of Saydabad would be tricky in the dark.

"It doesn't matter," said the platoon sergeant, Tim Cardinal, "these guys know the terrain much better than we do."

When Cardinal was satisfied everyone was in place, he told the American platoon leader, Lt. Nathan Bier, who gave the order to move out. Capt. Rembetsy had quietly joined the unit too, but barely said a word, confident enough to let his officers and NCOs do their jobs.

We spread out over the hillside and moved carefully down the slope toward the village, Americans in front, Afghans trailing behind. While I had spent a lot of time with Northern Alliance fighters in the past and had also gone on unilateral patrols with Afghan National Army troops, this was the first joint U.S.-Afghan patrol I had been on, and it was immediately apparent how differently each operated. The Americans were highly tactical in their staggered movements, a team of two going forward and providing cover from a protected firing position while the next team moved up. The Afghans almost sauntered across the terrain in clumps of four or five soldiers, easy targets for a short burst from an assault rifle. Some of them carried their weapons resting across their shoulder blades like farm tools, unready to use them if they came under attack.

I had seen Afghans fight, and they could be ferocious and effective. They didn't necessarily have to mirror American or NATO tactics to win; they just had to be better than their enemies. But were they?

Some were, to be sure, the ones who had been fighting their entire lives. But this was a new, volunteer army, many of the men former shopkeepers and taxi drivers who needed jobs and knew the Afghan National Security Forces provided the biggest employment programs for unskilled labor in the country.

But this group seemed eager to learn. They watched their American counterparts in action, and with some coaching from them, attempted to imitate their actions.

As dawn broke, the soldiers cast sharp shadows against the rose-colored mud-brick houses and walls they moved past. Boy shepherds began moving their flocks, stopping to look at the troops scurrying from one spot to the next. Shopkeepers stared, sometimes replying "*Va alaikum as salaam*," to the Americans' "*Salaam alaikum*," sometimes not."

We had passed through the village without incident when we saw a motorbike heading in our direction. Sgt. Randall Brown, the unit's forward observer, peered down the scope of his rifle.

"Two boys," he said to Bier, standing on the side of the road next to him. Another soldier held out his hand to tell them to stop. The driver looked about fourteen, his head covered with a *patu*—the Afghan shawl—against the morning cold; the passenger was about 10. The interpreter came forward and Bier asked the boys some questions before letting them pass.

"We good sir?" asked the soldier that had stopped them.

"They're good kids," Bier said.

"Yeah, they're fine," Brown agreed, and the fourteen-year-old kick-started the bike and headed down the dirt road between the soldiers walking on both sides.

The Americans called these daily operations "disruption patrols," a demonstration to the villagers that they were still around with their Afghan partners and weren't hiding behind the concrete blast walls and Hesco barriers of the COP. After a couple of hours, Bier was confident that the point had been made and began a carefully orchestrated exfil, or return to base. To do so, we had to cross Highway 1 and climb back up the slope, now fully exposed in the morning sun.

"This is the most dangerous part of the mission," said Choi when we found him in a covering fire position at the edge of a walled compound. "Getting home."

Nearby, Rembetsy had taken a knee and was talking to Bier about the mission. He looked up at Alex and me and gave us a carefree smile—as if he were attending his kid's soccer match rather than being in the middle of one of the most dangerous places in Afghanistan.

"Just having a word with one of my young Jedis," he said when he saw us looking in his direction. We laughed, then crossed Highway 1 and began the long climb to the COP.

Though there had been no contact on that morning's patrol, there was a palpable wariness on COP Soltan Kheyl since the Afghan boy had been killed. It was around 2 p.m. and Alex and I were just walking out of the dining facility after lunch when the round hit.

There was no whistling sound overhead, just the explosion when the 82-millimeter mortar hit the ground, a good indication that the point of impact was very close; we actually felt the ground tremble. We rounded the corner just in time to see three soldiers running into the combat aid station. One's face was covered with blood, and he was using his hand to apply pressure to a wound on his neck. The second soldier had no visible wounds. A medic was following closely behind them. When we try to go in after them, the base doctor simply pointed at the door and yelled, "Out!"

It had become a typical American military response to journalists trying to cover any U.S. battlefield casualties. They refused us access and even threatened and intimidated reporters to get them to put their cameras down. During my previous deployment, a colleague told me he'd gotten punched in the face by a Special Forces soldier for taking a photo of his wounded buddy. While it's a natural reaction to want to protect wounded comrades from the media, what most didn't seem to understand is that we weren't trying to exploit them; what we reported could show the sacrifices soldiers made in war. And while disturbing, it had to be reported: it is the truth of combat—people get injured and killed. The public needed to see that to understand war's costs. As embeds, we signed agreements preventing us from releasing any photos, video, or other identifying information about the wounded or dead until their next of kin had been notified, so family members would never be surprised by what we published or aired; they'd always hear any bad news about a loved one from an official military source first.

Instead of shooting at the combat aid station, we walked to where we had heard the detonation and found a small divot on the rocky ground next to the mortar—tail fins sitting upright, minus the nose that had contained the explosive charge.

Within a few minutes, two members from the base's Explosive Ordnance Disposal team arrived to study and photograph the impact point and the tail fins. They were gruff with us as well, basically telling us to fuck off, even though we'd been close to the incident and could've provided some helpful information.

We pieced together some details about the attack over the next few hours, but it took until the next day to get the whole story by interviewing one of the victims as well as the duty officer charged with responding to the attack.

Pfc. Brian Wintering and Spc. Shannon Kelley had been hanging around their MRAP when the round hit. Because it was hot, they'd left the back ramp and driver's side door open. The two were part of a quick-reaction team whose job is to respond if the COP comes under attack. But this time, they were the ones in the impact zone.

"I was playing Temple Run [a video game] and moved inside the vehicle so I could see [the screen] better. Shannon went out for a smoke," said twenty-one-year-old Wintering, lying on the bed in his hooch, his head still throbbing from the attack. "When the mortar hit, I just went to the ground. I felt a piece of shrapnel hit my neck. I was pretty much in shock. But then I heard Shannon screaming outside. He was on the ground, his face all bloody. I picked him up, and he said, 'We gotta get to the combat aid station,' and we just ran. That's about all I can remember."

The single 82-millimeter mortar had landed inside the gates, right next to them. There's no early warning system at the base, so at remote outposts like Soltan Kheyl, the sound of an explosion is likely the first indicator that it's time to find cover.

What the base does have, like so many other American bases across Afghanistan, is a high-tech "eye in the sky" gas-filled blimp tethered above it, known by another military acronym, PTDS, for Persistent Threat Detection System. The PTDS is mounted with a 360-degree video camera platform that can scan for miles. But the technology also has its drawbacks. While the blimp provides a constant view of the surrounding terrain, it also provides a nearly perfect target for Taliban mortar and rocket fire, one officer confided.

Still, the system archives the locations from which previous attacks have been launched so it can quickly acquire them as targets if they're used again. In this case, one of them had been. The PTDS locked on to two men, one carrying what looked like a mortar launching tube.

"We scanned the area and we saw the poo [point of origin of the attack], and two guys, one carrying the tube which he covered up in a red cloth," said Lt. Zachary Peterson, a fire support officer and the battle captain on duty that day. (A battle captain is the military's version of a police watch commander who monitors events from a tactical headquarters.)

Using the PTDS, they watched the man try to make a getaway on the back of a motorcycle driven by someone else.

"We tracked them back to their staging area, which we've seen them use before—a local mosque," said Peterson.

But along the way, the men passed behind some buildings and out of view of the PTDS. Somewhere en route to the mosque, the man on the back tossed the tube.

Meanwhile, on the COP, Wintering and Kelley, both bleeding, had still been able to scramble the 100 or so yards to the combat aid station within just minutes of being hit.

"Your training just kicks in after something like that," said Wintering.

Inside the aid station, medics quickly assessed the injuries of the two soldiers. Concerned that shrapnel might have penetrated vital organs, they bandaged Kelley's head and chest, and in just 26 minutes had him plugged into an IV saline drip, wrapped in a reflective Mylar coated blanket to keep him warm and prevent shock, and packaged on a stretcher on the back of Gator (a golf cart on steroids) heading to the helicopter landing zone for a medevac to the more advanced medical facility at Forward Operating Base Shank, about fifteen minutes away by chopper. Wintering was kept on base, treated for the blast concussion, and monitored for any hidden internal injuries.

While the injured soldiers were being treated, Lt. Peterson ordered artillery teams to stand by to respond to the attack with mortars of their own, but since the local men had disappeared from view, they couldn't be certain the two had been responsible and were wary of causing any accidental civilian deaths, something for which President Karzai had repeatedly and publicly criticized the U.S. military.

Peterson called up two A10 "Warthog" aircraft on station. The pilots located the dropped tube, and using an infrared camera, detected a white-hot heat signature from it that indicated it had likely been used to fire the mortar round.

"In an immediate show of force we dropped two 500-pound bombs on the tube," Peterson said. "It was an open area without potential for collateral damage, and we destroyed the weapon. That's a victory for us."

It seemed to be an expensive and perhaps empty message, but one that had to be sent to let the Taliban, or EOAs (Enemies of Afghanistan), as the military now called them, to let them know that they couldn't fire on the base with impunity: there would be repercussions, if not entirely effective ones. Some experts criticize what they deem overly cautious rules of engagement for the ISAF, complaining that it forces them to fight a war with one hand tied behind their back. But the military leadership had decided that the alternative—further accidental civilian deaths, which had been used very effectively by the Taliban in their propaganda war against the ISAF and the Afghan government—was even more unpalatable than having to pull their punches on the battlefield sometimes.

Kelley's injuries were not life threatening. He was treated and returned to COP Soltan Kheyl within the week. As for Wintering—"I still have a headache and ringing in my ears, but I guess I'm okay," he told Alex and me.

Mortar attacks are to be expected in a war zone, and the frequency of such attacks signaled how dangerous Afghanistan remained. Still, Wintering wondered—as those who survive lightning strikes, shark attacks, and other acts of very specific environmental violence must—how, out of all the real estate on COP Soltan Kheyl, this mortar fell so close to him.

"You're shocked, and ask you yourself, 'Why me?' I've seen them before, but you never expect it to be you," Wintering said. "When you get knocked down, you have to get back up again, but when I hear the explosions I still get scared." Understandably so, I thought. But maybe after this war is over and he's back home, he'll realize his luck really hadn't been bad at all.

One of the soldiers on that first patrol was Sgt. Adam Murphy, a beefy twenty-nine-year-old short-timer from Tacoma, Washington. Murphy had been a bartender in Reno, Nevada, before joining the army seven years ago, but after two tours in Iraq and one in Afghanistan, he had decided it was time to get out. His wife, who was also in the army, working supply, was pregnant and due in a month. Their dream was to move to Austin, Texas, and open a sports bar he planned to call "Murphy's Law."

"I know what it's going to look like already," Murphy told me as we sat outside the row of Conex storage containers that serve as living quarters at COP Soltan Kheyl for some of the 3-7. "The bar is going to be in the center and shaped like a giant football helmet, and we'll even have a courtesy taxi service," he said, smiling.

But first Murphy wanted to go to college and study business administration so he'd have a better chance at succeeding— maybe even franchise the idea. Before that could happen, he still had to survive a few more days here. And he couldn't relax, he said, until he was out of the country.

"You always hear that story about the guy that's about to go home, and then all of sudden, boom! Mortar attack. I call it," he said, "Murphy's Law."

Murphy was proud of his work as a squad leader, a top position within a platoon usually responsible for two fire teams of four men each.

"I haven't lost anyone under me as squad leader, even though four were killed in this unit so far. It's been a lot better than some of the earlier tours," he said, offhandedly.

"What happened on the other tours," I asked? Murphy didn't hesitate to answer.

"While I was in Iraq, one of the NCOs snapped and shot two others. Sgt. Bozicevich, he's serving life now," Murphy said.

"Why did he snap?" I asked.

"I'm not really sure," Murphy replied. "I was rolling in from a patrol when it happened. One of the NCOs was on the ground; a couple of guys had Bozicevich detained. Durbin was shot in the neck. Sgt. Dawson had internal injuries, but the birds couldn't fly because it was red air [dust conditions], so they couldn't get them medevac'd out right away."

I later researched the incident to learn the details. According to court documents, Sgt. Joseph Bozicevich, forty-one, of

Minnesota had shot and killed his squad leader, twenty-four-year-old S.Sgt. Darris Dawson of Florida, and Sgt. Wesley Durbin, twenty-six, of Texas, at a patrol base near Baghdad in Iskanderia, Iraq, on September 14, 2008.

Bozicevich admitted shooting them after they confronted him about mistakes he'd made during a recent operation. Prosecutors said that Bozicevich exploded after the two criticized him for leaving behind one of his men while on patrol. According to his platoon leader, Bozicevich had also lost one of his grenades, and Dawson was planning to replace him with Durbin as team leader. Durbin was found shot seven times at the base's communication station, and Dawson was shot six times while Bozicevich chased him; he fired the last two shots point blank, standing over him where Dawson had fallen. At his trial three years later, Bozicevich was found guilty of murder and sentenced to life without the possibility of parole.

I asked Murphy if the incident was one of the reasons he was getting out. He shook his head.

"Nothing that I've experienced in the army has influenced me to get out. I'm just tired," he said, "and the war's coming to an end. I think it was all worth it."

There was another patrol scheduled for 3rd Platoon the next morning, and though he'd officially completed his last one the day before, he said he still might got out. He shrugged when I asked him why. But before he goes, he will put his ear to a small, stuffed bear his wife sent him a few months earlier, as he has before every patrol since it arrived, to hear inside the recorded heartbeat of his unborn child.

Soltan Kheyl was a combat outpost where everything was focused on the kinetic: training, patrolling, and fighting—in
other words, violence and the potential for it. Everyone there
had to be prepared to fight—so there were no public affairs
officers around. That's why Sgt. Choi had been assigned to
deal with us.

Most 11-Bravos (the army designation for infantry soldiers) would rather empty latrines than babysit reporters, but
Choi, perhaps because of his extroverted nature and energetic
tempo, didn't seem to mind. It gave me the opportunity to
question him about why he was in Afghanistan.

"To be honest, I was bored—very bored," he said. "I did
one semester of college, hated it, and went to a recruiting station and signed up. My parents were against it. At first my
mother was really upset, but then they saw me graduate from
basic and their attitude changed. Now they're just worried."

Choi had been in the army for five years. He did one tour
in Iraq and was now on his second in Afghanistan. He was a
team leader, in charge of three other soldiers on a squad. He
said he loved the work, and he was so earnest, I believed him.

"In my deployments, I do make a difference," he said.
"These people had been oppressed in Iraq and we opened up
schools for girls there. In Kabul, we built a college for women."
He even had faith in the Afghan National Security Forces.

"The ANSF have been repelling attacks without help
from the coalition. It instills confidence in them and we have
to let them out, let them fly," he said. "My biggest concern
with ANSF is that they might feel we're abandoning them—

but we're not. There must be some cultural gaps, but we have a shared brotherhood."

Like a true believer, Choi doesn't feel the Afghan government will self-destruct or that the Taliban will take power again. But if they do, he will blame himself.

"If it does happen, I will feel like maybe I could've done more," he tells me. "I could've been working out less or putting my studies aside for a bit so I could have helped them more. I mean, how far are you willing to go to help out your friends? In the long term, Afghanistan will make a really good ally, and a good, good friend."

That sense of loyalty came in part from a feeling like he may have failed other friends in the past.

"The toughest part of all this is transitioning back to peacetime," he said. "The first time back from Iraq, thinking that no one understood, I bottled up everything inside, and there was a lot of alcohol use. The second time got easier; now the third time, I really understand, but the challenge is to make sure they understand, too—my soldiers. I've lost a lot of buddies, half of them to combat, half to suicide. Help was there to get, but we're alpha males, prideful—'I'm good buddy. I'll be okay.' You have to be able to cross over that line to help them."

Choi, like many other soldiers I've met, was grappling with life's thorniest questions prematurely: a twenty-four-year-old shouldering the burden of life and death, at one moment ready and committed to kill or die in combat, at another struggling to keep comrades from taking their own lives after the fighting is over.

Suicide has become endemic among American military veterans. According to a recent U.S. government study, veterans are killing themselves at the rate of 22 per day, or an average of one every 65 minutes. In 2012, suicides among active-duty personnel outpace the number of war deaths: 349 have taken their own lives, while 295 have been killed in combat.[*]

"Suicides are the biggest thing for me," Choi said after sitting quietly for a moment. "I'm a type-A personality: I like to control. I can't reach out to everyone, but when I do reach out, I know I can help."

The next morning we went out on patrol with 3rd Platoon again, and even though he didn't have to take the risk, Murphy came with us. This time there was a bit more coordination between the Afghans and Americans; U.S. troops provided outside security while the ANA searched inside houses and compounds.

The Afghans at first complained that they had searched these places dozens of times, but Lt. Bier insisted. He was particularly concerned about one local mosque, a building with white minaret constructed of progressively smaller sections like the layers of a wedding cake. Informants had said the mullah there might be a Taliban sympathizer. The ANA searched the mosque and, surprisingly, found an American

---

[*] U.S. Department of Veteran Affairs, Mental Health Services: Suicide Data Report 2012, by Janet Kemp, RN, PhD, and Robert Bossarte, PhD. http://www.va.gov/opa/docs/Suicide-Data-Report-2012-final.pdf.

military stretcher. The mullah and a group of teenage boys watched as the ANA, obviously pleased with themselves, confiscated the stretcher. But it was pretty thin evidence, and no one was detained.

It was still Ramadan, and the Afghan soldiers were eager to get back to their base and rest. Instead of walking over the hilly terrain, they took the more dangerous but flatter route, walking along the berm of Highway 1, easy targets for sniper fire. Soon they were so far ahead, the Americans couldn't see them anymore.

While they were looking for the ANA, the platoon's sergeant, Time Cardinal, noticed an Afghan man in the field, watching them. He didn't look like the other farmers. His *shalwar kameez* was clean and white, his hands weren't calloused, and his nails looked as if they had been manicured. Even more suspicious, the man was standing in the field with a shovel, while other farmers had hoes. Cardinal had his men bring the Afghan under the shade of some trees and questioned him through an interpreter.

Cardinal told one of his soldiers to BAT the guy. A biometric automated toolset looks like a large digital camera. American troops have been using the technology regularly since the war in Iraq to capture iris patterns, fingerprints, and facial images. The images are then compared to a massive database to determine whether someone has any criminal history or connections to insurgent movements.

U.S. and NATO forces have collected this kind of information on more than 1.5 million Afghans, according to a 2011 article in the *New York Times*; that's one out of every twenty residents and roughly one of every six military-age males.* In Iraq, the numbers were even greater. By the end of the U.S. military involvement there, they had compiled a database of three million—one in every fourteen people, or one in every four military-age men. The reason the numbers were so high was because the technology was also used on ordinary citizens as a screening measure in particularly violent cities in Iraq during the U.S. occupation. For example, after insurgents were pushed out of Fallujah, Iraq, in 2004, residents had to show special IDs and undergo biometric scans to reenter the city.

The Department of Defense had become very serious about biometrics, budgeting $3.5 billion for biometric programs for fiscal years 2007 through 2015. They even created the Biometrics Identity Management Agency in 2010 to manage the ongoing development of the technology and the ever-growing database.

Within minutes of sending the man's scans to be analyzed, Cardinal got word that he was on an insurgent watch list. He would be arrested and detained. But there was a problem. Because they had turned over responsibility for all detentions and detention facilities to the Afghans, they couldn't take him prisoner; only the Afghans had that authority—but they were nowhere to be seen, now halfway back to their base.

Cardinal informed the Tactical Operations Center at Soltan Kheyl of the situation and then sent his interpreter

---

* Rod Nordland, "Afghanistan Has Big Plans for Biometric Data," *New York Times*, November 19, 2011

ahead to find the Afghan squad leader. Twenty minutes later he showed up with a couple of his men, who looked perturbed. They nonetheless took the man into custody.

The next day, on our third and final joint foot patrol. we headed out with a different unit, the 3-7's first platoon, led by a young lieutenant and Yale graduate named Frank Piasta, who had decided to join the army instead of going to medical school. So far, he said, he hadn't regretted his decision.

From the start, Piasta was annoyed by the ANA squad assigned to patrol with them. They moved so fast that they were out of Piasta's sightline, just like the squad that had been with the 1st Platoon. Through his interpreter, he called the squad leader back and politely asked him to slow his guys down.

"Every hundred meters or so I need you to turn around and look at the element, and they'll help direct," Piasta told him, then waited for the interpreter to explain. "So we're good?"

"Good," the squad leader replied in English. And they set off again, at an easier pace.

It was a long patrol that wound through fields flush with clover and a lush parcel of golden summer wheat that the soldiers had to wade through. It produced an ethereal, painted quality that seemed to mitigate the menace of dozens of men dressed and armed for violence.

At a large *qalat*, or mud-walled compound, the Americans again pulled security while the Afghans searched inside. Through his interpreter, Piasta questioned a farmer named Zargul, who lived in the *qalat*. Zargul had a weathered face and a long beard tinged with gray at the ends; he wore a black turban.

"So, when is the last time you saw the Taliban?" Piasta asked.

"The Taliban come through here," Zargul admitted, "but they cover their faces and they have guns, so we can't talk to them."

Piasta wanted to enter the *qalat* to inspect some wires that Zargul said were found inside, but the ANA were adamant about keeping the Americans out because, they said, there were women inside. Piasta insisted, promising not to enter any of the rooms—he just wanted to see the wires. After some tense negotiations, the ANA reluctantly allowed their "partners" to enter. Piasta returned a few moments later, satisfied that the wires were just part of a makeshift aerial antennae.

After about four hours into the mission, Piasta decided it was time to head back, and 1st Platoon threaded through the narrow alleyways of a village. An A-10 Warthog, flying close air support, made a thunderous low pass overhead to discourage an attack. At the end of the village, they crossed Highway 1, weaving through the burned-out carcasses of a half dozen trucks that had been part of a convoy attacked earlier that summer.

On the walk back, one of the Afghan soldiers said that he had twisted his ankle and wanted a ride back on one of the MRAPs standing by for medical support. Piasta said his medics could bandage the Afghan's ankle but that no one would be hitching a ride on the vehicles. With that news, the Afghan, who had been limping seemed to recover; dismissing the offer of medical help, he sped off ahead with his comrades.

A day after Alex and I left Wardak Province and COP Soltan Kheyl to travel to our third embed stop, FOB Shank in nearby Logar Province, we received some disturbing news. At 8:30 a.m. on Tuesday, July 23rd, about the time the Americans and Afghans would be wrapping up their joint patrol around the mud houses and walled compounds of the Sayedabad district, a suicide bomber on a donkey rode between the units and detonated the explosives he was carrying. The blast killed three U.S. soldiers and their Afghan interpreter and wounded four Afghan National Army troops. The Taliban quickly took credit for the attack.

Alex and I wondered if any of the guys we knew were among those killed. Had Sgt. Murphy risked one last patrol and finally run out of luck? What about our patient babysitter Sgt. Choi, or Tim Cardinal, the platoon sergeant who loved bass fishing? Was it the forward observer Sgt. Randall Brown? Lt. Bier? Piasta? Or Capt. Rembetsy?

I felt a small surge of relief, quickly replaced by guilt, when I learned that the platoon that had been attacked was neither of the two we had been with. The loss was obviously no less great, but the deepest mourning shifts, unfortunately, to those who knew them best. The victims were from the 3rd Battalion, 15th Regiment, a unit we hadn't spent much time with. The dead were Lt. Jonam Russell, 25, of Arizona; Sgt. Stefan Smith, 24, of Georgia; and Spc. Rob Nichols, 24, of Colorado.

There's a whiplash of cognitive dissonance when news of violence disrupts your recollection of a place you remember as calm. During our patrols, we had walked passed animals, joked with boys herding sheep, watched a farmer load tufts of wheat on the back of a donkey. Each time we'd left the base in darkness, but as dawn broke over the mountains the sun painted the landscape a dazzling hue of gold, making it hard to imagine anything violent could ever happen there. But we knew it could—and then it had.

I was initially surprised by news of a beast-borne IED, but the absurdity of these killings seemed in keeping with the intensity of this vicious twelve-year war, where some of the world's most rugged and inhospitable terrain had forced a battle of both high and low technology—drones and donkeys were employed to achieve the same ends.

And this had not been the first use of a donkey IED. In April 2013, an Afghan policeman was killed at a checkpoint in Laghman Province by a bomb attached to a donkey. Three years earlier, in April 2010, a donkey carrying explosives blew up at a police post in Kandahar, killing three children and wounding four others. And the previous August, a policeman had been killed by a donkey bomb in Ghor Province.

General Abdul Raziq, commander of the Afghan National Army's 4th Brigade, responsible for Wardak and Logar provinces, warned his officers at a meeting the following morning that the Taliban would resort to almost anything to kill coalition and Afghan troops.

"They place IEDs on donkeys, they are using women with burkas—all kinds of tactics," he said. "They are using some that no one has seen before. Previously, we had a village elder that called out to get the attention of coalition forces, and as they came closer he blew himself up. They are using the darkness of the night and mealtime to conduct their attacks. We are facing the enemy all the time. We have to be alert. We have to keep our minds, our eyes, and our ears open."

Despite the American retrograde, the deaths at Soltan Kheyl underscored that the danger to U.S. troops was still very real. Their war was winding down, but the Taliban's was not. There was a popular saying in Afghanistan: "The Americans have the watches, but the Taliban has the time."

I later had a chance to ask Col. Kimo Gallahue, the commander of the 4th Brigade's combat team, which operated in eastern Afghanistan, how he could expect his soldiers to continue to fight and die when they knew their war was almost over. He paused, then explained what every soldier seemed to know: it's not about the cause, but about each other.

"Those kids walk outside the wire every day because they walk out together," he said.

But while they remained loyal to one another, I knew the soldiers wanted their sacrifices to be meaningful. That meaning was eroding day by day by the bad news coming out of Iraq.

When the U.S. and Iraq failed to sign a bilateral security agreement, America had pulled all its troops out of the country, the last ones leaving in December 2011. The U.S. was threatening to do the same in Afghanistan. Since the withdrawal from Iraq, violence had increased, culminating in the summer of 2014 when the Sunni militant group the Islamic State of Iraq and Syria began capturing wide swaths of northwestern Iraq including Tal Afar, Qaim, Mosul, and earlier that spring Fallujah. News that militias connected to Al Qaeda had retaken the city of Fallujah in Al Anbar Province was heartbreaking to American soldiers and marines who had fought there.

Two of the biggest battles of the war had been fought to wrest Fallujah from insurgents; in 2004, as many as fifteen hundred Americans were killed in the restive Al Anbar Province, more than one-fourth of all the Americans killed during the entire war. In an article in *Business Insider,* former marine turned journalist Paul Szoldra wondered if the sacrifices his friends had made in Iraq were in vain:

It shouldn't be such a surprise the place my friends fought for is falling back into civil war. I shouldn't be surprised when the same thing happens in Afghanistan. But it still is, because I don't want it to happen. . . . I'll never know why they died. It wasn't to stop the "mushroom cloud" or to defend the nation after 9/11. It sure wasn't for freedom, democracy, apple pie, or mom and dad back home. The only reason they died was for the man or woman beside them. They died for their friends. I'm just not satisfied with that.[*]

At the end of summer I learned that the leader of the 3rd Kandak on COP Soltan Kheyl, Col. Atrafy Mulinkadin, had been relieved of his command. The move angered his mentor and key American supporter, Maj. Rob Howard, who said in a *USA Today* article that after Mulinkadin was fired, convoy attacks once again increased, with a total of forty-four trucks burned in ten days.[†]

---

[*] Paul Szoldra, "Tell Me Again, Why Did My Friends Die In Iraq?" *Business Insider*, January 3, 2014.

[†] Victor Blue, "Highway 1 shows the difficulties ahead in Afghanistan," *USA Today*, December 5, 2013.

BOTH WINGS BROKEN

Love draws a dagger and pulls me close.
Lock and key. Bird with both wings
Broken. The love religion is all that's
written here. Who else would say this?
You open me wide open. Or you tie me
tighter. The ball waits on the field
to be hit again. You push me into fire
like Abraham. You pull me out like
Muhammad, "Which do you like better?"
you ask. All the same, if it's your hand,
troubles or peace. Friends become enemies,
faithful faithless. Some knots tighten;
some loosen. Unruly tangle of caution and
rebellion, ropes and uncombed hair, no one
can tell. Then comes the sure attention of
a mother's hand for her hurt child.*

---

* "Both Wings Broken," from *The Soul of Rumi: A New Collection of Ecstatic Poems*, translation by Coleman Barks (Harper One, 2001).

PART V
THE LAST EMBED

U.S. Army soldiers from the 6-8 Cavalry return to base after an afternoon patrol in Logar Province.

25
SUICIDE VEST

||||||||||||||

Afghan local police and Afghan National Army soldiers arrest a man
they say was helping a suicide bomber in an aborted attack.

While Combat Outpost Soltan Kheyl had felt like a small, hastily constructed shantytown on the edge of the frontier, Forward Operating Base Shank in Logar Province felt like a large, well-constructed town on the edge of the frontier. Because it came under mortar attack on almost a daily basis, Shank had earned the nickname of Rocket City.

It was home to the 4th Infantry Brigade Combat Team, Task Force Vanguard, which was comprised of five battalions and their support units—more than two thousand soldiers in all. Also on the base was the Afghan National Army's 4th Infantry Brigade. Between them, they were responsible for all of Wardak and Logar provinces, two of the most volatile in the country.

Shank had everything you might expect from a FOB of its size: a busy heliport, an even busier drone airstrip moving million-dollar Shadow observer drones that flew six to eight sorties a day, a high-tech artillery weapon called the Interceptor that shot down mortars and rockets in midair with a burst of high-explosive 20-millimeter rounds, a PX, and perhaps most important to those deployed there, a fully equipped and certified CrossFit gym.

FOB Shank also had a public affairs office headed by an affable and efficient major named Matt Fontaine. Fontaine was the kind of public affairs officer journalists actually liked. He responded quickly to information requests and didn't try to sell you bullshit puff pieces. And he was honest. When he knew something, he told you, and when he didn't, he told you that as well. His work engendered the kind of trust necessary for two professions often at odds with each other to coexist constructively.

Fontaine set us up with one last embed. We would join an American platoon at the nearby COP Baraki Barak for one more chance to see a joint U.S.-Afghan patrol. Before we went, I asked the top commanders at Task Force Vanguard the question that had nagged at the American military leadership since the announcement of the 2014 withdrawal: could the Afghan National Security Forces sustain themselves without American help?

Even many NATO countries couldn't do that. There was no country better equipped than the U.S. to move machines and manpower great distances and in unforgiving environments. French forces needed U.S. airlift support to get their troops into Mali when they intervened there in 2013. The British and French needed American air support during NATO's military action in Libya that had helped overthrow Muammar Gaddafi in 2011. If some of the world's richest nations need military logistics support, how would the world's third-poorest nation fare without continued U.S. assistance?

While military leaders tried to be optimistic, their answers provided little assurance. Lt. Col. Justin Hadley, commander of the 6th Squadron, 8th Cavalry, said he hadn't provided any supplies or assistance to his Afghan army counterparts since

February 2013, and that they hadn't really asked for any—
not for much, anyway.

"I can count in single digits the number of times they've
requested something from me," Hadley said. "I'm not providing them any food, ammunition, or fuel. I'm not providing anything. But sustaining the force is a real issue. They've
been able to feed and fuel themselves, but operational ready
rates don't look so good."

I got to see this firsthand during the daily morning staff
meeting of the Afghan army's 4th Brigade, when the chief logistics officer responded to the a question from the brigade's
commander about missing supplies.

"With each *kandak*, I gave them seven tents. I don't know
why they report they do not have them," he said. "I have the
paperwork in my office. I don't see any tents out there."

Capt. Jeremy Dillard, a U.S. army intelligence officer charged
with mentoring his Afghan counterparts in the Afghan army's
4th Brigade, said that even getting operational maps printed was
a hassle, and many had no idea how to read them, anyway. Some
couldn't read at all.

"We've had to develop classes in map reading using six-
digit grids without a protractor. It's a challenge," he said,
"but they're eager to learn. They want to know how we do it
and how they can do it better. We get along really well, but it
gets frustrating when they're about to cross the finish line and
then they fall back."

The task force commander, Col. Kimo Gallahue, was also
uncertain if the Afghans could sustain themselves.

"Our concern in 2009, as we were making an army, is the same as it is now; until they can sustain themselves in the field, they're not an army." Sustainment, parts, systems—the jury is still out on whether we've given them the right tools to sustain themselves."

By the time they find out, I wondered, would it be too late? Or was it too late already?

The Blackhawk ride to Baraki Barak took only ten minutes, but I saw why we were flying instead of driving. The geography was an insurgent's dream. There were hundreds of irrigation canals and waterways dividing swaths of farmland filled with clover, summer wheat, and watermelons, providing cover for the enemy in every direction. While beautiful from the air, it was hell on the ground for the soldiers who had to patrol it.

Baraki Barak made Soltan Kheyl look luxurious. The base had officially been turned over to the Afghans, but an understrength platoon of American cavalry and Special Forces troops still occupied a few of the rundown wooden structures at one end. In an outdoor workout pit, a bench fitted with a barbell of rusty metal plates gave the place the feel of a state penitentiary. David Mennig, the first sergeant of the 6-8 Cavalry's 3rd Platoon, met Alex and me at the landing zone and took us to the Tactical Operations Center.

Mennig was an old hand—he'd been through two tours in Iraq during some of the heaviest fighting there. He was a plain-talker with little time for bullshit or bullshitters. This would be his last tour before retiring, he told us, although he hadn't given any thought to what he'd do next: he'd given himself over completely to army life; what came afterward was a mystery.

We were introduced to the unit's fire support officer, Lt. Jeff Hart, a friendly, talkative guy who knew the area of operations well. They weren't conducting many mortar missions in order to avoid injuring civilians, so Hart spent his free time studying the area like a social scientist.

He told us that before his unit arrived, the Afghan security forces were like turtles: they stayed on base and covered up, becoming a target for enemy mortars. And the Afghan National Army had little contact with the national or local police. The Special Forces had been brought in to train the local police, and the 6-8 Cavalry to mentor the army. They made their presence known immediately, doing two joint patrols each day: one in the morning, one in the afternoon; one headed east, and the other west.

"They weren't used to seeing patrols outside the base, but now we were in contact with the enemy five times a week," Hart said. "Now it's down to once or twice a week."

Hart said the new operational tempo had pushed the insurgents back about 3.5 kilometers to the south and at least 3 kilometers to the west.

"I see the insurgents here as two different types of cells," said Hart, "I call one the 'doomsday preppers.' These are

people who are just very conservative; they've been here forever and they'll fight anyone occupying their territory. The
others are the foreign fighters—Taliban. The two used to
work together, but I think they've quit that since we've been
here."

Before we went on the afternoon patrol, Hart asked one of
the base's interpreters to work with us. The Americans called
him "Double-O-Seven"; they didn't know his real name, or
the names of any of the other interpreters. Instead they all
had monikers like "Dragon" or "Boss"; it was safer for them
that way. Still, it was strange to hear soldiers yell, "Where's
Double-O-Seven? Get Double-O-Seven!"

Double-O-Seven had been an interpreter for the American military for five years. He had lost plenty of friends
during that time; that he was still alive attested to either his
luck or his cautiousness. Some of the Americans joked about
how quickly he dove for cover when they took contact. He
shrugged it off: they came to Afghanistan for nine months,
but his deployment never ended.

Patrolling on the outskirts of Kotub Kheyl, I walked with
him along the river that irrigated the patchwork of wheat and
clover fields near the village of Baraki Barak. He told me
he wanted to get a visa and come to the United States. (The
availability of a special expedited visa for military and government interpreters in Afghanistan is why many of them do
this dangerous work.)

"If all the educated Afghans leave for America," I asked
him, "who will be left to run this place? Just the warlords?"

He paused, and then shrugged. "I'm not that educated," he said.

In between our conversations, he listened to radio chatter from some of the Afghan National Army soldiers and the Afghan local police who trailed behind this worn and weary platoon of American soldiers from the 6-8 Cavalry.

Carved into the plywood ceiling of one of the buildings back at the combat outpost was the sentence "There's no reason to hide how we feel." When I read it, I thought of the manpower shortages caused by the retrograde. The drawdown of American forces meant that when soldiers died, got injured, or went home, they weren't replaced. In this unit, the platoons, squads, and fire teams were now functioning at about half strength.

But if there was disillusionment, no one showed it. Every day they patrolled on foot—vehicles were useless in terrain crisscrossed with irrigation canals—and fueled themselves with energy drinks, dip, and the knowledge that their time here, at a little over four months, was almost half done. But their job—training and assisting the local Afghan security forces—seemed far from complete.

I had embedded with the American military many times on my trips to Afghanistan. This time, I needed to see what legacy they were leaving behind. There was certainly blood: more than twenty-one hundred American service members had been killed in combat here, thousands more injured. But had they created a sustainable army that could fight the Taliban? One that believed it had gained something worth fighting for in the last dozen years? It didn't seem so.

Double-Oh-Seven told me about the ANA radio chatter.

"They are saying they are tired—and hungry," he said, laughing. Maybe it was an unprofessional thing for soldiers to be talking about on the radio, but why *wouldn't* they be tired and hungry, I thought. It was Ramadan, when most Muslims were fasting. It was also the middle of a summer afternoon with temperatures in the mid-90s. I found it hard not to suck down the contents of my own canteen in front of them.

We walked along one of the many small nameless rivers, even wading through them in places. It reminded me of pictures and news footage of American troops crossing rivers in the jungles of Vietnam. The Afghans, on the other hand, bypassed the water, taking shortcuts or going through fields, doing almost anything to avoid getting their boots wet. I alternated between thinking they were being lazy and being smart.

After an hour, we pushed off the river and walked north under the cover of a narrow line of trees that ran parallel to the road. We heard a single shot, then a three-round burst behind us. We dropped to the ground.

There was shouting and confusion from the Afghans. The American platoon leader, Lt. Michael Hourihan, called up Dragon and Double-Oh-Seven to translate as he spoke with the ANA by radio.

Within minutes, some of the ANA and local police led a short, bearded man in his late twenties up the road toward the Americans. His hands were bound behind him with a scarf—probably his own.

The ANA said he was the driver of a motorcycle—the man riding on the back had jumped off the bike and run away when they shot at them. The ANA radio operator said he'd heard Taliban radio chatter that the passenger was wearing a suicide vest.

"I shot in their direction so we could capture them," said an Afghan army squad leader named Zabiaullah, "but there was also a woman nearby, and I didn't want to hit her." He said the men on the motorcycle hadn't fired first, nor did he see any weapons, but they could've been hidden under their clothing.

The Afghan radio operator said that after they'd captured the motorcycle driver he had heard more chatter: the mission had been aborted. Their prisoner told the ANA soldiers he had just been giving the other man a ride. He didn't even know him, he said. The ANA led him away, back in the direction of their base.

The American platoon leader, Lt. Hourihan, thought the motorcycle might be rigged with explosives, and he wanted to blow it up where it was parked.

"No, no," said one of the Afghans who waved the lieutenant off, while the other got on the bike and prepared to start it up.

"Do *not* start that bike," Hourihan said firmly.

They looked at him defiantly, rolled it ahead a few yards, then kick-started the engine and rode away. Hourihan shook his head.

When we returned to the base an hour later, we saw the two Afghans on the commandeered motorcycle, cleaned up, out of uniform, and heading off base, probably on their way to the *iftar* meal to break the Ramadan fast. Double-Oh-Seven looked at me and rolled his eyes.

"Those guys," he said.

The Americans and Afghans weren't working together very well, and there was plenty of suspicion—and maybe even a little contempt—on both sides. But maybe that didn't matter anymore. Their on-the-ground partnership was about to end anyway, and most military experts agreed that the Afghans didn't have to fight like Western armies to win this war; they just had to fight better than the Taliban. While American assets like airpower, high-tech weaponry, and logistical support certainly provided an edge, the time remaining to take advantage of it was waning, and if President Karzai didn't sign the Bilateral Security Agreement, it would disappear altogether.

To hold their own or beat the Taliban, the Afghan National Security Forces had to find a reason to fight. Maybe they already had, and I had just witnessed it. Had their cowboy tactics just prevented a suicide attack against the American patrol? Or had I just watched them steal a motorcycle so they wouldn't have to walk all the way back to their base? I just couldn't be certain.

Uncertainty. It was a strange place to be after a dozen years of war and the $600 billion—and more than twenty-one hundred lives—the U.S. had spent here. Most would expect a better return on an investment of so much blood and treasure.

But who was to blame? The Afghan government for corruption so bold that it levied a departure tax on American military vehicles withdrawing from the country? Or was the American government at fault for dispersing military and humanitarian aid here as if it were coming out of the end of a fire hose, not vetting whom they gave it too nor accounting for it once it had been dispersed? That was not a recipe for corruption—it was an invitation.

And there were military shortcomings as well. While the Taliban's atrocities were well documented, the ANSF, ISAF, and the Americans had also wracked up more than a few of their own: torture at black prison sites, extrajudicial killings. There were also the really ugly stories that threatened to taint the entire mission, like the extracurricular killing spree of S.Sgt. Robert Bales, who murdered sixteen villagers in Kandahar in March 2012, and the former U.S. soldier turned freelance mercenary and suspected psychopath Keith "Jack" Idema, who pretended to be a journalist to get into Afghanistan and then kidnapped Afghan citizens and tortured them in the basement of his rented house in Kabul.

Despite missteps and even tangible evil resulting from the war, the ISAF had helped stand up a national army and police force, which in the last year had acquitted themselves quite well on the battlefield, fighting bravely, absorbing a great number of losses, and inflicting a fair amount on the Taliban as well.

And while the scale of fiscal mismanagement was mindboggling, the American and other international aid had done much good, too, taking Afghanistan from the third-poorest nation on earth to an improved if dubious position as tenth-poorest. According to the U.S. Agency for International Development, 3,000 wells, 2,000 kilometers of roads, and 615 schools had been built; 8 million students were in primary and secondary school, nearly 40 percent of them female; infant and child mortality rates had declined by 57 and 62 percent, respectively; and more than 27 percent of Afghan parliament seats, 1 provincial governorship, 3 cabinet posts, and 120 judicial positions were now held by women.

One Afghan friend told me that "Americans have changed the lives of everyone in Afghanistan, even the Taliban." And there was some hard evidence that he was right. Despite all of the violence, corruption, unemployment, and other problems the nation faced, a recent poll found Afghans were actually optimistic about their future.

An annual survey by the Asia Foundation[*], a nonprofit international development organization, revealed that 57 percent of Afghans believed their country was moving in the right direction. That number has been rising steadily over the last three years, from 46 percent in 2011 and 52 percent in 2012. The survey cited five reasons for Afghans' optimism: the reconstruction efforts, better security, an improved education system, opening schools for girls, and the increased presence of the Afghan National Army and the Afghan National Police.

---

[*] Asia Foundation, *Afghanistan in 2013: A Survey of the Afghan People*, 2013. Expert survey teams were deployed from July 17 to July 25, 2013, to gather the opinions and perspectives of a representative sample of 9,260 Afghan men and women from all 34 provinces in face-to-face interviews .

But maybe it was simpler than that. Maybe Afghans just liked their music, their mobile phones, television, dancing, that their sisters could go to school and their mothers could leave their home—all the things the Taliban frowned on or outlawed. They didn't all have to love their current government—that's certainly not the case in the U.S. or most other democracies—but they now had the right to fight to choose it, as they would again in the April 2014 presidential election.

Regardless of what they may have achieved, America hadn't come in 2001 to save the Afghans; it had come on a mission of vengeance and national security to smash Al Qaeda and overthrow the Taliban. Under the narrow scope of those early goals—mission accomplished. As for the goals of nation building and creating a stable, secure Afghanistan, America has obviously fallen far short.

That a group as universally despised at the Taliban could make a serious comeback in post-9/11 Afghanistan says something about how wrong the experiment has gone. The Taliban's rise to power in Afghanistan was born of a national frustration with the warlords and their corruption. Their return, it seems, is born of much the same thing.

While the U.S. and Afghan governments have not lost the military war, they are losing the battle of ideas: that a central government must provide its citizens with justice as well as security, transparency as well as opportunity. In a dozen years, neither the fearsome power of America's military nor the formidable depth of its pockets had succeeded in convincing the Afghan people that their national government is worthy of their trust and support.

That failure to forge a sense of national identity among disparate people through common values and principles is Afghanistan's worse broken promise. Regardless of the optimistic Afghan opinion polls, intelligence predictions for Afghanistan's future are bleak.

In January 2014 a classified report, the "National Intelligence Estimate,"* which is comprised of information from sixteen U.S. intelligence agencies, predicts that chaos will engulf Afghanistan without ongoing U.S. military and financial aid—and that even with an ongoing investment of $8 billion a year, the Taliban will likely take over the country by 2017.

So is all lost? My journeys tell me no. Hope both political and economic remains. Youth movements are forming, pushing back against both the government's corruption and the Taliban's extremism. Experts also say that Afghanistan could one day sustain itself with properly managed mineral and other natural resources. China, India, and other nations are already investing.

There's little doubt that 2014 will be a disruptive year; in addition to the withdrawal of international forces, Afghans will have elected a new president through a peaceful transition of power for only the second time in their history. It will

---

* Many U.S. political and military experts say the National Intelligence Estimate report is overly pessimistic and did not account for the improved effectiveness of the Afghan National Security Forces.

be a chance at a clean slate, to begin again the massive effort of building a stable Afghanistan—on the Afghans' own timetable and by their own design.

Will they succeed in establishing a national identity strong enough to harness the power of their ethnic diversity, to face down their corrupt warlords, their massive drug problem, and the Taliban? Maybe what I saw in Baraki Barak was evidence that they can and will do it, in their own imperfect way, without American help. Or maybe what I saw was evidence that they've already failed and are simply headed for a rendezvous with their dark Taliban past, riding there on a stolen motorcycle.

I don't know. I just can't be certain. After all these years, lives, and money, that such uncertainty can linger may be the worst crime of all.

America has profoundly changed Afghanistan just as America has been forever changed by this once (and perhaps future) failed state that gave Osama bin Laden and Al Qaeda safe haven to launch the deadliest foreign attacks on American soil in history. So much has been wagered in the last dozen years because of 9/11, so many questions raised. Was our response to 9/11 worth the price that we've paid? Have we helped build a better Afghanistan, or have we helped to destroy it?

Afghanistan has certainly changed me; indeed, it has defined me for one-fifth of my life. I have become intertwined with its myth and magic, lost friends and colleagues—as well as my innocence. It is a beautiful and brutal place, infuriatingly incongruous, a place where the world's most generous hospitality and most horrifying honor killings coexist, a society with the propensity to shroud its women in burkas and dress up its boys as dancing girls, a people strong enough to defeat outside invaders but unable to stop fighting themselves.

It is a perfect reflection of the good and bad in us all.

Epilogue
EXIT

IIIIIIIIIIIII

Twelve years after checking out of the Hotel Intercontinental Kabul, I return their key. Desk clerk Farhad is politely unimpressed with the historical relevance of the now useless chunk of metal and my efforts to see it home.

There were two things I needed to do before leaving Afghanistan, and both were about getting some closure. The first was to return a key. The second was to say goodbye.

When I'd rolled out of Afghanistan and over the Pakistan border on my last ride onboard the Tora Bora Bus in late December 2001, I brought a few things with me: the strange illness I'd picked up after spending the night in the dead man's bed at the Spinghar; a Russian helmet liner with the words "This is the jihad of the Taliban" scribbled on it in black marker that I'd found in the ammo dump at the bombed-out Al Qaeda camp at Reshkhor; and the key to Room 435 at the Hotel Intercontinental in Kabul, which I'd inadvertently forgotten to return.

Of those three things, I had kept only the key, which was attached to a heavy steel rectangle with the words "Hotel Intercontinental Kabul" etched in high relief that I liked to rub my fingers across when I sifted through a box of mementos in the following years.

While it was a poignant reminder of that first journey to Afghanistan, I felt it was time to return it, and I brought it with me when I again crossed the Amu Darya in 2013. The hotel, in the Karte Parwan neighborhood of western Kabul, was the nation's first international luxury hotel when it opened for business in 1969, and it had ridden the waves of Afghanistan's conflicts ever since. The two-hundred room, three-star hotel served as officers' quarters during the Russian occupation from 1979 to 1989, was extensively damaged, like everything else in the city, during the civil war from 1992 to 1996, and was filled with journalists like me after the fall of the Taliban in 2001, when there was neither running water nor electricity.

The Intercon, no longer affiliated with the chain, went through a $25 million dollar renovation after the fall of the Taliban. But in June 2011, nine gunmen, some of them wearing suicide vests, killed as many as a dozen guests and staff members before being killed themselves in a six-hour gun battle during which NATO helicopters and New Zealand Special Forces troops were called in to support the Afghan National Police. The Taliban claimed credit for the attack.

The hotel had been repaired and the renovations completed when Haroon brought me to the front desk to return the key. There we met a young clerk named Farhad who, though extremely polite, seemed neither surprised nor overly impressed when I handed him back the now useless hunk of metal and key that had long ago been replaced by an electronic keyless entry system. Nonetheless, he gamely agreed to give us a tour of my old room to satisfy a nostalgia that, in this group, was obviously mine alone.

The layout of the Intercon was the same—the hotel entrance, the front desk, the restaurants. But the detail and the mood had changed. In 2001, everyone had been scurrying back and forth in the loud, dirty lobby, trying to get a grasp on the history shifting in front of us. There had been a small bookstore in the lobby, and I remember browsing through it when I first arrived only to discover the Taliban had either scratched out or taped over every book with a human or animal depicted on its cover.

Now the lobby was empty, only the sound of innocuous music filling the space. We rode the mirror-paneled elevator to the fourth floor and headed down the hallway, the worn and ratty red carpeting replaced with a new red carpeting that looked astonishingly similar. On the way to my old room we ran into a member of the cleaning staff, a tall, slender man named Jameel who had been with the hotel for almost twenty years. I asked him what he remembered from 2001.

"I remember the Taliban moved out and all of the journalists moved in," he said. "There was CNN, BBC, NHK, NBC—it was very crowded, and all of them put their generators on the roof."

We had done that, in the absence of hotel electricity, to power our cameras for our rooftop live shots and for our satellite feeds. Eventually, the leaking fuel from all the generators caused a fire that Jameel and other staff tried to extinguish by carrying buckets of water up six flights of stairs.

Farhad handed the key card to Jameel, who opened the vacant Room 435. It looked dark and drab, just as it had in 2001. When Jameel opened the drapes, it didn't look much different—just better lit. It still had heavy curtains and two single beds, both covered in maroon bedspreads with fake wooden headboards. There was at least new carpet, and a loveseat and television that hadn't been there in 2001. And the room once again had running water and electricity.

I looked around, remembering the times I would drag myself back to the cold, dark room and wash my face and brush my teeth with bottled water, and flush the toilet with a bucket of water filled from a ground floor spigot. Still, it had been a nice, clean refuge from the dust and rain that besieged us in those early days in Khoja Bahauddin at the House of Massoud.

I asked Jameel, who had been the better tippers, the Taliban or the journalists.

"The journalists," he said, laughing, after Haroon had translated.

Before we departed the hotel, leaving the key and my 2001 memories behind, I asked Jameel what he hoped for the future.

"I wish for peace," he said, without hesitation "and I hope the Taliban don't return."

"Why," I asked, "because they were bad tippers?"

"Not just the tips," he said, laughing again, "they had a lot of other issues, too."

"They were messy, I bet," I joked, "but they couldn't have been worse than the journalists."

On my last night in Afghanistan, Haroon, Hakim, and I met up with Hakim's cousin Shafiq at the rooftop hookah bar at the Safi Landmark Hotel.

Shafiq had also been one of my fixers in 2001, and despite his less-than-fluent English, he successfully helped me navigate a Taliban mortar attack that nearly killed us, as well as a score of other close calls. He had studied medicine at university, but had focused his post-2001 efforts on a contracting business, building roads and infrastructure for the International Security Assistance Force and other international entities. Haroon had told me Shafiq had done a job at Bagram but underestimated his costs and lost money on the job.

Shafiq was a regular at the Safi's rooftop hookah bar. Weeks earlier we had run into each other in the lobby—it was the day I checked in after leaving Dost's apartment. While I had grown gray and my face creased from endless hours of sun and harsh weather, Shafiq still had his boyish looks.

On the roof, we all squeezed into a booth. The waiter brought us pots of hot tea and a meter-high hookah pipe that he quickly and expertly prepared. He filled the bowl with a moist, mint-flavored tobacco, then placed smoldering coals on top of a perforated foil lid that would heat the tobacco from the top as we sucked the air through the pipes, drawing it down through the bowl, through the bubbling water, and finally into our lungs. Smoking shisha, hookah, hubbly-bubbly— whatever term you preferred—was a Middle Eastern tradition that had only become popular in Kabul with the influx of foreigners and foreign money. It was just as unhealthy as cigarettes but seemed less so because of the mellowness of the water draw and the social act of sharing the pipe.

We pulled from the pipe, recounted old stories, laughed, and enjoyed each other's company. Haroon, Hakim, and I had decided to try a little prank on Shafiq. We came up with the idea after I learned he'd asked Haroon if I might be able to help get him another foreign building contract. As a journalist, I had no such influence—I didn't even have any contacts. Still, while we sat around the pipe, I teased Shafiq with the false notion that I wanted to get an airplane runway built in Tora Bora, an absurd idea on every level, including a complete lack of need, security, or even level ground there.

He took the bait and began his sales pitch, assuring me that his company could provide everything necessary to get the runway built, from securing the construction site—an outlaw frontier overrun with Taliban—to the construction itself. As he became more excited, the prank make a hard turn south, from funny to mean. I was repaying the guy who had safely guided me through a minefield by raising and then destroying his expectations for my own amusement. When I told him I was just joking, his smile faded, and disappointment replaced the enthusiasm in his eyes. It was still there when we embraced and said goodbye at the end of the night.

The next day Haroon and Hakim brought me to the departures area of Kabul International. The goodbyes were brief, unemotional, and tinged with uncertainty, as so much else on this journey had been. I wondered what the next year would bring for my friends. Hakim was single and I knew would never leave Afghanistan, but Haroon had three young daughters and was afraid of what lay ahead for his family.

When Haroon had returned to Afghanistan after his year of study in the United States, everyone asked him why he'd returned—he had made it to America, the dream of so many Afghans. But he had also made a promise to return to his country when his education was complete. And so he had.

But now, like so many other educated Afghans, using his knowledge and skills meant either working in a government office where he would be expected to take bribes to offset an unlivable wage, or taking a well-paying but likely unsustainable project job funded by USAID or an NGO; the latter would leave him slightly better off but marginalized in the long run, outside the sphere of government power without the ability to contribute to meaningful change in his country.

His other option was to get an American visa and leave Afghanistan and its uncertainty behind. His paperwork, he told me, had already been submitted.

I shook their hands, embraced them both, and walked away.

At a security checkpoint in the parking lot before entering the airport terminal, a lone Afghan security guard scanned my luggage in the X-ray machine and saw a small pocketknife in the luggage I'd checked. He offered to let me keep it—for a price.

"*Bakshish, bakshish*," he said, rubbing his thumb back and forth over his fingers—the universal sign for "money."

I looked at him and shook my head no, but he persisted. I continued to refuse and felt my anger reaching a tipping point.

Not one more dime, I wanted to tell him. My country had spent more than $600 billion, more than 2,100 lives, and a dozen years here, I thought. Thousands more were injured and maimed on Afghan soil, and they and their families would never be the same; just paying for their long-term health care was likely to jack up the price of this war and reconstruction to more than a trillion dollars, a debt that by itself could bankrupt America. I had lost friends and colleagues in the course of the war and had even come close to buying it myself. So no. Not one more dime, not one more minute, not one more thought. I picked up my bags without giving him anything and walked inside the building.

Once inside, I took a deep breath and did a reality check.

He was a security guard, not a warlord. He hadn't robbed me, merely asked for a small tip on top of what was most certainly a pitiful salary. He, like the rest of his countrymen, hadn't asked for this war nor America's help. We'd come uninvited, and now we were getting ready to dump it all back in their laps because we were done with it. We had turned in our key, made some jokes and vague promises, raised expectations, broke a few things and fixed some others, and now we were saying our goodbyes.

The least we could do was leave a little tip. And so I did, and it was this:

Trust no one, and good luck.

Afterword
AMERICA'S POST-9/11 LEGACY IN SHAMBLES

||||||||||||

U.S. soldiers on early morning patrol in Eastern Afghanistan. The legacies of America's wars in Afghanistan and Iraq have left neither country more stable, nor America confidently secure itself.

As I write this on the eve of the Fourth of July, America has nothing much to celebrate regarding its post-9/11, war-on-terror legacy. Iraq has all but imploded with a Sunni militant coalition declaring a new Muslim caliphate in the regions it has captured, shortening its name from the Islamic State of Iraq and Syria (ISIS) to simply the Islamic State and demanding immediate allegiance from all Muslims worldwide.

In the same week in Afghanistan the news was just as bad. Taliban forces had launched major offensives in northern Helmand Province, focusing on the district of Sangin, considered the spiritual birthplace of the Afghan Taliban. Initial reports said that more than one hundred Afghan security forces and fifty civilians had been killed.

The Taliban's attack underscored a growing queasiness both in Kabul and in Washington about Afghanistan's rapidly expanding instability as American troops continue their withdrawal.

This was the grim scenario as reported by the *New York Times*:

> Already, areas once heavily patrolled by American forces have grown more violent as the Afghan military and the police struggle to feed, fuel and equip themselves. The lackluster performance of the Afghan Army so far in Helmand has also evoked comparisons with Iraq, raising ques-

tions about whether the American-trained force can stand in the way of a Taliban resurgence.[*]

This "resurgence" also seemed to exploit the presidential political crisis that followed the June 14 runoff elections between former Afghan foreign minister Dr. Abdullah Abdullah and former Afghan finance minister Ashraf Ghani.

Abdullah, part-Tajik with strong support in the north, declared he would boycott the vote count, claiming the results were tainted and that he had evidence of ballot stuffing in favor of Ghani, a Pashtun. Ghani denied the election had been corrupted.

In the 2009 presidential election, Abdullah relented in favor of President Hamid Karzai, after making similar allegations of fraud, but warned that he would not do so again, adding the specter of renewed ethnic violence to an already shaky security environment.

Regardless of all the events that forced the simultaneous crises in Afghanistan and Iraq to a head in the same week of July 2014, it seemed doubtful that the U.S.-led wars in both countries had achieved its goals of "exporting" democracy to other parts of the world. Both countries remain deeply unstable, and America can't consider itself much more secure than it was before 9/11 in the wake of such looming disasters.

---

[*] Azam Ahmed and Taimor Shah, "Taliban Mount Major Assault in Afghanistan," *New York Times*, June 27, 2014.

As all of this was happening, I was emailing and videoconferencing with Haroon, my friend and fixer in Kabul. He shared some disturbing news about one of the individuals he had introduced me to in Kabul, the female dentist Farzana Nawabi, whom I wrote about in Chapter 16.

Farzana lived with her mother and father and extended family in a nice neighborhood in Kabul. But in the spring of 2014, ten men, armed with Russian-made Makarov pistols, ransacked their home and robbed them of nearly everything of value, including their computers, cellphones, jewelry, and entire life savings in cash. They also badly traumatized her parents, putting pistols to their heads and beating them. Farzana wasn't home at the time.

In an email from Haroon:

> Farzana said to me that since the robbery took place, all of them are shocked. Mr. Nawabi and his wife are having bad trauma. She is seeking ways to get out of the country. She told me that she's afraid she may lose her life for no reason one day. She definitely wants to get out and work for Afghan women and Afghan society from overseas. She said when she goes to work, she feels very insecure, worried about her parents and her life even more than during the time of the Taliban.

Haroon sent me photos of the interior of the house after the robbery. Clothes were everywhere, furniture and carpets overturned. It looked like it had been hit by a tornado. It was devastating to see the savagery and easy to imagine from the photos that the thieves had taken more than just the Nawabis' possessions. They had also stolen the most precious thing anyone can have in Afghanistan, their hope.

And to this story, Haroon added one more thing. He was leaving Afghanistan. Haroon's work for both the U.S. and British governments in Afghanistan had put him and his family in constant danger. The risks had become significant enough to qualify them for U.S. immigration visas under a special assistance program.

In a few months, he and his wife and three daughters would be coming to live in America. We talked about options for his resettlement and agreed that the Washington, D.C., area would be best in terms of possible job opportunities with his language skills as well as good access to other Afghan immigrants in the region to help ease the transition. I asked him how he and his family felt about leaving Afghanistan and if he had told his best friend, Hakim?

I talked to my wife. She told me that she has a feeling, a taste of something like a mix of sour and sweet together. She is happy that she will be able to improve and get education that she missed, as well as she is happy for her kids that they will have a secure and good future, but she is worried that what does the U.S. look like? She does not know the language, how long will it take her to learn? What do the people look like? Culture and so many other issues? She is happy that I will be secure at least. I have not told my kids that we are leaving yet.

He continued:

I am worried about a job and I will be very busy for the first year as I have to act as a father, husband, and translator to my family and guide for four ladies of different ages (my wife and kids). It is hard to manage, but not impossible. I hope to find good residence with good people and a good job to make enough money to look after my family and myself. I hope I can do something for peace in Afghanistan and for women and children rights. My life will be very much different than in Afghanistan. It takes time to orientate my family and myself but I hope to be successful to have my dreams come true.

Haroon, as always wisely cautious, said he had not told any other family or friends about the visas and the move.

I HAVE KEPT EVERYONE IN DARK ABOUT MY TRANSITION until I get my ticket and am aboard in plane with my family. Hakim will be very upset, but I assume he agrees with my plan. He will be alone, but never apart from me. He is my brother.

In the past, when he first mentioned his interest in possibly moving to the U.S., I told Haroon that I was worried that if all the young, educated Afghans emigrated no one would be left to take the country back from the warlords and the Taliban. But now I know that was the thinking of someone who's never faced the prospect of living a life of perpetual insecurity. I want a better future for Afghanistan, but I also want what is best for my friend and his family now. That means leaving Afghanistan. One day, if he decides he's ready and he wants to, Haroon can always return. One thing I do know is that while hope is mightily tested, often beaten, battered, and sometimes stolen, it never really dies in the hearts of most Afghans.

But there was, I realized, one final irony to all of this. While America's post-9/11 legacies were seemingly in shambles in both Iraq and Afghanistan, it still provided the promise of a more peaceful future for those who had to flee their own countries because of America's outside experiments in democracy.

—*Kevin Sites*
July 1, 2014

ACKNOWLEDGMENTS

|||||||||||||

I've loved and feared Afghanistan from the first moment my feet touched its soil more than a dozen years ago. I've borne witness to its dark secrets and its aspirations. But they would have remained an impenetrable mystery had it not been for the Afghan people who guided me on my many journeys—physical, spiritual, and historical— through their country.

I'm deeply indebted to Abdul Matin Sarfraz, my former student at the University of Hong Kong, who became my teacher and friend while traveling and reporting from his home region in northern Afghanistan. I'm also grateful to his cousin, Dost Muhammad, owner and driver of the un-forgettable Bahmani-mobile and an unforgettable character himself. As always, many thanks to my good friend Muham-mad Haroon Khadim, who has been by my side for nearly every step I've taken in Afghanistan. Also my appreciation to Hakim, who has also been a part of the adventure from the very beginning. Thanks to my friend Hayot Tuychiev for a last-minute assist getting me through Tajikistan on this last journey, as well as to my colleague Alex Pena for allowing me to piggyback on his *Stars & Stripes* embed to RC-East.

I'm proud that Harper Perennial has published all three of my books and grateful to associate publisher Amy Baker, who has guided each from concept to publication. She's been a supportive, creative editor and an encouraging friend. My gratitude also to the rest of the Harper Perennial team involved with *Swimming with Warlords* including production editor Keith Hollaman, copy editor Andrew Miller, and publicist Amanda Ainsworth. My thanks goes as well to my literary agent, Paul Bresnick.

This book began as an article for *Vice* magazine, and I want to thank my supervising editor there, Wilbert Cooper, for seeing the value of the idea and giving me the freedom to explore it. Additional thanks to *Vice*'s editor in chief, Rocco Castoro, and senior editor Wes Enzinna, who both weighed in on the story, providing insights that helped me develop and expand it from a five-thousand word article to an eighty-five-thousand word book.

I want to thank my boss, Ying Chan, the director of the Journalism and Media Studies Centre at the University of Hong Kong, for providing a stable and creative environment from which I get to enjoy the best of both worlds: teaching the next generation of journalists while practicing the profession I've loved for more than twenty-five years.

Finally, my love, respect and gratitude to my wife Anita and my "bonus" daughter Cam, who bear the brunt of my long absences in difficult places as well as my often rocky returns from them. Your sacrifice and endurance hold a special place in my heart.

ABOUT THE AUTHOR

||||||||||||

Kevin Sites traded in his career as a network news correspondent/producer (NBC, ABC, CNN) to become a pioneering backpack journalist on the Internet. He covered nearly every war in one year for Yahoo! News, earning the 2006 Daniel Pearl Award for Courage and Integrity in Journalism. He is the author of *In the Hot Zone* and *The Things They Cannot Say*. He was selected as a Neiman Fellow at Harvard and an Ochberg Fellow at Columbia and currently serves as an associate professor at the University of Hong Kong's Journalism and Media Studies Centre.

BOOKS BY KEVIN SITES

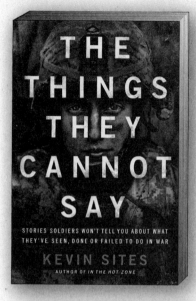

THE THINGS THEY CANNOT SAY
Stories Soldiers Won't Tell You About What They've Seen, Done or Failed to Do in War
Available in Paperback and eBook

Eleven soldiers and Marines display a rare courage that transcends battlefield heroics—they share the truth about their wars. For each of them it means something different: one struggles to recover from a head injury he believes has stolen his ability to love, another attempts to make amends for the killing of an innocent man, while yet another finds respect for the enemy fighter who tried to kill him. Award-winning journalist and author Kevin Sites asks the difficult questions of these combatants.

"Absolutely brilliant! Kevin Sites is a masterful storyteller."

—Sean Parnell, *New York Times* Bestselling Author of *Outlaw Platoon*

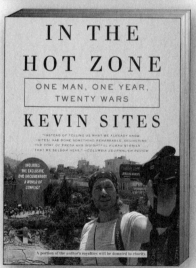

IN THE HOT ZONE
One Man, One Year, Twenty Wars
Available in Paperback and eBook

Kevin Sites is a man on a mission. Armed with just a video camera, a digital camera, a laptop, and a satellite modem, the award-winning journalist begins his journey with the anarchic chaos of Somalia in September 2005 and ends with the Israeli-Hezbollah war in the summer of 2006. Sites talks with rebels and government troops, child soldiers and child brides, and features the people on every side, including those caught in the crossfire. His honest reporting helps destroy the myths of war by putting a human face on war's inhumanity. Personally, Sites will come to discover that the greatest danger he faces may not be from bombs and bullets, but from the unsettling power of the truth.

"These images and dispatches form the numberless rooms of hell have an undeniable cumulative power." —*Kirkus Reviews*